Water supply surveillance

A reference manual

Water supply surveillance

A reference manual

Guy Howard

Water, Engineering and Development Centre,
Loughborough University,
Leicestershire, LE11 3TU, UK

© WEDC, Loughborough University, 2002

ISBN 13 Paperback: 978 1 84380 004 0
ISBN Ebook: 9781788533744
Book DOI: http://dx.doi.org/10.3362/9781788533744

A catalogue record for this book is available from the British Library.

A reference copy of this publication is also available online at:
http://www.lboro.ac.uk/wedc/publications/

Howard, A.G. (2002)
Water Supply Surveillance: A reference manual
WEDC, Loughborough University, UK.

WEDC (The Water, Engineering and Development Centre) at Loughborough University in the UK is one of the world's leading institutions concerned with education, training, research and consultancy for the planning, provision and management of physical infrastructure for development in low- and middleincome countries.

This edition is reprinted and distributed by Practical Action Publishing.
Since 1974, Practical Action Publishing has published and disseminated books and information in support of international development work throughout the world. Practical Action Publishing trades only in support of its parent charity objectives and any profits are covenanted back to Practical Action (Charity Reg. No. 247257, Group VAT Registration No. 880 9924 76).

This document is an output from a project funded by the UK
Department for International Development (DFID)
for the benefit of low-income countries.
The views expressed are not necessarily those of DFID.

About the author

Guy Howard is a Programme Manager at WEDC, Loughborough University and was previously Research Fellow and Head of Overseas Projects at the Robens Centre for Public & Environmental Heath, University of Surrey. He is involved in the revision of the WHO Guidelines for Drinking-Water Quality as the Co-ordinator of the Monitoring and Asessment component of the Working Group on Protection and Control of Water Quality. He was based in Uganda for 3 years working with the Ministry of Health on the DFID Research Project (R6874) which produced many of the lessons reflected in the manual. He has undertaken long and short-term assignments in over 20 low and middle-income countries in Africa, Asia, Latin America and Central Europe, including working for ActionAid in Sierra Leone in the early 1990s. The main focus of the editor's work in the monitoring of water supplies and development of risk assessment and risk management methods in relation to environmental health.

Acknowledgements

The Editor would like to thank the following for their valuable contributions to this publication:

John Hubley, Health Education Consultant, Leeds, UK
(contributions to chapter 14)

Margaret Ince, WEDC, Loughborough University, UK
(contributions to chapter 7)

Joanna Teuton, Centre for Applied Psychology, Leicester University, UK
(contributions to chapter 9)

Heikke Wihuri, IRC, Delft, Netherlands
(contributions to chapter 1)

The approaches outlined were developed by a project team working in Uganda, Bangladesh and Ghana between 1997 and 2001. Grateful thanks are due to following for their input into this research:

Paul Luyima, Assistant Commissioner for Health Services-Environmental Health Division, Ministry of Health, Kampala, Uganda
Robert Odongo, Senior Health Environmentalist, Environmental Health Division, Ministry of Health, Kampala, Uganda
Caroline Hunt, London School of Hygiene and Tropical Medicine, University of London, UK
John Lewis, Data Processing, Aberdare, UK
Joanna Teuton, Centre for Applied Psychology, Leicester University, UK

Han Heijnen, Environmental Health Advisor, World Health Organization, Dhaka, Bangladesh
Sarit Datta Gupta, Chief Engineer, Rajshahi City Corporation, Bangladesh
Gul Bahar Sarkar, Chemist, World Health Organization, Dhaka, Bangladesh,
Jonas Jabulo and colleagues, Ghana Water Company Ltd, Accra, Ghana
Wisdom, Aditey, Lynda Osafo and Carrie Bell, Accra Metropolitan Environmental Health Initiative, Accra, Ghana

The photograph on the front cover shows a public tap in Lusaka, Zambia
(Source: Guy Howard)

Contents

1.

Introduction

The purpose of this manual is to present the methods employed in the implementation of surveillance of water supplies in urban areas, particularly those of developing countries and to outline the strategies necessary to ensure that surveillance is effective. It is also concerned with developing linkages between surveillance and improvements in water supply.

The layout of this document is intended to reflect the key activities in water surveillance programmes and the use of such data in urban areas. The first Chapter provides an introduction to surveillance, and Chapter 2 discusses the nature of urban areas in developing countries and the implications for the development of surveillance and improvement strategies. Chapters 3, 4 and 5 review the basic institutional and planning issues and the indicators used in surveillance programmes. The following chapters then cover the procedures used in the collection of information. Chapter 6 covers sanitary inspection with Chapters 7 and 8 discuss analytical ranges and sampling design for water quality analysis. Chapter 9 reviews social surveys within surveillance programmes and Chapter 10 covers information management and analysis. The final four chapters deal with the use of surveillance data in variety of settings. Chapter 11 reviews the role of regulation, Chapter 12 reviews the use of surveillance in policy making, Chapter 13 discussed technical and environmental interventions to improve water supplies and Chapter 14 discussed surveillance and hygiene education. The Annexes at the end of this document provide examples of the tools that may be used in surveillance programmes within developing countries.

1.1 Target audience and links with other documents

This document is designed for managers of surveillance programmes and aims to provide material on a wide-range of issues related to the surveillance and improvement of drinking-water supplies. It is part of a series of documents that deal with different aspects of surveillance and which have different target audiences. There is a short guide for the implementation of surveillance activities in the field, which concentrates on practical issues relating to field-based collection of surveillance data. There is also a guide for co-ordinators that deals with the day to day management and planning issues for surveillance, which is available at the watermark web-site (www.lboro.ac.uk). This web-site also contains of teaching materials to support the delivery of basic training in water surveillance techniques.

The purpose of this guide is help programme managers plan and implement surveillance programmes and to guide them in the use of the data generated to improve water supplies. It provides a detailed overview of the issues related to surveillance and aims to provide a comprehensive discussion of approaches that may be adopted to assist in the decision-making process.

The document was developed as a part of a project to develop low-cost, decentralised system of water supply surveillance in urban areas in Uganda, which was supported by the Department for International Development (UK) under the Knowledge Action Research programme of the Infrastructure and Urban Development Department. Additional support came from WHO Uganda and WHO Geneva. The material was further tested in programmes in Bangladesh and Ghana and was also used in Kosovo. Whilst the focus of this document is on the development of surveillance programmes in urban areas, it is hoped that the information contained in the document will also help managers planning surveillance programmes in rural areas.

1.2 Water and health

Water has a profound effect on human health both as a means to reduce disease and a media through which disease-causing agents may be transmitted. The impact of water on health derives principally from the consumption of water containing pathogenic organisms or toxic chemicals and the use of inadequate volumes of water that lead to poor hygiene. In turn, these are influenced by a number of factors that can be directly measured as indicators of water supply adequacy: continuity in supply; access and distance to recognisable (usually public) water supplies or sources; the cost of water purchased; and, the amount of water lost within the supply.

In the 2nd edition of Guidelines for Drinking-Water Quality, Volume 1, published in 1993, WHO define surveillance as being: 'the continuous and vigilant oversight of drinking water supplies from a public health perspective'. In the 2nd edition of Volume 3 of the Guidelines, published in 1997, a further definition is given as 'investigative activity that is designed to identify faults in water supplies, evaluate their importance to health and identify appropriate actions to improve the water supply'.

Water supply surveillance is therefore designed to protect public health through the identification of inadequacies and by promoting timely implementation of action to control risks. Surveillance must, therefore, take into account that there are a wide range of influences on health derived from water supply and that a broad-based system of data collection and interpretation is needed. A focus on any single issue alone will not be adequate to provide the information required to protect public health.

Surveillance programmes are also designed to provide an independent verification of the degree to which the water sector is meeting basic right on people to a safe and adequate water supply is being met. Access to safe and adequate water supply may be restricted due to prohibitive charges, daily or seasonal fluctuations in availability or failure to extend supplies to low-income or informal settlements. The cost of water purchased from neighbours or from public facilities may represent a significant proportion of family income and limit the amount of water that may be collected each day. The continuity of supply may be poor due to weak operation and maintenance of the supply, thus forcing families to use reduced volumes of water and store water. Elsewhere, seasonal, geographical and hydrological factors may deny individual households or entire communities a continuous, reliable supply of drinking water. During dry seasons, spring sources may dwindle, reservoirs may empty and excessive demands by one group may compromise the needs of their neighbours.

Surveillance may also be used to assess whether certain groups are disadvantaged or are particularly vulnerable to risks from poor supply. Access to services in urban areas of developing countries is often highly inequitable, with a few areas receiving high quality services, with other (usually low-income communities) having very limited access to water supplies and where at best only communal facilities are provided. Where water is provided through communal facilities, such as public taps and point sources, volumes of water collected may be limited and the use of multiple sources is likely, some of which may be highly contaminated. Water from such sources may need to be stored within the home and this may represent a particular problem in maintaining high quality water.

1.2.1 Health implications

The provision of water was one of the eight components of primary health care identified by the World Health Assembly in Alma Ata in 1978. The Alma Ata Declaration on Primary Health Care expanded the concept of health care to include broader concepts of affordability, accessibility, self-reliance, inter-sectoral collaboration, community participation, sustainability and social justice.

In most countries the principal risks to human health associated with the consumption of polluted water are microbiological in nature, although there are significant concerns about chemical contamination. As indicated in Chapter 19 of 'Agenda 21' of UNCED:

'An estimated 80 per cent of all diseases and over one third of deaths in developing countries are caused by the consumption of contaminated water and on average as much as one tenth of each persons productive time is sacrificed to water-related diseases.'

The risk of acquiring a waterborne infection increases with the level of contamination by pathogenic micro-organisms. However, the relationship is not simple and depends on factors such as infectious dose and host susceptibility. Drinking-water is only one way for the transmission of such pathogens, some agents may be transmitted from person to person, or through the contamination of food. In many cases, poor personal hygiene may lead to the transmission of pathogenic organisms through contamination of water stored within the home or by preparation of food. Excreta disposal is also critical as a first barrier to disease transmission.

Therefore, the reduction of morbidity and mortality from infectious diarrhoeal diseases requires improvements in the quality and availability of water, excreta disposal and general personal and environmental hygiene. Different aspects of environmental health improvement may be critical in different circumstances and will be determined by the current health burden, economic development and availability of services, as well nutritional and immune-status.

Water quality control is critical in reducing the potential for explosive epidemic events as contaminated drinking water supply is one of the most effective methods for mass transmission of pathogens to a large population. However, water quality may be critical to control during times of epidemic outbreaks, but no more important than other aspects in controlling endemic disease. Equally important to improvement in health is to recognise that different interventions may yield the greatest impact in different urban communities and at different times within the same community. Surveillance of water supply can contribute to this by addressing the health consequences of poor quality of water and poor hygiene in relation to water storage, as well as identifying the need to reduce faecal loading in the environment as means to prevent contamination of water.

Surveillance programmes collect data on indicators of water supply service quality and has been found to be useful in orientating improvement programmes. In addition, indicators of hygiene practices should also be used by surveillance programmes. Such indicators should be based on simple, standardised observations in order to identify particular high-risk behaviours and thus inform hygiene education programmes. Surveillance has an important role in promoting participatory approaches to hygiene education which have been shown to be one of the most effective means of learning.

1.3 Water quality

The quality of the water consumed is important in the control of infectious diseases and other health problems. The overwhelming priority for drinking water supplies of all types is the control of microbiological quality and in particular reducing the number of pathogens (disease-causing microbes) in drinking water. It is these agents that lead to the outbreaks of infectious water-borne disease that affect millions of people world-wide leading to high mortality and morbidity rates, particularly in vulnerable groups such as the very young, old and immune-compromised.

Some aspects of water supply (such as colour, odour, taste and turbidity) are also critical as consumers may reject water of otherwise good quality that is unpalatable and use other sources of much lower quality and greater risk to their health. Chemical quality of water is generally a far lower priority as the majority of the impact of poor chemical water quality is chronic rather than acute. There are some exceptions to this and some chemicals, notably nitrate, arsenic and fluoride, are often included in routine surveillance or monitoring programmes.

To ensure that a supply of drinking-water is at relatively low risk of containing pathogenic organisms, it is important that samples should be examined regularly for indicators of faecal pollution, in general *E.coli* or as a substitute, thermotolerant (faecal) coliforms, as discussed in Chapter 7. However, care should be taken when interpreting the results of microbiological analysis based on such indicators as their absence does not provide complete proof of absence of pathogens, but rather that the risk of large numbers of pathogens being present is relatively low.

The WHO Guidelines are based on the risk to health from contaminated water supplies and do not address with issues of achievability. In general, these Guideline Values are only likely to be achieved by chlorinated water supplies, although deeper point sources may perform well. In urban areas of developing countries, the use of point sources is common amongst the urban poor and these sources may represent the principal risk to public health from poor water supply, as many will not meet Guideline Values on a sustained basis. In these circumstances, the use of interim water quality objectives may be more effective in improving water quality progressively than trying to apply stringent standards.

In piped water supply, the Guidelines Values should generally be achieved. However, poor treatment, interruptions in supply, large levels of water loss and back-siphonage may make piped water supply of poor quality. Water quality often deteriorates within distribution due to leakage, biofilm development within pipes and loss of disinfectant residuals that provide ongoing protection. The control of drinking water quality in distribution remains a major challenge in many urban areas of developing countries.

Many households in low-income communities will not have piped water supplied to their home and thus will use a variety of communal sources where protection and maintenance will be required. Of particular importance is the maintenance of sanitary protection measures around sources (including public taps) and ensuring that systematic preventative maintenance is carried out. These tasks will typically involve monetary contribution in urban areas, as the donation of labour may be less feasible. Therefore, critical to the maintenance of good water supplies is to ensure that communal sources are well-maintained and financially viable.

When water is collected from communal sources, the contamination of good quality water during transport, storage and handling is common. Therefore, it is essential that interventions for maintaining good quality water also focus on the improvement of water management in the home. This will typically take the form of health education activities, but may also involve the promotion of treatment within the home.

As the principal risks to human health associated with drinking water are microbiological, there is a greater reliance on relatively few water quality parameters in order to establish the hygienic safety of these supplies. This may be referred to as 'minimum monitoring' or 'critical parameter testing'. This approach assumes that health authorities will be aware of other specific sources of risk in each area such as chemical contamination and will include these in the monitoring scheme as appropriate. However, there is a basic principle that it is much more effective to test for a narrow range of key parameters as frequently as possible with complementary sanitary inspection, rather than conducting comprehensive but lengthy and largely irrelevant analyses less frequently.

Other water quality parameters may be included by the surveillance body if these are known to be present in the source waters and represent a risk to health or cause rejection of a supply. Some chemical substances are of particular concern, however, in particular nitrate, arsenic and fluoride.

Nitrate is linked to methaemoglobinaemia in children. The presence of nitrate in water may be due to excessive applications of fertilisers, on-site sanitation and the leaching of wastewater or other organic wastes into surface and groundwater. The lack of solid waste management in countries where large volumes of organic waste are produced (as for instance is common in most African cities) may lead to rapid increases in nitrate in drinking water supplies.

Exposure to high levels of naturally-occurring fluoride can lead to mottling of teeth and (in severe cases) skeletal fluorosis and crippling. Similarly, arsenic may occur naturally and exposure via drinking-water may result in risk to health. In areas with aggressive or acidic waters, the use of lead pipes, water fittings or solder can result in elevation of lead levels in drinking-water which may, after long term exposure, affect the mental development of children.

1.4 Water quantity

As well as acting as a carrier for microbes which can cause disease, a reliable, safe water supply plays an important role in prevention of disease, especially by facilitating personal, domestic and food hygiene.

The diseases which are most affected by provision of adequate quantities of water for hygiene purposes are referred to as 'water washed'. The diseases that are affected by availability and use of water for hygienic purposes may be classified into three groups:

(i) the faecal-orally transmitted diseases such as Hepatitis A, bacillary dysentery and many diarrhoeal diseases. Improved hygiene contributes to their control by preventing the transmission of pathogens from dirty hands directly to the mouth, to food or into water;

(ii) infections of the skin and eyes such as trachoma and fungal skin diseases;

(iii) infections carried by lice or mites. Good personal hygiene can assist in the control of these. Examples include scabies and louse-borne epidemic typhus.

The quantity of water that is used will be largely determined by the level of service provided and there is strong evidence that once a water source is beyond the immediate home area, the volume used will drop significantly. The cost of water may similarly also affect the quantity of water used, as may regular interruption to the supply.

Improving the quantities of water available will be dependent on ensuring that water supplies are close, affordable and reliable. Improvements in both quality and quantity will inevitably incur costs and this may at times be translated into higher prices for consumers. It is critical that improvements in one aspect of water supply (for instance quality) does lead to greater problems due to increased costs. An example of this is when water quality improvements in piped water supplies lead to increased tariff and increased numbers of people utilising other, less safe and convenient sources.

1.5 Organisational issues in surveillance and monitoring

There is a need for both independent monitoring of drinking water supply by a surveillance body and for monitoring by the water supplier. Evidence suggests that these are essential and complementary activities. However, the objectives and scope of each programme will be different. This manual covers issues of use to both water suppliers and surveillance agencies and collaboration between surveillance and supply agencies is important to promote better control of drinking water supplies in urban areas.

The aim of surveillance is to undertake routine, independent monitoring of the water supply from a public health basis. This means that surveillance activities will include collection of a wide range of information of variables that may affect public health such as water quality, quantity, access, cost and use patterns. The surveillance body will take responsibility for monitoring all water supplies within the urban area and will include assessments up to the point of consumption. The surveillance agency, therefore, will undertake a wide range of activities and interact with a variety of organisations, including community groups and water suppliers and aim to influence and initiate interventions on a wide range of issues.

The lead agency for surveillance at a national level can be either a Ministry of Health or Ministry of Environment. However, the lead agency should contain environmental health professionals with a broad range of skills and expertise in the water and environmental health activities and able to apply their knowledge in a number of fields. Implementation of surveillance should be carried out at the local level using cost-effective approaches that allow easy collection, dissemination and use of data at local levels. Local environmental health staff in most countries work closely with the communities that they serve and who have skills in participatory approaches that allow improvements to be sustained. Typically local surveillance includes water quality analysis and sanitary inspection as well as social surveys and hygiene evaluation. Surveillance should not be restricted to a physical science or engineering activity, but address social, economic and environmental issues.

Monitoring by water suppliers should be ensure compliance with current national standards and norms covering water supply provision. The water supplier has a duty of care to ensure that the water produced is safe and wholesome for consumption and undertake water quality analysis, sanitary inspection as well as preventative maintenance and proper operation of head works and distribution networks. Water suppliers will also be expected to ensure that losses of water from the system are kept to a reasonable minimum to ensure both efficiency and environmental sustainability.

In addition to the development of surveillance and supplier quality control monitoring, the promotion of community participation in both monitoring and improving water supplies is critical. In many communities, the water sources available may be point sources managed by community organisations and it is important that the surveillance body supports the development of the community participation in monitoring risks in their supply and in ensuring good operation and maintenance. Where piped water is primarily used, community participation in managing public taps and the environment through which pipes pass and taps are erected is also important. Developing the links between communities and suppliers for fault reporting is also an important component of improvements in water supply and surveillance.

1.6 Objectives for surveillance in urban areas

In common with all monitoring programmes, it is important that surveillance programmes are able to provide information that is useful for management decisions. It is therefore important to define objectives for surveillance programmes. There are three key objectives for surveillance can provide the overall direction in developing the surveillance programme:

1. To assess the adequacy of water supply and to identify the potential risks to health derived from poor water supply(s) or water handling;

2. To assess whether certain groups are particularly disadvantaged from inadequacy of water supply;

3. To identify what actions would lead to improvement in the water supply and likely health gain or reduce social disadvantage.

These overall objectives help define what data needs to be collected and the information needs required. They also help in identifying target audiences, who may be expected to include health professionals, water suppliers, policy makers and planners and communities.

Further objectives and questions can be identified to provide further refinement of the monitoring programme. These may include aspects such as compliance with standards and norms, environmental health trends, trends in water supply adequacy and evaluations of specific interventions in water supply or hygiene.

1.7 Surveillance and improvement of water supplies

Surveillance activities should be linked to a process of improvement in water supply and not simply a data collection exercise. However, the purpose of surveillance should be to promote decisions that are well-informed and rational and therefore there is often a need to develop convincing arguments based on significant amounts of data. Immediate reactions to single assessments are often inadvisable, as there may serious concerns about how representative the data collected has been.

A monitoring and surveillance strategy which aims at step by step improvement in water supply is more likely to bring sustainable improvements than a strategy that is academically correct, but requires a major leap in technology, management or financing and does not coincide with the daily reality of the service users. As a result, improvements are likely to be incremental and not restricted to a single type of intervention or water supply.

Surveillance should contribute to the improvement of water supply at several levels through policy, technical, environmental, social and institutional mechanisms. One approach to improving urban water supply is through the development of regulatory frameworks and enforcement of existing standards and legislation. The urban water sector is in many ways more amenable to such approaches than rural water supplies as the service provided to at least a significant proportion of the population is likely to be done by a utility. However, in areas where significant use of community-managed water supplies is found, the role of regulation may be less important, as such supplies are not amenable to regulation and standards. Regulation should also cover a range of issues and integration is important to prevent conflicts arising. The unnecessary enforcement of standards of limited importance to health may create greater health problems as the cost of water increase and access decreases. Enforcement of legislation regarding social provision and environmental protection is often as effective as enforcing compliance with standards.

Surveillance can influence policy in water supply by providing reliable information about the risks to health that result from practices and policies in water supply and by making recommendations regarding changes in policy that will promote improved water supply and act as an incentive to suppliers and users of water services. This may include the improvement of non-piped water sources to meet short-term needs as well as financial arrangements for piped water supply. Surveillance programmes should facilitate the process of establishing national, regional and community priorities and actions.

Technical improvements in the design, operation and maintenance of sources should also be improved through surveillance activities that identify faults and recommend specific actions. Such technical interventions will apply equally to utility supplies and community-managed sources, including both point sources and public taps. Environmental interventions may be required to protect and manage sources used and to ensure that sources used for domestic supply are sustained both in terms of quantity and quality. Environmental interventions may also be required at community levels to reduce contamination of water supplies.

Surveillance should also lead to appropriate social interventions that promote improved management of water up to the point of consumption. The development of appropriate hygiene education programmes that maximise the potential for participation by community and individuals may be informed by data collected through surveillance activities. However, other social interventions may be needed such as improved community management of communal sources, better financial management of communally owned water sources and promotion of community-based interventions that promote safe water chains such as provision of household water treatment chemical and devices.

In the long-term, surveillance and monitoring should be geared towards improvement and maintenance of water supplies that represent a limited risk to the health of the users. It is an ongoing activity whose focus and data collection methods may vary with time and in different countries, reflecting the changing nature of health risks.

1.8 Costs of surveillance

Any activity that involves the collection of data tends to incur costs. In surveillance programmes, such costs will include the staff time involved in collecting and reporting data, transport for staff to collect data, purchase of consumables for water quality analysis, electricity to run incubators and costs of printing and copying forms and reports.

The costs of surveillance can be reduced if it is decentralised as this can reduce the costs of staff time and transport. Where centralised approaches are used, costs will inevitably rise as distances that must be travelled will increase. Costs of water quality analysis can be reduced by using portable on-site testing equipment. This has many other benefits as it reduces the potential for sample deterioration where laboratories are located far from the sample site and because they can used as a hygiene education tool. Water quality analysis costs can be further reduced by maximising the use of sanitary inspection and developing realistic programmes of water sampling.

The use of decentralised approaches will also help to maximise the use of data and in particular to promote local solutions to problems. This may be particularly important when community-based approaches are required and when using surveillance as part of hygiene education.

Surveillance must be cost-effective and linked to the needs of communities and decision-makers in urban areas to retain relevance. Therefore, it is essential that the information generated is of use to planners, communities and water suppliers. This means that objectives should be regularly reviewed and discussed with stakeholders and that data should properly managed and analysed.

2.

Urban areas

The definition of what constitutes an urban area varies significantly between different countries and regions. Such definitions reflect the nature and range of sizes of human settlements and population size within each country. The way in which urban areas are defined often has an impact on the development of surveillance and improvement of water supply. Urban boundaries may also reflect boundaries in terms of access to funds, the types of service that are provided and the ability of users to demand and manage their own services.

Urban areas include a wide range of settlement sizes and types from the small rural town, through local towns of populations of several tens to hundreds of thousands, to large centres of one million or more inhabitants up to the mega-cities of tens of millions of people. The different types of urban settlement – extreme, large, medium and small all have difficulties in water supply provision and surveillance due to population and physical size, complexity of communities, incomes and water source availability. In reality there is a continuum between rural and urban areas that show gradual changes both in population density and in the economic outlook and nature of the population.

Urban areas are often seen as being better served with basic services such as water supply, sanitation, education and health services than their rural counterparts. Access to services often varies enormously, depending on the legal status of dwellings. In many towns and cities, the majority of the population frequently lacks access to services of a higher level than their rural counterparts and often live in more contaminated environments. There is often great inequality in service access and socio-economic status between different parts of cities and between different urban areas.

2.1 Urban growth

The proportion of the global population that resides in urban areas is increasing rapidly particularly in developing countries. The growth of urban populations occurs through two, often complementary, processes: natural increase due to high fertility rates; and, rural-urban migration. These processes often interact as migration leads to increasing numbers of urban residents, which leads to greater natural increase in the urban population. This may be further enhanced where migrants are young, leading to an overall younger urban population in comparison to its rural counterparts and hence greater fertility. Both may also lead to increasing urbanisation as differentials in age structure between rural and urban areas and ongoing migration result in an increasing proportion of the population that is urban.

Rapidly increasing urban populations place a strain of service provision. Demands are often not easy to predict nor to satisfy without major capital investment. Factors such as legality of tenure and poverty often further hamper service provision. The way in which services are charged in particular may make access to water supplies difficult where these are very different from the income patterns. Households that have insecure incomes find difficulties in paying bills that require them to save money over several weeks or months. Equally, initial capital investments may be difficult to make where incomes are low and access to credit is limited or non-existent. This may be exacerbated in some countries where migrants to urban areas do not perceive the move to be permanent and they prefer to spend accumulated capital in their home rural areas. Many poor households live in rented accommodation. If water supply provision does not take this into account, the net result may be an increase in rents that cannot be afforded and results in the household being forced to move to another area with lower rents and few services.

However, service provision to the poor is achievable. What is perhaps of greatest importance is that water supplies and other services are provided in response to the demands and desires of the urban poor. Many poor people already spend more on gaining limited amounts of water from sources or poor quality and reliability and therefore show that they are willing and able to pay for water services. What is important is that the water supplies that are provided in way that meets the demands and capacities of the urban poor. This means that flexibility in service provision is essential and often incremental improvements in water supply or water hygiene lead to significant health and socio-economic gains among the poor. Surveillance can assist in this process by generating information that supports flexibility in service provision by identifying current failures in water supply and offering solutions to overcoming these.

2.1.1 Meeting the needs of the poor

The low-income areas in most cities and towns in developing countries are where health burdens are greatest because of poor service provision and contaminated environments. The populations in such settlements typically pay comparatively more for poorer water supplies, largely because they are unable to access services that provide lower ongoing costs because the capital investment is high. Typically services are communal and as a result lower volumes of water are used, compromising hygiene. Water quality is often worse both at the source and within the home. These areas should be priorities for surveillance activities and improvement of water supply and not those areas served by services at higher levels.

There is growing recognition that community involvement in the delivery of services in urban areas is essential for sustainability of water supplies. In the past, community participation was primarily considered a rural approach with urban populations expected to be supplied through utilities. However, the lack of progress in increasing access to safe and adequate water supplies and the significant problems found in sustaining publicly provided facilities has emphasised the role of the community in taking responsibility for maintaining water supplies.

It has often been concluded that because urban populations are heterogeneous with people from many different ethnic, religious and socio-economic backgrounds living together that the potential for community participation in service delivery was difficult in urban areas.
However, although when taken overall the population of urban areas tend to be very heterogeneous, most urban areas are actually composed of a variety of small communities within an administrative boundary, which are often relatively homogenous. Migrants frequently move to areas where others from the same area or ethnic/religious group already live. Such settlements often represent areas where community-based activities can be implemented.

One important element in surveillance is to approach urban areas from the perspective that they are large aggregations of small communities rather than a single large entity. The involvement of communities in surveillance and improvement of water supplies is therefore possible and highly desirable, particularly in low-income communities where the provision of services may be limited to public facilities and communities may have to take a significant amount of responsibility for management, operation and maintenance. In addition, as much of the water available may be provided through informal sale of water by vendors or households with a direct connection to the utility supply, community-orientated approaches will be essential to ensure that costs of water are affordable and the quality of water is good.

There are several major economic, technical, institutional, and legal problems in serving the urban poor with fresh drinking water. The Water Supply and Sanitation Collaborative Council (WSSCC) Working Group on Urbanisation came to the conclusion that achievement of sustainable progress in the extension of water supply and sanitation coverage to low-income urban and peri-urban areas has been hampered by two issues, which have largely been neglected in the past:

1. Knowledge of the low-income urban sector, coupled with failure to appreciate its importance, which has caused technological, economic and institutional mistakes.

2. Enabling sector institutions to recover both capital and operating costs and to gain access to financial resources is crucial.

The following table presents a categorisation of different low-income urban areas, the text in bold in table 2.1 shows the type of water supply and sanitation problems in each type of settlement.

Location	Legally occupied areas	Semi-legally or illegally occupied areas
Central city	Inner city slum. Poor living conditions result from poor maintenance and repair, and overcrowding. Congestion may hamper service provision, but offers economies of scale for piped water.	Small squatter areas on redevelopment sites and public land. Very low security of tenure. Improvements will have to be community-based, but insecurity of tenure may influence sustainability.
Within official boundaries of urban area	Low-income housing areas of different types. Poor environmental conditions result from poor planning and deterioration of existing services. Improvement of O&M and encouragement of community involvement required.	Old squatter areas unsuitably located. Poor environmental conditions due to flooding, inadequate service provision, and poor layout. Community-based approaches required, technical and environmental problems may limit technology choice.
Outside official boundaries, but fully occupied	Low-income housing areas of different types. Poor conditions result from inadequate and irregular service provision and institutional problems. Improve supply performance and encourage community-based approaches.	Squatter areas and passively urbanised villages. Not serviced. Deterioration of conditions with gradually increased densities. Provision of community-managed public taps and point sources.
Urban fringe, in process of urbanisation	Planned but unserved plot development. Environmental conditions not necessarily poor. Potential for successful service provision at higher levels and public facilities.	Unplanned and unserved plot development. Often with poor layout. Environmental conditions not necessarily poor, but high potential to degradation through unplanned development. Community-based approaches emphasise environmental maintenance and lobby for service provision.

Table 2.1: Low-income urban areas

2.2 Urban zoning for surveillance

One of the constraints facing health bodies in low-income countries when trying to develop routine surveillance is that the population to be covered is diverse, unevenly distributed and is likely to use a wide range of water sources of different quality, susceptibility to contamination and service level. In addition, in larger towns, there are high populations and the physical area to be covered may be large. For instance in Kampala, Uganda the administrative area is $160km^2$ and is home to roughly 1.2 million people in Parishes whose equivalent population densities range from over 30,000 people to 600 per km^2 and whose total population ranges from 3,000 to 21,000.

A critical role in developing surveillance, particularly where resources are limited, is to target activities on those communities with the least access to higher service levels of water supply and who are at greatest risk from infectious disease. In many urban areas of low and some middle income countries, relatively few people have access to water supply at least a yard level and the urban poor will typically collect water from communal sources. Multiple sources of water may be used because of distance, cost and reliability factors. In these circumstances, it is more effective to divide the urban area up into discrete zones taking into account factors such as socio-economic level, population density and water source use patterns. When applied systematically, such zoning can categorise each community and can group different communities in terms of similar category. These can be ranked in terms of their priority for surveillance, thus allowing activities to focus on the urban poor.

Zoning of urban may be achieved through a variety of means using either qualitative or quantitative measures of socio-economic status and risk. In Bangladesh and Ghana, priority areas were selected on the basis of previous studies of urban poverty and through local knowledge.

In Peru in the early 1990s, a rapid process of 'zoning' of urban areas was achieved through a qualitative exercise involving technical staff 'walking' an area. This allowed the street arrangement and housing to be verified against whatever maps were available. A sample of households (one house per 'side block') which were visited to determine the means of provision of drinking-water. On the basis of the results obtained the urban area was divided with respect to dominant means of water supply provision, which bore little relationship to administrative boundaries. One effect of this zoning was to bring small often 'informal' urban settlements often of very high density, low service provision and perceived high vulnerability into the surveillance programme.

For public health reasons greatest attention was paid to urban fringe areas where the greatest populations depended on unpiped supplies. In some cases this was through 'vertical' targeted activities that were outside the simple flow of organised surveillance. An example of this concerned a direct assessment of the effectiveness of tanker truck deliveries (which support a large proportion of the population without access to piped water in some areas). These activities lead directly to improvements in volumes of water supplied through simple measures.

2.2.1 Zoning in Uganda

In Uganda, zoning was achieved through use of a quantitative index based on data on the following:

1. Socio-economic status

2. Population density

3. Water availability and use (the 'water economy')

When combined, these factors can provide a robust mechanism for planning surveillance and for prioritising activities in most vulnerable areas. Essentially they work in 3 levels of stratification with socio-economic status defining the first level of stratification, population density the second level and water economy the third level. Effectively, socio-economic status is used to broadly define different areas into high, medium and low income. As activities should be targeted in low-income groups this provides the first step in the stratification. The population density can then be used to categorise different low-income areas into high, medium and low density. The water economy is used both to categorise similar low-income population density areas by their water economy in order to identify those areas likely to be at greatest risk, usually related to the level of use of non-piped or poorly protected point sources.

Socio-economic status is used because risks to health are closely related to the socio-economic status of a household. Studies have show that poorer the family, the greater the likelihood of suffering from an infectious disease. This is likely to be due many factors including the use of inadequate volumes of water where this must be collected and/or paid for, use of unsafe water sources as well as poor nutrition, lower education levels and limited access to services. Furthermore, the nature of many such settlements makes them more prone to unreliability in the piped supply and more likely to be disconnected where aggressive disconnection policies are followed.

Population density is important, as contamination may be expected to be greater given the larger numbers and concentration of pollutant sources and pathways within the community. Where direct connections are low, the numbers of people using a particular source or tap may increase, as proximity is likely to be a driving force in source selection. Furthermore, higher population densities clearly will increase the possibility of pathogen transmission by person-person and contamination of food from poor hygiene. Thus if a pathogen is introduced through the water supply not only can it be expected that significant numbers of people will be exposed but also its subsequent transmission is easier.

The water economy is important because it helps to define the vulnerability of different communities to disease based on the level of services, the types of water source used and the quality, reliability and cost of water from these sources. It also informs where samples for water quality analysis should be taken from. The water economy measure is composed of assessments of the level of direct connection, the availability of different source types and the use of different sources both in terms of the type of use of the water and in terms of relative priority for consumption.

2.2.1 Socio-economic status
It is important to define socio-economic status if a focus is to be maintained on the urban poor. In general, the income earned by the household is of little use when defining socio-economic status as this may have little relevance in terms of access to services. For instance, government workers may receive what appear to be very low wages. However, many are

provided with subsidised housing of a far higher quality than they could afford on the open market. These houses may often include services for which the occupiers do not pay the full market price. Furthermore, such workers may access to other subsidies such as transport, food or allowances that make their wages incidental. Equally, many families may earn relatively large sums of money but because full market rates are paid for rent, food and transport, they cannot afford to live in well-built houses or well-planned areas. It should also be noted that as many low-income families operate at least partly in the informal economy, it will be difficult if not impossible to obtain a reliable figure for earnings.

Socio-economic status is therefore best defined by using a multi-factorial index that draws on recent data such as a census. There are no hard and fast rules about the selection of factors that should be incorporated within any particular index as this will vary between countries and may also be determined by the availability of data. In Uganda, the index used a total of 6 factors. These factors were selected on the basis of discussion with professionals working in urban areas as to which were most associated with the socio-economic status and were drawn from the most recent census to allow a quantified approach to be adopted without the need for additional data collection.

Within the variables selected, some were felt to be better proxy measures than others and therefore were weighted accordingly. The weights allocated to each variable are an indication of the sensitivity of that proxy to socio-economic status. The higher the weighting score, the greater the sensitivity of the proxy to socio-economic status, with a weight 1 indicating relatively low sensitivity. The groups were asked to initially rank the variables in relation to their sensitivity to socio-economic status and discuss the strength of difference between variables in terms of their sensitivity. The variables and weights are shown in Table 2.4.

The next stage was to provide scores within each variable to reflect the range of conditions from low, through medium to high socio-economic status. The basic purpose of this is to reflect the socio-economic condition that, for instance, the use of tiles, iron sheets and grass for roofing indicate. The range of scores allowed for a variable was −5 to +5, with −5 reflecting very low income, +5 reflecting high income and 0 representing an average condition. The conditions within each variable and the weighted score of each is shown in table 2.4.

A score for each Parish was then calculated by multiplying the percentage of households in each Parish that had the characteristics of the conditions in each variable by the score given to that condition and then summing these to provide a cumulative score for the variable. These were converted into proportions and transformed into a weighted score by dividing the cumulative score by the total percentage. The mean (average) weighted score for all Parishes was then obtained by adding the cumulative scores for all of the Parishes and dividing this by the total number of Parishes. The standard deviation of the weighted scores for all Parishes was also calculated.

Using the average and standard deviation of the weighted scores, a standardised score was calculated for each variable in each Parish by subtracting the mean value from the weighted score and dividing it by the standard deviation. The purpose of the standardisation was to ensure that a score was equivalent across all variables in terms of reflecting a socio-economic level. The scores for each variable for each Parish were then added up to provide a final index score.

Estimates of socio-economic status are important if a focus is to be maintained on low-income groups. For instance, those Parishes in Kampala that were categorised as high income were not routinely covered by the surveillance programme and medium socio-economic status Parishes received a far lower frequency of water quality analysis and sanitary inspection than low-income areas. This approach was followed as resources were limited and a strong focus was required on the poor. The higher socio-economic groups already enjoy a wide range of services (including water) at much higher levels of service than the poor. Furthermore, such groups would receive protection through routine water quality analysis programmes followed by the water supplier.

Variable	Variable weight	Conditions	Score
Roof material	4.0	Iron sheets	0
		Tiles	5
		Asbestos sheets	1
		Concrete	5
		Papyrus	-3
		Grass	-4
		Banana leaves/fibre	-5
		Other	-5
Floor material	4.0	Concrete	-1
		Brick	1
		Stone	4
		Cement screed	0
		Rammed earth	-5
		Wood	3.5
		Other	-5
Persons per room	2.5	<1.7	1.5
		1.8-2.1	1
		>2.1	-1.5
Educational attainment	2.0	None – male	-3
		None – female	-3
		P1-P7 – male	0
		P1-P7 – female	0
		S1-S4 – male	2
		S1-S4 – female	2
		S5-S6 – male	2
		S5-S6 – female	2
		University – male	3
		University – female	3
Main source of livelihood	2.0	Subsistence farming	3.5
		Commercial farming	4
		Petty trading	-4
		Formal trading	1
		Cottage industry	-1.5
		Property income	4.5
		Employment income	0
		Family support	-5
		Other	-4.5
Average household size	1.0	<3.4	1.5
		3.4 – 4.3	1
		4.4. – 4.7	-1.5
		>4.7	-1.5

Table 2.4 Socio-economic index variables and conditions with weightings

2.2.2 Demography

As already discussed, population density and population totals are important components of the zoning process. Population density may need to be estimated unless there has been a very recent census (i.e. within 1 year). Where the census was some time ago, the population at any given years can be calculated using the recorded population growth over a 10 year period to the power of the number of intervening years.

This will only be estimate as often city-wide growth rates have to be used, whilst growth may be more concentrated in particular areas of the city or town. However, it provides a simple mechanism for determining population without the need for expensive data collection. Density of population can then be calculated provided the area of the Parish or settlement is known or can be estimated.

2.2.3 Water economy

The water economy is a key component of the zoning process. This approach helps inform which sources should be sampled and the likely importance of testing household water. It is important to review data relating to a series of factors including:

- Direct household connection rates

- Availability of sources to the unserved population (this may include protected and unprotected point sources as well estimates of the likelihood of piped source use based on connection figures)

- Water use patterns covering the use of different types of source and the numbers of people using multiple sources and supplementing water at a household level through rainwater collection or purchase from vendors. When multiple sources are used it is essential to known whether all sources are used for drinking and cooking or whether there is a differentiation between different sources in terms of use.

Household connection rates are best collected from water suppliers where records are kept up to date. If this data is not available, it will be very difficult to make any estimates of this without undertaking a census style survey. If this is not possible, great caution should be taken before trying to estimate numbers of connections from a sample. There can be very significant differences between areas of similar socio-economic score in terms of connection (e.g. in Kampala this ranged from 2.5% to 50%). Even within one small area, connections may be concentrated in certain parts, making identification of total connections difficult.

An inventory should be undertaken as the first stage of the surveillance programme, as discussed in Chapter 4. The inventory should identify all the sources that are available for people not served by their own connection. This will usually include taps, both public and individuals with their own connection who sell water to their neighbours, as well as protected point sources such as springs or boreholes and unprotected sources.

It is possible at this stage to categorise each area on the basis of this information to give an initial zoning pattern. In Uganda, the zoning was done at a Parish level as this was the lowest level for which detailed data was available. If possible, zoning should be carried out at lower levels (e.g. individual communities) provided reliable data is available or resources are adequate to undertake field studies. Certain initial assumptions can be made of relevance to the surveillance programme at this time. The population in low-income Parishes of any density group where no protected point sources are recorded can be deemed to rely primarily on piped water. This can be justified because the majority of people will use sources that are close to them. Although there may be some use of sources outside the area, it is likely that would be a relatively small proportion of the population as proximity is likely to a primary reason in source selection.

However, the use of inventory data alone is unlikely to be adequate to determine which sources the low-income population is using most often. Sources may exist, but this does not equate to their use. For instance, a large numbers of taps may be available, but only used by a small number of households. In Kampala protected springs represented roughly 26% of all available sources, with taps representing 58%. However, in low-income areas, whilst the first choice of water source followed a similar distribution (33% protected springs, 59.5% taps), the total proportion of households using protected springs for at least part or all of their domestic water needs was 62%. In some areas, the use of protected springs, as a first source was over 50%, the highest being 63%. Therefore it is clear, that some attempt must be made to identify the relative importance of different water sources when zoning the urban area.

Furthermore, it is important to clarify which sources are used for activities involving consumption of water – drinking and food preparation. As water quality analysis is carried out on the assumption that water will be consumed, there would be little point in testing sources that were only used for other activities such as cleaning and laundry. When the data on use of different sources was analysed more reliable systems of zoning of the urban area is possible.

2.2.4 Creating the zones

There is a wide range of zones that could be defined using this approach which would provide differing degrees of accuracy in the classification of different areas and in assessing vulnerability. One approach to this is shown below in Table 2.2 for Kampala, Uganda.

Category	High income	Middle income (1)	Middle income (2)	Low income (1)	Low income (2)	Low income (3)
Piped supply, continuously available	Zone 1a	Zone 1b	Zone 1c	Zone 1d	Zone 1e	Zone 1f
Piped supply rationed, no alternatives used	Zone 2a	Zone 2b	Zone 2c	Zone 2d	Zone 2e	Zone 2f
Multiple sources of water; piped water reliable, limited use of alternatives	Zone 3a	Zone 3b	Zone 3c	Zone 3d	Zone 3e	Zone 3f
Multiple sources of water; piped supply erratic; significant use of other sources	Zone 4a	Zone 4b	Zone 4c	Zone 4d	Zone 4e	Zone 4f
Single point protected source, protected < 50m	N/A	N/A	N/A	Zone 5d	Zone 5e	Zone 5f
Single point protected source, protected > 50m	N/A	N/A	N/A	Zone 6d	Zone 6e	Zone 6f
Multiple point sources (protected/unprotected) <50m	N/A	N/A	N/A	Zone 7d	Zone 7e	Zone 7f

Table 2.2: Potential zones identified in Kampala, Uganda

However, if the methodology is designed as a working tool, it is often better to reduce the number of available categories to as few as possible. The detailed classification given above may be useful in defining vulnerability and describe accurately the water supply situation within an urban area, it may be overly complex for the use in surveillance planning as it incorporates 33 different zones. Such a complex method of zoning would be primarily effective when undertaking specific assessments, for instance in response to outbreaks of disease.

In order to refine monitoring programmes and target actions it is preferable that a more simplified approach is adopted with a more limited number of zones, thus making prioritisation of activities easier.

A simplified version of zoning that is useful for development of surveillance operations is show below in Table 2.3. These are the zones determined for Kampala, with their relative priority for the monitoring programme.

Zone	Description	Parishes	Priority
LHMX	Low income, high density, mixed water source use	22	1
LMMX	Low income, medium density, mixed water source use	10	2
LHPP	Low income, high density, principally piped water use	5	3
LLMX	Low income, low density, mixed water use	7	4
LLPP	Low income, low density, principally piped water use	3	5
L/MMMX	Low-medium income, medium density, mixed water use	2	6
L/MLMX	Low- medium income, low density, mixed water use	5	7
L/MMPP	Low-medium income, medium density, principally piped water use	2	8
MEDM	Medium income, direct connections and use of communal piped water use	16	9
HIGH	High income, direct connections coverage very high	17	10

Table 2.3: Urban zones from Uganda

This table illustrates that using relatively simple data, the urban area can be divided into smaller units. Using the zones define above, the monitoring programme was focused on those Parishes at greatest risk from poor health and where equity in access to water supplies is least. In terms of vulnerability to disease, the highest priority zones are those that are most at risk from epidemics of infectious diseases. A comparison of the zones in relation to the numbers of cholera cases recorded in each Parish during the outbreak in 1997/98 showed a significant association with zone type and numbers of cases recorded ($R = 0.650$, $p = 0.01$). This illustrates the value of this approach in establishing water quality monitoring programme for control of potential epidemics.

It should be noted that where there are only very few alternative supplies, a simplified system of zoning could be developed based on predominant service levels or the reliability of the piped water supply.

The advantage of this zoning approach is that it directs the surveillance activities on those areas where the population is at greatest risk from water-related diseases. It allows improvements to be focused on those areas of greatest need and an initial evaluation to be made as to what type of intervention will be most appropriate. It should be noted that the degree to which an urban area is divided up into discrete zones depends on the size. In small towns, they may be little point in dividing the town up further, although a greater emphasis should be placed on low-income areas and areas water source use includes both piped and non-piped sources.

3.

Institutional issues

As the purpose of water supply surveillance is to promote the improvement of water supply services, it is important that the organisational arrangements intended to facilitate this pay due consideration to the important and complementary roles of both independent surveillance and monitoring by water suppliers. It is also essential when establishing or reviewing the institutional arrangements of the sector with respect to surveillance and monitoring functions that the most appropriate institutions takes responsibility for different functions. The institutional framework at both national and local levels should be clearly defined. Attention should also be paid to the level at which surveillance and monitoring activities should be carried out and how local implementation of surveillance relates to a national framework.

3.1 Complementary roles of surveillance and supply

In principle, it is better that the two functions of surveillance and supply control are carried out by separate institutions to provide a mechanism for checks and balances in the generation and use of data. Where only one sector functions, there is always a risk that the information generated may be biased and therefore decisions may not be the most appropriate responses or be focused on the areas of greatest need.

The separation of roles at national levels should be relatively straightforward. However, at local levels, resources may dictate that distinct separation of roles may not be feasible and there has to be far greater integration of surveillance and quality control. Where separation is possible it must be stressed that there always needs to be close collaboration between surveillance and supply bodies in order to promote improvements in water supply.

It is also important to identify the limits of institutional responsibility for water supply and quality at a practical level. Surveillance bodies are expected to undertake monitoring and assessment of all water supplies that are used by the urban population and should undertake such monitoring up to the point of consumption. This means that point sources, piped water supplies and water stored within the home will be included in monitoring and assessment programmes. The surveillance body may also take responsibility for improvements in water supplies outside the responsibility of a water supplier, for instance community-managed point supplies and are likely to take a responsibility for hygiene and environmental health education in communities. Where community-managed water supplies exist, responsibility for operation and maintenance will lie with the community body established to manage the supply, although support may be given by both the surveillance and water supply agencies.

The water supplier, by contrast, only has responsibility for the system that they are charged with operating and only up to the point where supply infrastructure connects to the household infrastructure (typically at a meter or on the boundary of the property where supplies are not metered). The nature or extent of supplies falling within the remit of the supplier will depend on how the water supply sector is developed. In some cases, particularly where water is provided by urban authorities or water user associations, all supplies in a town may fall under the remit of the supply agency who then has a responsibility to ensure that all supplies are properly maintained and provide water of a safe and wholesome nature. In this situation, the supplier will be expected to undertake periodic monitoring and assessment of all water supplies. In other cases, responsibility may be limited to the piped network operated by the supplier, who then retain no responsibility for any other water sources used and thus monitoring is restricted to the piped water system.

3.2 National framework

There are a numbers of issues in allocating institutional responsibility for different monitoring functions. When allocating responsibility, it is important that the purpose of each function is clearly defined and matched against the overall remit of the institution. It must borne in mind that because surveillance is a broad-based activity, there are a number of areas where expertise and responsibility may overlap.

There are a number of key players within the water sector who have an interest in the outputs of surveillance or who have responsibility for implementing interventions in the water sector.

The key stakeholder institutions are as follows:

- Environmental health departments charged with ensuring that a healthy environment is created that reduces the risk to health of the urban population;

- Water supply and sanitation agency(s) or Government departments, who plan, develop, operate and manage drinking water supplies;

- Water resource management bodies departments responsible for the allocation of available resources between competing needs;

- Economic and development planning departments that oversee the allocation of monetary resources for water supply and who may have a responsibility for ensuring targets regarding access to water supply are met.

3.2.1 Surveillance agency

The surveillance agency should have a proper legal mandate to undertake surveillance. This is usually linked to the broader policy framework for the protection of public and environmental health. There are a number of potential lead agencies for surveillance, but in general it is usual for these to be located within either the Ministry of Health or Environment. Ministries of Water or Local Government are usually less appropriate. In the case of the former, this is because they are likely to be involved in the provision of services and therefore should support the development of quality control monitoring by water suppliers. In the case of the latter, there is often limited expertise and capacity and frequently direct involvement in service provision.

In some countries the Ministry of Health is the preferred lead agency, because of the role of surveillance in protecting public health. In Uganda, for instance, water supply surveillance has always been an activity undertaken of Environmental Health staff and has been included both in the minimum health services package and in the health policy. However, in some countries the capacity of the Ministry of Health to fulfil this role is limited and therefore the Ministry of Environment is preferred. If the Ministry of Environment adopts the role of surveillance agency, it is important that links are made to the health sector to ensure that information of importance to health is made available.

The national lead agency should co-ordinate and supervise the implementation of surveillance programmes at local levels. This includes providing training, support supervision to field staff, provision of materials for health and environmental education and technical advice on the development of surveillance programmes and use of surveillance data. The lead agency should also operate a national water quality and sanitary risk database and support local surveillance bodies in developing local programmes of surveillance data collection, data storage and reporting. They should provide national overviews of drinking water quality and supply from a public health perspective and guide interventions.

The national lead agency should set policies relating to the implementation for water supply surveillance at local levels, for instance by requiring that local Public Health Departments undertake routine surveillance and provide regular reports of surveillance findings. The national lead agency can also provide an important link to the donor community to support the development of surveillance where internal resources may be inadequate. This would typically include attracting funding for equipment, training of staff and development of guidance materials.

The national lead agency may also provide a link to other key stakeholders in the water sector and influence the development of policies that address the needs for water and sanitation in an equitable and health-promoting fashion. They also can facilitate the collection and dissemination of other data needed for surveillance bodies such as rainfall and coverage data that is not always easy for local surveillance bodies to gain access to. The lead agency should also provide advice on conducting social surveys at local levels to collect data on aspects such as coverage, costs and quantities used and provide technical assistance in the development of routine water quality monitoring programmes.

3.2.2 Water supply agency

The water supply agency has a responsibility to ensure that the water that they supply is fit for human consumption and meets all prevailing national norms and standards applicable in the sector. Ultimately it is the supplier who is responsible for the quality of their water supply and who must safeguard this through proper operation and maintenance of water supply infrastructure and through quality control procedures that will encompass the range of information discussed within this manual.

The water supplier should undertake frequent routine monitoring of the quality of the water supplied to provide a systematic and comprehensive overview of the water supply. At a national level, the role of the water supply agency will depend largely on how water services are provided. Where there is a single national water supply body (e.g. parastatal, Government Department or Water Company) the national level should provide support to local level staff in undertaking monitoring through training, support supervision and technical advice. They should also provide national overviews of the quality of water supplied to surveillance and other key bodies. In some countries such an organisation may only be responsible for relatively small number of supplies and therefore the head office staff will provide the same functions as noted above, but purely for their own supplies.

3.2.3 Other agencies

The other key agencies in the sector are the water resource management agency and the body responsible for the control of tariffs and provision of social services. In the case of the water resource management agency, it should ensure that drinking water needs are prioritised in terms of resource allocation and that abstractions for other uses do not limit the availability of water to supply drinking water systems. They should also control pollutant discharges into source waters and ensure that neither increased abstraction nor discharge into water sources will lead to significantly greater treatment requirements. The link to the surveillance body and water supplier is both through the definition and enforcement of source protection measures and through routine monitoring of source waters and notification of changing conditions or trends of concern.

The body responsible for tariff control and social provision will set the standards or targets for the water supplier to meet in terms of charges to be levied, numbers of people to be served and usually on financial sustainability. This will usually be undertaken by a Ministry of Finance and/or Economic Planning. In addition to establishing the tariff norms to be followed, this body may also take responsibility for allocation of national and donor funds to different towns and monitor the use of funds provided to ensure that they have been invested in the most cost-effective manner. Links may be made between the surveillance agency and the tariff control body on the prices paid by households for water from communal sources and in sharing data on water quality and operational performance. Sharing of water quality may be particularly important as investments to improve water quality may have impacts on the tariff and likewise, the tariff may inhibit water quality improvements being made if this is set too low.

3.3 Local-level implementation of surveillance and quality control monitoring

Both surveillance and quality control monitoring by the water supplier are best undertaken at a local level. This is in part due to reasons relating to sample deterioration for water quality analysis as discussed in the next Chapter and in Chapter 7, but also because of using surveillance data to generate local solutions to local problems.

In general, the local institutional arrangements will effectively mirror those at a national level. However, it is likely that the two principal organisations actively involved at local levels will be the surveillance body and the water supply agency. It is unlikely that the financial management body will operate at local levels, although there may be some very limited local-level control of tariffs and costs. The water resource management body may also lack local representatives, although it is preferable that there is at least one staff member operating at a local scale.

The inter-action between surveillance and water supply agency staff is particularly important at local levels as this is the area where action will be urgently required in the event of failures and where realistic strategies can be developed to improve water supplies. The roles are briefly outlined below.

3.3.1 Local environmental health institutions

The most appropriate local-level bodies to undertake the routine collection of surveillance data are Municipal health or environmental health departments. This was followed in Bangladesh, Ghana and Uganda. The principal role of the local-level body is to implement surveillance programmes and develop local intervention strategies to improve poor water supply and hygiene. This may include aspects such as rehabilitation of water sources, provision of new water sources, hygiene education programmes and support to communities to maintain communal sources effectively.

In some towns the local authority have responsibility for the provision of water services and thus clearly have a duty of care to ensure the water provided are safe and wholesome as a water supply agency. However, the Municipal health department should also undertake surveillance of all water supplies including those not directly managed by the authority as well as water stored within the home. The public health department should also carry out surveillance of the Municipal water supply as they would for any other water supply agency. In general this approach would be most appropriate when the outputs of surveillance are not primarily driven by the need to check and enforce compliance with standards under a system of regulation. In many situations, the need for surveillance is not primarily driven by a regulatory function but rather as a means to promote improvement and at this level there is no real conflict of interest.

Where compliance with standards is the principal basis for surveillance of water supply in urban areas, then it is preferable to completely split the supply and surveillance functions and in this case, usually the supply function would move out of the local authority remit. However, it may still be possible to operate supply and regulatory functions within the same overall institution provided that these are separated up to the most senior executive level.

Surveillance staff
It is important that one person in the local health department takes responsibility for co-ordinating surveillance. This may be a Chief Health Inspector/Environmental Health Officer or the head of the department. The role of the co-ordinator is to ensure that field staff undertake the surveillance activities planned, provide technical and administrative support and to represent the surveillance programme within the local authority, the Ministry of Health and with water suppliers. The co-ordinator should also take responsibility for ensuring that funds are allocated to support surveillance in annual budgets.

The staff who are best placed to undertake surveillance activities in the field are those with an environmental health background such environmental health officers, health inspectors and health assistants. These are staff who should have background training in environmental health and already have many of skills required for surveillance. They would usually have a good knowledge of the importance of different aspects of the environment on health and understand the basic transmission routes of infectious diseases. However, it is also important that such staff spend a considerable time in the field working with communities. This is important, as a key role in surveillance is to ensure that information can be made accessible to communities and advice given on ways to improve water supply and hygiene behaviour. If staff are not field-based, it may be much more difficult to implement community-based actions and to make surveillance activities relevant to the communities within the urban area.

The staff selected for surveillance activities should be involved in all stages of the programme. The key element in surveillance is to build capacity in local staff to undertake information collection, dissemination and use with communities. In addition, they will be expected to use the information that they generate to inform policy-makers and planners about priorities and interventions required.

Co-ordination of surveillance is important. Field staff need support from supervisors in planning activities and overcoming problems. Co-ordinators will need to provide support supervision, training and take responsibility for the preparation of reports on activities undertaken and interventions to improve water and hygiene. Good co-ordination will make sure that surveillance is implemented effectively and encourage field staff.

3.3.2 Local water supply agencies

As with surveillance, actual implementation of supply agency quality control activities is best at the local level. Thus it is usually most effective to have at least basic equipment at the headworks or office of each water supply. This will usually be possible where a water supply agency covering several towns is responsible for water supply provision. In small towns where the water supply is provided by local Government or other bodies such as water users associations, it may less feasible to have facilities for routine quality control. In these circumstances it may be necessary for the surveillance body to carry out basic quality control monitoring as part of their wider surveillance remit.

Each major works should have at least one water quality technician with access to facilities to be able to undertake critical parameter testing as well as an expanded range of chemical parameters. For small supplies, the operator should be provided with equipment for basic analysis of critical parameters (including if possible microbiological testing equipment). The operators should be supported by water quality technicians responsible for larger supplies who should undertake regular monitoring visits.

For community-managed supplies, water quality analysis is unlikely to be feasible for the community to undertake, but routine sanitary inspection and other forms of monitoring may be implemented. In some countries simplified testing kits have been developed that are designed for use by communities. However, these often only test for total coliforms, which if the water sources is untreated may provide little useful information and may be difficult to integrate into the broader surveillance context.

3.4 Inter-Agency Collaboration

The links between different sector agencies are important to promote informed decision-making in improving water supply. Unless the different agencies collaborate with each other, information generated by one agency may not be available or used by other agencies and therefore decisions may be made that are not based on the complete and reliable information.

Collaboration must include sharing of information between different sector agencies and developing joint strategies towards problem solving wherever possible. Where the surveillance agency identifies problems in the quality of supply from the water supplier, it is important that this is discussed with the water supplier. When the water supplier themselves identifies a failure in supply the surveillance agency should be notified.

Even where the principal basis of surveillance is for regulation and enforcement of standards, it is more effective for the regulator and supplier to work closely together to resolve water supply problems in a collaborative manner as this tends to produce more successful and sustainable solutions.

Collaboration should also include other agencies including the resource management body and the tariff setting body. Again this should include the sharing of data and a dialogue in protecting water resources and sources and promotion of efficient use of available water resources. In terms of financial management and social provision, close collaboration with the surveillance agency should identify the areas in greatest need for improvement in the water supply based on the risk to public health. The surveillance agency should also have say in any changes in tariff that may reduce the ability of the poor to access better services.

3.5 Institutional issues in regulation

Institutional responsibility for regulation must be clearly defined when a regulatory body is being established. The details of available approaches for regulation of the water sector is discussed in Chapter 11 and only institutional roles in regulation are discussed here.

Whilst surveillance would typically include a broad range of data collection and the health sector should take and overall responsibility for surveillance, it does not necessarily follow that the health sector should be the regulator of water supply, although it may take responsibility for part of the regulation. There are issues such as tariff control and social provision that must take into account issues other than health (including requirements of international loan agreements, financial sustainability and broader socio-economic development plans). The health sector will not necessarily retain the expertise to be able to regulate such aspects adequately and whilst it should lobby for decisions in tariff control and access that promote improved health, it would not be appropriate for the sector to regulate such issues. The health sector, however, should take some responsibility for the regulation of drinking water quality as this directly affects health and may be a source of an epidemic. Such responsibility may take the form of direct regulation or indirect involvement through the setting of health-based standards.

As Government water departments are usually involved in facilitating the provision of water supplies there are weaknesses in their ability to perform a role as regulator. This is particularly the case whether ownership of infrastructure is retained by the Government (as is usually the case even where the private sector undertake operation of part or all of the water supply). In these cases, failure to meet standards may result from Government inability to provide the improvements or investments required. There is therefore an inherent conflict of interest in a Government department responsible for water supply to regulate the sector, unless it does not play any role in the facilitation or provision of services.

It is often more effective to establish a regulatory system that draws on the expertise of all the relevant sector but which is not under the direct jurisdiction of one institution. Bodies such as public utility regulatory commissions (PURCs) can pull together the necessary expertise from different sector and programmes, but are able to function independently. This approach also allows more cost-effective regulation and can ensure that integration of the different aspects requiring regulation occurs. Such a body would therefore be composed of professional either seconded or directly employed from each sector and would engage in a process of dialogue with all sectors to ensure that water supplies are provided in the most efficient and effective manner and provide services that are of adequate quality and reliability that promote health.

4.

Planning Surveillance Programmes

The successful implementation of surveillance and monitoring programmes is largely determined by whether the programme has been properly planned, taking into account existing surveillance activities and infrastructure, financial resources, scope of the work to be covered, available human resources and institutional arrangements.

There is no simple blueprint about how quickly a surveillance programme will develop, but in general terms it is important that the development of surveillance programmes is done in a systematic and rational way. Critical to this process is to ensure that the legal basis and institutional arrangements for surveillance are resolved as discussed in the previous Chapter 11.

Where surveillance activities are not currently implemented within urban areas, a new programme will need to be designed. In this case, it is preferable to adopt a phased approach to surveillance development with some initial pilot areas selected for implementation. These should broadly reflect the range of towns found in the country and there should be a reasonable geographical spread of towns throughout the country. Both factors are important as there may be issues that are specific to the size of town or area where the town is located that requires modification of the approaches and tools used. For instance, in smaller towns zoning may not be necessary or may only require identification of lower income areas and source use, with population density being largely unimportant. As the numbers of samples to be taken are likely to be relatively low in any case, there is little point in dividing up a small community. In other towns there may be specific issues related to water shortages, different water supply administration or water quality that require a slightly different emphasis in approach. For instance, arsenic or fluoride may be identified as particular problems in certain areas served by groundwater and the monitoring of these parameters would be important.

4.1 Development of surveillance programmes

Implementation of surveillance is more effective at local levels, however, the planning of programmes will be a responsibility of the national level as this may require a progressive approach to be adopted. The development of surveillance programmes should start with a pilot phase for tool and methodology development, followed by progressive expansion to cover the whole country. Such an approach allows lessons learnt in early stages to be built in to subsequent larger programmes.

4.1.1 Pilot stage

The pilot stage should be the time that the different tools and approaches for surveillance will be developed, tested and refined as necessary. Examples of sanitary inspection, reporting and questionnaire forms are provided in the annexes of this manual. However, it is recommended that these be modified in each country to reflect prevailing local circumstances. The testing of such tools and approaches in a pilot programme will ensure that any weaknesses have been identified and rectified, thus ensuring that their subsequent use in a larger programme is effective and efficient.

During the pilot stage, considerations must be given to a range of activities that will facilitate surveillance. The staff required to undertake surveillance at local and national levels should be identified and their training needs assessed. Suitable courses will have to be designed and delivered to ensure that staff are competent to undertake surveillance activities.

The current courses available for training of environmental health staff should also be reviewed to ensure that surveillance techniques are covered. It is important that key aspects of surveillance are covered such as indicators of water supply adequacy indicators, water quality parameters, sanitary inspection and using surveillance data to improve water supplies. Training should also address community involvement in surveillance and improvement and the presentation of information to different target audiences. If graduates from courses in environmental health are able to carry out sampling and analysis of drinking water and can perform sanitary inspections, then surveillance will become more cost-effective. Ongoing training needs should be considered and the supporting materials required for staff and users of the information developed. Materials to support training events (overheads, sessions plans and background materials) can be found and downloaded from the watermark web-site (www.lboro.ac.uk/watermark) and from WHO (www.who.int/water_sanitation_health).

4.1.2 Expansion of the programme

Following the pilot stage, the programme should expand progressively to cover the other urban areas. Where resources permit, this may be an expansion to cover the whole country, but limitations in availability of staff to undertake support supervision and to undertake training must be carefully considered if national expansion in a single phase is proposed. A progressive approach may be more appropriate to ensure that a balance can be struck between the need to provide surveillance services in safeguarding public health and cost-effectiveness. Where a more progressive approach is adopted, it is recommended that this uses pilot areas as nodes to maximise the potential for local networking and peer support and supervision. Therefore, during the first stage of expansion, urban areas close to those included in the pilot programme should be included, with subsequent expansions based on moving out from established centres to new areas.

In some cases surveillance programmes will already exist but there is a need to refine these. Again, if changes are proposed in any of the approaches adopted or tools used, it is always more effective to undertake an initial pilot phase in order to test these. This allows subsequent modifications to be made without incurring excessive costs. Where surveillance programmes are being modified, it is often possible to expand of the new programme to a national level once the pilot stage is completed.

4.2 The implementation cycle

When a programme is being developed in a town, there are a number of critical stages to be gone through as indicated in Figure 4.1 below. The process of acquiring information is often lengthy, but should be done systematically to ensure that it is reliable and that the information required for each stage of programme development is available.

```
┌─────────────────────────────────────────────────────────────────────────────┐
│                                                                               │
│  ┌──────────────────────┐                    ┌──────────────────────┐         │
│  │ Assess staff training│                    │   Feedback data and  │         │
│  │ and infrastructure   │◄───────────────────│ implement improvements│        │
│  │      needs           │                    │                      │         │
│  └──────────────────────┘                    └──────────────────────┘         │
│           │                                            ▲                       │
│           ▼                                            │                       │
│  ┌──────────────────────┐                    ┌──────────────────────┐         │
│  │ Carry out inventory  │                    │   Water use study or │         │
│  │ and connection       │                    │ projection from other│         │
│  │      reviews         │                    │       areas          │         │
│  └──────────────────────┘                    └──────────────────────┘         │
│           │                                            ▲                       │
│           ▼                                            │                       │
│  ┌──────────────────────┐                    ┌──────────────────────┐         │
│  │ Training in          │                    │   Feedback data and  │         │
│  │ surveillance         │                    │ implement improvements│        │
│  │ techniques           │                    │                      │         │
│  └──────────────────────┘                    └──────────────────────┘         │
│           │                                            ▲                       │
│           ▼                                            │                       │
│  ┌────────────┐   ┌──────────────┐   ┌──────────────────────┐                 │
│  │Zone urban  │──►│Carry out     │──►│ Routine monitoring   │                 │
│  │   area     │   │assessments on│   │ design and           │                 │
│  │            │   │sources and   │   │ implementation       │                 │
│  │            │   │household water│  │                      │                 │
│  └────────────┘   └──────────────┘   └──────────────────────┘                 │
│                                                                               │
└─────────────────────────────────────────────────────────────────────────────┘
```

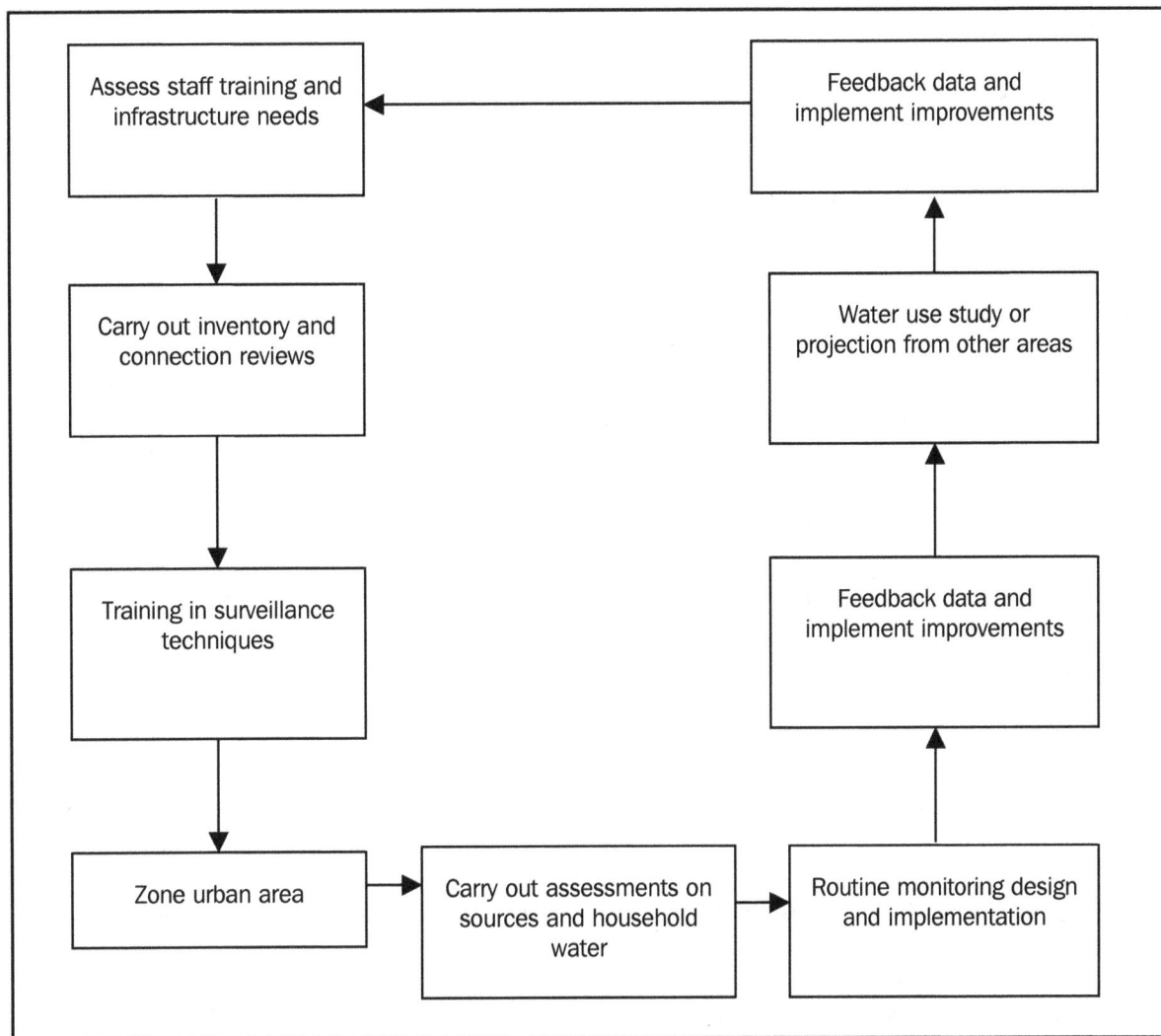

Figure 4.1 Surveillance development within an urban area

The first stage is to undertake an inventory and review of access data in order to understand what types of water supply are available to the population. The primary focus of the inventory is to collect information on the sources used by the population not served by a direct connection. It is likely that there will a variety of different types of water sources available to the unserved population from which domestic water may be obtained. These may include:

- Public taps

- Individuals with a direct connection who sell water to their neighbours

- Taps serving several houses or compounds provided by the landlord

- Boreholes

- Protected springs

- Dug wells (with and without handpumps)

33

- Unprotected point sources (including springs, scoop wells)

- Surface water sources

The purpose of the inventory is to identify all the available sources within the urban area that serves the needs of the population without a direct connection and therefore a census approach is adopted. This means that the whole urban area should be covered and all available sources recorded. This will usually require staff to visit each area and through both a process of observation and questioning identify the sources available. In some areas the data may be available already for protected point sources and public taps, but would be unlikely to cover unprotected sources or individuals who sell water. The latter are very common in many urban areas with a formal piped water supply. During the inventory, information should also be collected on:

- The ownership of the source

- Responsibility for supervision, operation and maintenance

- Whether users must pay for water and if so how much for what volume

- When the source was constructed, by whom and with support from which organisation

- Whether any rehabilitation or major repairs have been undertaken and if so, what these were, when they were done, who did them and how was it paid for

- Whether restrictions on volume are applied to users (excluding issues related to payment) and if so why

- Whether there is ever interruption in supply and if so how frequently and for how long (e.g. regularly for taps, seasonal for groundwater sources

An example of an inventory form is shown in Annex 1. Before the inventory is undertaken, it is essential that field staff receive training in filling the inventory forms and in identifying the sources. This will typically involve one day to review the form and to pilot the use in the field. The inventory data should be stored on a database to allow easy analysis. In Uganda, EpiInfo was used as the data could be stored in a questionnaire format and setting up an appropriate database is reviewed in the co-ordinators manual.

In addition to the inventory, a review of the population served by a direct connection should be carried out using data from the water supplier. Where possible this should be done in relation to the socio-economic status of different areas as part of the zoning process, but if this is not possible, it should be carried out at least in relation to populations in defined areas. Aggregate statistics for the whole urban area are not useful, as they will inevitably be a skew to higher-income areas, thus the access data should be broken down into the smallest possible administrative unit available.

At this stage an initial zoning of the urban area can be carried out based on the water supply availability and population density. However, if possible, at this stage socio-economic data should be analysed and the town zoned according to the process previously described.

Following the inventory, the surveillance staff should be trained in surveillance techniques. It is likely that most environmental health staff will have received some training in surveillance techniques during their formal training. If this is not the case, then the formal training courses require revision and improvement. Even where staff have received training, if they have not been actively undertaking surveillance, it is recommended that at least refresher training is provided to ensure that they are competent to undertake routine field work.

The initial training of field staff should focus on practical issues in the implementation of surveillance activities, use of the surveillance tools, data analysis and reporting and using data to initiate improvements in water supply. Such initial training can be provided to staff through short (one to two weeks) courses on surveillance that includes significant field and practical work. Example of timetables for such training is provided at the watermark web-site (www.lboro.ac.uk/watermark). Where surveillance staff undertake or arrange for construction or upgrading of water supplies, training will need to be longer and possibly take the form of several modules covering design, construction techniques and health education.

Ongoing training should be available to surveillance staff to provide them with an opportunity to upgrade their skills, share experiences and develop and refine surveillance and intervention strategies. Unless specific upgrading of skills are required, ongoing training is often best done by bringing together groups of staff from different towns or parts of towns and carried out in a participatory manner. For instance in Uganda, ongoing training was primarily carried out through participatory refresher training courses in which the participants defined the areas of importance and the agenda to be followed. A key element of these training courses was that it facilitated a process of local networking that allowed lessons learnt in one area or town to be shared and discussed with other staff. This facilitates the process of developing local solutions to local problems.

Further training courses may be undertaken which focus on specific issues of relevance. This may include the use of new equipment or on certain aspects of the use of data. An example of such training needs may include development and training in the use of participatory health education materials and tools. In Uganda this included the development of water quality specific PHAST tools and training in their use. Other specific training needs may include training in new construction techniques or use of new designs in water supplies or in managing small contractors undertaking works on community water supplies.

Following the inventory and training in surveillance techniques, a baseline water quality assessment can be undertaken. This is designed to provide information on which to base subsequent monitoring programmes to reflect the importance and likely variations in quality of different sources. Household water will also require assessment in order to determine current practice in ensuring good quality water stored in the home and where water quality is poor to identify health education needs. Unprotected sources would be a low priority for testing because the quality can be expected to be poor and more importantly, the action required can be identified without the need for water quality testing – it should be protected or an alternative source of water provided.

The assessment of protected point sources, piped water and water stored within the home should be carried out over a short period of time to ensure comparability of results between water sources of the same type. For piped water, the timing of the assessment in relation to climate may not be critical, unless the source is considered particularly vulnerable to contamination (for instance a spring source feeds a gravity piped system with no chlorination). The assessment of point sources (springs, dug wells etc) should be carried out at a time when quality is most likely to be poor, usually during wet periods. When assessments are performed on the sources of water, household water quality should be assessed and the source of water identified at each household. The assessment data should be analysed and routine monitoring programmes developed following the process outlined in Chapter 8. The numbers, frequency and locations of sampling points should be decided upon to ensure they are representative.

Water usage studies may be required in some towns in order to refine the zoning process and to collect data on costs and quantities of water used. These studies will also provide a good mechanism to evaluate health education messages regarding the use of safe sources or treatment of water within the home, when pre and post intervention water use studies provide quantifiable measures of behaviour change. These may be broad-spectrum studies, participatory studies or combination of techniques to triangulate the information gained. Water usage studies are discussed in more detail in Chapter 9.

An essential element in the surveillance cycle which is essential if the programme is to be successful is the reporting of results to key stakeholders. Without proper reporting and feedback, the development of remedial strategies will not be effective and therefore from the outset of the programme it is important to establish appropriate systems of reporting to all relevant bodies. Indeed, the ability of the surveillance programme to support the interventions to improve water supply outlined in Chapters 11 to 14 are highly dependent on the ability of the surveillance bodies to analyse and present information in a meaningful way to different target audiences. The target audiences for surveillance information will typically include:

- Public health officials at local and national levels

- Water suppliers

- Local administrations

- Communities and water users

The appropriate mechanisms for reporting to each target audiences will vary and are discussed below.

4.3 Reporting of surveillance data

The reporting of results to key institutions is important to ensure that the data generated can be effectively used. There may be many demands for surveillance data from planners, water supply bodies and health officials who want information regarding the quality of water sources and water stored in the home during an epidemic or for identifying vulnerable groups. Local administrative officials may also require information on activities undertaken by staff as a means to ensure that funds allocated have been used appropriately. The reporting of such data should consider carefully what the target audience is, what the use of such information will be as well as the level of understanding of water supply issues.

The reporting of different types of data may take different forms. Data on inventories, including cost and connection rates, would typically be reported after the data has been collected but as this data is generally collected infrequently at the outset of the programme and at low-intensity after this, the reporting frequency will be low. In general such reports would include an assessment by area of source availability, average and range of costs of different types of water supply as well as other key data from inventories such as average age of sources or numbers of seasonal water sources.

Water quality and sanitary risk data (including discontinuity) will be collected frequently and therefore the reporting of such data will equally need to be frequent. For routine reporting the format must be simple, comprehensible and short. Where reports are lengthy or require a detailed understanding of water quality issues they are unlikely to be appropriate for anything but a small technical audience. One of the key purposes of surveillance is to provide information to non-specialists for use in planning and other exercises. Typically such reports will include where samples were taken from, the water quality found and sanitary risk score. Additional information may include the number of samples failing to meet standards or average contamination found for point sources and household water. Some examples of monthly report forms generated are shown in Annex 2. Such reports would be sent to health officials and local administrative officials. Reporting to water suppliers may be less frequent, for instance quarterly or only in the event of a failure being noted. Where a regulatory body exists, routine monthly reports should typically be submitted for review.

It is often also desirable for the national surveillance body to prepare a more detailed annual report that provides a review of activities at the national level and includes more in-depth discussion of the results and their implications. An annual report should highlight the major issues of concern, such as low rates of access to direct connection, high costs of water, poor reliability in supply. It would also discuss the results of water testing and the likely causes of water quality failure and indicate how these may be prevented in the future.

4.3.1 Community feedback

A critical component of the analysis of data and reporting on surveillance activities is to ensure that the users of the water supply have access to information about their water supply. Reporting is particularly important as part of the routine collection of water quality data, as the users of water supply have a right to know the quality of the water they consume and the risk to their health. They will also want to know the major problems noted with both the supply and in-house storage and the recommended actions that they can take to improve the quality of the water they drink.

Feedback to communities represents certain problems in reporting. Clearly, most community members are not water or environmental health professionals so the information that is reported back to them must take into account comprehensibility. There may also be an overall lack of education that makes understanding of pathogens and their transmission difficult and this must be taken into account when planning information feed back to communities. Although in many cases, the actual causes of microbiological contamination of water may be solved within communities with little or no outside financial support, communities may perceive that resolution of the problem is the responsibility of someone else. Again this may be an important issue to address through the feedback of information.

Reporting to communities has to ensure that the information provided is in a format that allows them to easily understand the risks to their health and which can support a process of community decision making. There are a number of ways in which water quality surveillance information can be relayed back to users and the selection of the method adopted is dependent on a number of factors such as; the presence of community organisations, literacy and the type of water supply and water management system.

One of the problems with feedback of information to users is that there are usually very many people within the community and to ensure that each person received information directly from the surveillance body is not feasible. Thus it is better the use community organisations where these exist to provide an effective channel for feedback of information to users that is cost-effective. Local organisations will usually have regular meetings with the communities that they serve and can therefore provide a mechanism of relaying important information to a large of number of people within the community. Furthermore, by using local organisations it is often easier to initiate a process of discussion and decision-making within the community concerning improvements in the water quality.

Local organisations may be local government structures, as was the case in Uganda where urban areas had been divided into 'zones' covering a relatively small number of households with each zone having a 'village' or LC1 committee, responsible for administration of the zone. As these zones were small, the households within them often utilised a particular public tap or point source. A simple report in the format shown in Annex 2 allowed information that was relevant to the target audience to be provided. This report provides simple information as to where samples were taken, whether any faecal contamination was found in the water, the major problems noted in the supply and recommendations for community action. Such feedback mechanisms provided not only a useful, simple and cost-effective means of providing information but also allowed communities to come to their own solutions of the problem. Reporting to the LC1 was supported by periodic attendance by environmental health staff at community meetings to discuss water quality and supply issues and to facilitate a process of problem identification and solution. In addition to attending LC1 meetings to discuss water quality issues, environmental health staff also utilised a number of participatory tools to facilitate communities to improve water supply.

Whilst local councils represent one way of involving communities in the feedback and use of water surveillance information, they are not the only type of organisation that can play this role. In some circumstances where such organisations do not exist or are weak, alternative organisations may be more useful. This may include local community-based organisations (CBOs) or other NGOs, as well as womens groups, church groups, mosques and schools. The most important element in using local organisations to provide a mechanism for information feedback is to ensure that the organisation selected can access the whole community and have the ability on the ground to initiate discussion around the results of surveillance.

Community meetings
One of the most effective mechanisms for feedback of results to users of water supplies is through holding community meetings to discuss the results of surveillance activities and the resolution of problems. Community meetings are particularly important where communal sources are used and water is stored within the home. The advantage of community meetings is that they allow communities to clarify points on which they are uncertain and to gain access to technical advice on improving their water supply that may not be readily available within the community itself. However, community meetings take extra time and may involve staff attending meetings at weekends and evenings and this must be taken into account when using these as a means of information feedback. Furthermore, communities may not respond positively to over-frequent meetings to discuss water supply or quality issues. Thus it is often

more effective to plan and hold community meetings at a lower frequency in order to discuss issues in greater depth than to use community meetings simply to relay information.

When planning to attend or to call a community meeting, it is vital to be clear as to purpose of the meeting, the way in which you wish the information to be relayed and the desired outcome of the meeting. Without proper planning by the surveillance staff member who facilitates the meeting, the discussion of surveillance data may be limited, superficial and not lead to any definable outcome. Furthermore, in some cases there may be a particular group within the community that is being targeted. This may be women as water managers or water user committees.

Therefore, there are a series of key questions that should be answered before holding a community meeting:

1. What is the objective?

2. What outcome is desired?

3. How will the meeting be conducted – how do you want to get your message across and what kind of response are you looking for?

4. Are there particular groups that you wish to target and how will you ensure that these participate in the discussion?

Whilst the objectives of each meeting should be determined in the context of the particular community to be met and the area to be discussed, in general there are some key objectives and approaches that should be considered. The objectives may include to:

1. Increase awareness of the quality of the water being consumed (whether relating to sources or to water stored in the home) and the risk to health that this represents

1. Discuss and identify with the community the major causes of water quality failure and the underlying problems leading to these problems (for instance poor operation and maintenance of a source or poor cleanliness of water containers)

2. Identify how these problems may be overcome and who is responsible

3. Determine a timetable of action

Depending of the amount of time and resources to be spent in one community, some or all of the above objectives may be included for one or for a series of meetings held with a community. In most cases, the process of community decision-making will dictate that the first two objectives are most readily covered from the start with objectives 3 and 4 addressed at a later meeting. Several meetings may be required to reach objective 4.

The outcome desired is improved water source management and maintenance and ensuring a safe water chain up to the point of consumption. Thus the outcome is unlikely to be realised until the full process has been completed and interim objectives and milestones may need to be set to allow the surveillance agency and the community to measure their progress. Interim outcomes will be aspects such as an agreed timetable of action or establishing a water source committee.

The most appropriate approach to community meetings is to make sure they are as participatory as possible and to maximise the opportunity for communities to reach conclusions themselves. This is likely to deliver more sustainable improvements than directing communities to conclusions. The role of the surveillance staff is to provide information otherwise not available to the community and to facilitate discussions about this information. In order to ensure that all the concerns of all groups are addressed, ensuring that participants are provided an opportunity to contribute is important.

Other community feedback mechanisms include the regular posting of results of surveillance at key points within a community such as a health centre, school, church, and mosque or community hall. This can again be effective provided that the community are aware that this information can be found at this location, the information is clear and comprehensible and that the information is posted where it is easily seen. In some countries, this process is simplified by categorising the water in terms of its risk to health and in South Africa this included a colour-coding scheme. This can be an effective way to feedback results, but like all education materials should be thoroughly pre-tested with a sample of the target group to ensure that the message that you wish to transmit is the one that is understood by the target group. Such an approach should be supported by community meetings to allow greater discussion of the issues identified.

5.

Indicators of water supply and data collection

As noted in Chapter 1, there are six key areas of water supply for service indicators can be developed. These are:

1. The quality and in particular microbiological quality and may be done in relation to the number of supplies meeting WHO Guidelines or national standards;

2. Continuity – the percentage of time that water is available from the supply;

3. Cost – the price paid by consumers for domestic water at the point of purchase;

4. Quantity – the average volume of water used by consumers for domestic purposes

5. Coverage – the percentage of the population that has access to a recognisable water (usually public) supply. This would typically be those that have some sanitary protection or treatment;

6. Unaccounted-for water. For water suppliers this may be a significant component of monitoring. For surveillance agencies monitoring may only be with respect to risks to water quality or to ensure that the supplier does monitor unaccounted-for-water.

These different factors provide a reliable overview of the water sector, but have very different methods of collection and analysis and may require different approaches to data collection depending on the degree to which each is likely to change with time and different urban areas.

When deciding how data should be collected and analysed for each factor, the following points should be borne in mind. Certain indicators may vary significantly in short periods of time and over short distances and these require frequent and comprehensive monitoring if surveillance is to be effective. Other will not show significant variation in the short term and thus only require relatively infrequent periodic assessment. A further element to keep in mind is that for a number of the above indicators, sampling approaches can be used to collect the data.

Table 5.1 summarises the data collection needs and approaches for these different indicators and some broad indication of the use of the information provided by the indicator is shown. Detailed discussion of how these data will be collected, analysed and used is given in the following sections. These focus on the collection of data on continuity, quantity, cost, coverage and unaccounted-for-water. As water quality is composed of a far greater range of parameters and requires more frequent analysis given that changes in quality may be rapid and occur within a short distance, the material on data collection methods and sampling frameworks for water quality is covered in Chapters 6,7 and 8.

Indicator	Type of activity	Frequency of data collection	Data collected	Data collection method	Outputs
Quality	Routine monitoring	Critical parameters – frequent;	Numbers of bacteria and concentration of substances in water	Analysis of water samples	Risk to health
	Periodic assessment	Chemical parameters, usually infrequent unless specific problem noted	Sanitary risk data	Sanitary inspection	Identify of principal causes of contamination
					Evaluation of O&M performance
			Wide range of chemicals means careful selection required		Recommendations on performance improvement
					Health education
Continuity	Routine monitoring (piped)	Frequent (piped)	Percentage of time water unavailable	Sanitary inspection	Assessment of performance
	Periodic assessment (point)	Infrequent (point)	Percentage time supply non-functional	Rationing data	Assessment of sustainability
				Inventory	Investment required in water supply to reduce unreliability
				Water usage study	Training and support needs to communities
				Assessments of functional status	
Cost	Periodic assessment	Infrequent usually precipitated by changes in price	Costs charged by utilities	Inventory	Identify bottle-necks to increasing coverage
			Costs paid by consumers	Water usage study	Recommendations on costs
			Cost components	Utility tariff reviews	Review of connection fees and creation of incentives
				Contingent valuation	
Quantity	Periodic assessment	Infrequent	Per capita volumetric assessment	Water usage study	Analysis of equity in water use
			Service level	Consumption analysis from household meters	Focus resources to improve water supply and health education in priority areas

Indicator	Type of activity	Frequency of data collection	Data collected	Data collection method	Outputs
Coverage	Periodic assessment	Usually infrequent	Access to different service levels	Census	Overall assessment of progress in providing social services
			Percent of households receiving continuous water of adequate quality	Connection data analysis Water usage study	Assessment of progress in meeting policy targets
					Assessment of adequacy of infrastructure to meet demand
					Identify vulnerable groups and target investments
					Identify capital investment needs
Leakage	Routine monitoring	Frequent	Physical losses of water from piped network	Preferably leakage detection and monitoring based on meter readings	Assessment of physical losses
				Minimum qualitative assessment through sanitary inspection	Improved efficiency in water production
					Improved repair and rehabilitation strategies
					Assessment of water quality risks

Table 5.1: Monitoring requirements for indicators of water supply by surveillance agencies

43

5.1 Continuity

Continuity is a measure of system reliability and is expressed as the proportion of the time on a daily, weekly or monthly basis that water is available in the water supply.. The continuity of supply has important implications for consumers and water suppliers. When water supplies are discontinuous or intermittent, households may be forced to use alternative sources that may be less good quality and less convenient. Discontinuous supplies may also lead to reduce volumes of water collected, leading to poor hygiene and increased risk of diarrhoea and will mean that water must be stored, which may increase the risks of contamination. Where piped water is discontinuous, it is more susceptible to contamination through back-siphonage. Continuity is therefore a crucial element of health-based surveillance.

5.1.1 Piped water

Piped water supplies often suffer from discontinuity. Discontinuity in piped supplies may result from a number of causes but in most cases it is indicative of weak operation and maintenance and/or poor design. However, one of the principal causes of discontinuity world-wide is high levels of leakage that lead to the inability of the supply to meet demands for water. This may be particular problem during peak demand periods. In some cases, the inability to supply peak demands reflects population growth creating demands that cannot be met by current supplies and therefore requires capital investment in the extension and expansion of water supply. However, in very many cases, the reduction of leakage may resolve the discontinuity problem or at least reduce significantly the investment requirements. In addition to physical losses, high rates of commercial losses may exacerbate discontinuity as funds are not re-invested in maintenance.

One of the other common causes of discontinuity in supply may be interruption in the power supply. In some cases, no back-up power source is available and therefore water cannot be pumped during the power-cut. Where stand-by generating sets are available, they are not always used because of a lack of fuel or because the generating sets have developed faults or are non-functional.

Discontinuity exerts an impact on water quality through allowing back-siphonage and it should always be included in sanitary inspections of piped water supplies. When water is flowing under typical mains pressure, the pressure gradient will run from the pipe to the soil, thus any holes in the pipe will allow water to flow out rather than into the pipe, although contamination may still occur as pumping of water often results in pressure fluctuations. However, when there is discontinuity, this pressure gradient reverses as the pipes will be likely to be at a lower pressure than the surrounding soil. Thus, when distribution systems have no water or pressure is significantly lowered, there is potential for contaminated water to enter the pipes from the environment.

Measuring discontinuity in a sanitary inspection may be done through a number of ways. In most cases, the best way to monitor discontinuity is to ask consumers during the sanitary inspection whether they have suffered any interruption in supply in the recent past. If this is kept to no more than one week, recall should be reasonably reliable. This is particularly useful where discontinuity is unpredictable both in terms of frequency and in location within the distribution system. Where interruption in water supply is very predictable because of rationing and records are kept of which parts of the system have received water at which

44

time, this data will provide a good overview of discontinuity within piped water supplies. Indeed, this may be essential in order to plan monitoring activities in the field.

Discontinuity affects different groups to different degrees. The poor who only have access to communal piped water sources are worst affected as they have more limited capacity to store water in the home. As a large number of households may rely on a few taps, discontinuity in supply may lead to restrictions regarding how much water that each household may collect to ensure that as many people as possible can get water. Given the limited ability to store water, discontinuity often means that the poor have to collect water from alternative sources that are often of far poorer quality increasing the risk to their health. Wealthier families may be less affected as they may have cold water storage tanks allowing continued use of water during the interruption.

Discontinuity that continues for extended periods of time has the greatest impact on health, as under these circumstances there will be little choice for households other than using alternative supplies. However, very unpredictable interruptions also have very negative effects. When interruption is reasonably predictable, many households can plan for periods of discontinuity and may not have to resort to alternative sources.

5.1.2 Point sources

Discontinuity is point water supplies will tend to reflect seasonal water shortages and would be typical of development of seasonal springs or where boreholes have been sunk into perched aquifers. Seasonal discontinuity is most effectively measured through an inventory or water usage study when households are asked whether the supply ever dries up and with what frequency.

Boreholes may be further affected by breakdowns and discontinuity is reflected as a 'downtime' – the amount of time taken before operation is restored. This is clearly easily measured during periodic surveys of functional status. Such assessment should include estimates of the downtime experienced. In Uganda, this ranged from 3 months to several years. In general, discontinuity in point supplies may have a limited effect on quality and thus does not to be included in a sanitary inspection.

5.2 Cost

The cost of water supply may exert a profound influence on the use of water supplies. Where water is expensive, the use of other socially acceptable sources of water may be the norm. The cost of water may also prevent the use of sufficient quantities of water for good personal hygiene. The monitoring of purchase costs of water that the urban population is expected pay is an important component of surveillance programmes. Attempts should be made by surveillance agencies to ensure that costs of water do not become prohibitive.

Very often, the monitoring and control of costs of water supply is only carried out in the context of establishing tariff structures for piped water supply. Social or differential tariffs may be established and usually lower costs are charged by the water supplier for lower-level services such as public taps than for domestic or institutional connections and commercial uses of water. However, very often there the price of water purchased by poor households may be far greater than the tariff charged by the water supplier. In some ways this is inevitable as public taps may have additional costs associated with their use such as payment of community members to collect fees for water and to remit these to the supplier.

In many urban areas, the population not served with their own direct connection purchase water from their neighbours or vendors. These costs will typically be several times higher than the actual utility tariff rate. An example from Kampala is shown in table 5.3 below.

Service level	Utility cost per Jerrycan	Average purchase price/ per Jerrycan
Public tap	USH 9.36	USH 33.33
Domestic connection	USH 14.41	USH 14.41
Purchase from neighbour	USH 14.41	USH 50.00
Institutional	USH 17.78	USH 17.78
Industrial (1st 500m^3)	USH 24.71	USH 24.71
Industrial (501-1500m^3)	USH 29.58	USH 29.58
Industrial (> 1500m^3)	USH 33.32	USH 33.32

Table 5.3: Purchase price of water, Kampala

This table illustrates that purchasing water from a neighbour is the most expensive form of piped water supply and is 5.3 times higher than the utility charge for a public standpost, 3.5 times higher than a direct connection and 1.5 times higher than the maximum charge levied by the utility. Even water from public taps is on average, the same price as high volume industrial water users.

To investigate the purchase price of water from communal sources, two approaches may be adopted. In Uganda, during the inventory of sources, details on charges for water at all taps was collected. This data was later supplemented by questions asked during a water usage study that highlighted that little change in the price of water was seen over a period of 2 years.

Where the numbers of household connections is low, then there may be specific components of the tariff that discourage poor families from acquiring their own connection. A critical problem may be the capital investment costs required. These are often high and may discourage a household that could afford the recurrent cost of the tariff from purchasing a connection.

A further problem may be the way in which payment of utility bills is demanded. As there tend to be relatively long periods of time between bills (usually minimum of one month and sometimes longer), this means that money must be saved to set against a bill for water used. For poor families with insecure incomes and little access to banking facilities, this may be difficult and acts as a disincentive to connect to the supply. Surveillance bodies can play a significant role in identifying these problems by working with communities and suppliers to identify bottlenecks in improving supplies.

5.3 Quantity

In the first section, the importance of the quantity of water was discussed in relation to health and it was noted that the use of inadequate volumes of water may lead to poor hygiene and increased incidence of diarrhoeal disease. The volumetric use of water by households is also important for planners or supply operators when reviewing investment decisions regarding extension, rehabilitation or upgrading of water supplies as this will be key factor in design and will have significant cost implications.

The quantity of water used is a factor that does not require routine monitoring quantity but requires periodic assessment, as significant variations are unlikely to occur within short periods of time. Supply-side measurements, for instance in terms of daily, monthly or yearly per capita production of water, whilst relatively easy to calculate have little meaning for surveillance bodies. For health-based surveillance, it is actual quantity of water used that is important rather than that which is potentially available.

The volume of water used is primarily a function of proximity and it has been shown in a number of studies that once the source of water is located outside the home environment, the volume of water used decreases significantly. In general, the evidence suggests households collect around 20 litre per capita per day of water or less from communal sources. From water supplied to a single tap in the yard, a figure of around 50 litres per capita per day is quoted. For water piped into the home 150 to 300 litres per capita per day may be used, as more water-hungry devices will be used such as flush toilets, showers. Payment for water may also lead to reduced volumes of water used..

Table 5.2 provides information from studies in Uganda.

Level of service	Consumption (l/c/d)
Non-piped sources, Jinja	15.8
Communal taps, Jinja	15.5
Yard tap, Jinja	50
Water within home, Jinja	155
Non-piped source, Kampala	17
Communal piped source, Kampala	18

Table 5.2: Consumption by service level, Uganda
NB: Data for Jinja taken from the Guidance Manual on Water Supply and Sanitation Programmes (Well, 1999) and for Kampala based on water usage studies

Given the studies that have been undertaken in the past, there is strong argument to suggest that rather than focusing on actual volume use by households, service level and time to water source can be used as surrogates. However, this will only produce relative results and no empirical evidence of how much water is being used each day. This may adequate for many uses.

In some circumstances there is a need to gain a more reliable picture of how water is being used by households enjoying different levels of service. Most governments have policies that define the target for water supply access in the country and this is likely to include a figure for quantity of water to be supplied. Therefore to assess the degree to which such targets are being met, it will be essential to gain a reasonably accurate idea of how much water is actually being collected and used. Other examples of times when actual figures of use are required will include the planning of new water supplies where demand must be forecast to ensure that the supply is neither under nor over designed. It may also be of use when evaluating the health education programmes that promote better hygiene through increased use of water.

Although measuring quantity usage is not simple, it can be done through a variety of means. However, perhaps the critical point to note is that trying to assess how much water each household is using would be time consuming and unnecessary. A sample of households will be taken that is representative of the population. Whilst imperfect, such an approach is useful in gaining reliable results within a reasonable cost and time framework. A minimum sample size can be estimated by using standard approaches to sample size calculation or by using appropriate software.

Where piped water supplies are metered, the volumes used by households with a direct connection can be relatively easily assessed, provided some data is available on the demographics of the area. This is clearly easiest for households with their own connection, whether in the yard or in-house. The average volume of water used can then be calculated from a sample of households with either a yard or an in-house water supply. The volume of water used over a 12-month period can be measured based on metered consumption and a per capita consumption obtained by dividing the total consumption by the average household size for the area. If there is uncertainty about which residences have water only at a yard or in-house supply, then it may be necessary to check the households in the study to ensure that it is clear which level of service is enjoyed.

Where supplies are not metered, then estimates of volume use will be difficult to determine without carrying out a more detailed study into the water use patterns. Such a study may use a variety of methods, including water use diaries, but would be time-consuming and not necessarily of value to a surveillance agency.

Measuring quantities of water used is most difficult for communal supplies is because the number of users may not be known. Design figures of people using the sources should not be used as this is likely to lead to highly inaccurate estimates. Where there is good record keeping by the source caretaker about the purchasers of water and number of units of water sold then a reasonable estimate can be made, provided this identifies repeated collection by the same household in one day. However, many families may use more than one source and therefore care must be taken that assessments of metered water use at a public tap does not under-estimate volumes of water used.

If data is required on the volumes of water used for domestic purposes by the population served by communal sources, then this should be collected through surveys of the target population. This data will be useful in determining the volume of water likely to used from a new communal facility, for instance a public tap, which will provide indications of the financial viability of the installation. Such data may help communities and field staff investigate how many taps are required in an area and whether the revenue from the tap will support the operational costs. Assessments of quantities of water used at different service levels should allow planners of new infrastructure to base investment decisions on more sound knowledge of the demand for water in different parts of the city.

5.4 Coverage

Coverage is a measure of the number of people who have access to a recognisable water supply, although this may be converted into a figure for the population served by an adequate and safe water supply. In many ways, coverage should represent an overall performance assessment that takes into account issues such as quality of water, quantities used by consumers utilising different service levels and the continuity of supply.

Coverage estimates should not be based purely on the presence of infrastructure as this may bear little relation to actual usage of different types of water supply. Assessing the extent of distribution networks alone, for instance, has limited meaning for the surveillance agency as a measure of coverage. It may, however, have other purposes such identifying what type of action (i.e. investment in infrastructure or marketing of services) is required and whether limited infrastructure is a critical constraint in extending services. It is also useful to look at rates of disconnection, in particular in relation to socio-economic status, as a measure of equity in water supply.

5.4.1 Measuring coverage as an indicator of access

Coverage is often assessed as the number of people with access to water at different service levels and source types and does not take into account any other factors. This may be done for instance to assess whether defined national and international targets on access to water supplies are being met and what shortfalls exist, leading to the identification of priority areas requiring services and the targeting of resources on those who lack adequate services. Furthermore, coverage terms can also include assessment of whether the available infrastructure is able to meet current and projected demands and whether capital investment is required.

Using census data

The determination of access to different service levels is not necessarily simple within urban areas. The easiest and most reliable method to collect this data is during a national census, making sure this includes data on the level of service provided at each house. However, some caution should be used in the use of these data, as many censuses only record the principal source of water. Thus while the data on people with water piped within the home or to a yard level of service may be reliable estimates, the data relating to those using communal services may be inaccurate. Where water supplies are unreliable, the extent to which multiple sources will be used can be expected to increase and this should be taken into account when estimating coverage.

Where a variety of communal or public sources are available, it is likely that households will use more than one source and subsidiary sources may receive significant use. For instance, in Kampala 50% of the low-income population with easy access to more than one source at a Parish level utilise at least two water sources and up to two-thirds supplement this with rainwater collection. Using data from a water usage study, it was calculated that 33% of this population used protected springs as their first choice water source, but overall use of protected springs was in the region of 63%. Given that 430,000 people live in Parishes that have easy access to springs, the Kampala aggregate use of springs is at least 40% of the population.

Where the census data is deemed to be unreliable or is felt to be greatly out of date, there are several alternative approaches that can be followed:

- Large-scale survey of the whole population

- Sample survey of the urban population

- Reviews of utility/supplier data

Large scale survey of the whole population

Undertaking large-scale surveys are unlikely to be realistic in most cases, as the expense involved would be very high in any reasonable sized towns. Unless specific programmes are initiated to greatly increase the number of direct connections, the changes in percentage terms may be minimal over short time periods. Therefore, the figures gained from a survey may be valid estimates for some time. If a major initiative to increase direct connections is implemented, then changes in access would be more easily carried out through a review of utility connection data.

Survey of the urban population

Other sample surveys may include demographic health surveys (DHS) where a certain number of towns or regions within a country are included and data collected. Clearly, as with all social studies, care should be taken to make sure that the sample sites selected are representative of country as a whole and the findings can be broadly applied to those town not included within the study. A sample of areas within an urban area could also be taken, with same caveats as above.

Reviews of utility/supplier data

Where good records are maintained by the utility or water supplier, the numbers of people with access to water at a yard or in-house level of supply can be determined on a rolling basis. However, in many cases record keeping is poor and there may be limited up to date data. Furthermore, it cannot be assumed that where records are kept that there will be a differentiation between yard and in-house water supply. Utilities may commonly only keep records of numbers of direct connections to a household and possibly the pipe size. Whilst for assessments of coverage, the differentiation between in-house and yard level of services is important, from the utility point of view is not necessary as they are simply concerned with keeping a record of their customer base and to bill and collect revenue for water that has been used. Where good records are available for new connections, disconnections and reconnections, a rolling annual assessment in connection rate is possible.

5.4.2 Providing an estimate of coverage

When data is collected on access, a summary will be appear as follows:

1. Percent population with individual connection (preferably broken down into within-house and yard)

2. Percent population using solely piped water from communal taps (public or neighbours)

3. Percent population using piped water from a communal source supplemented by a second non-piped source

4. Percent population using a non-piped source supplemented by a second piped source

5. Percent population using solely a non-piped source

Summing these figures will give an estimate of coverage with piped water supply. If an estimate of the number of people receiving a safe and adequate water supply is required then this must take into account the water quality and continuity data. To do this the number of people served by piped water supply would be multiplied by the annual compliance rate (i.e. number of samples with no detectable microbiological quality) and the frequency of supply interruption.

This may be expressed as follows:

$$P = Ps \times CR \times D$$

Where Ps is the percentage of people using the source
CR is the compliance rate (expressed as a percentage of the total samples)
D is the percentage of sanitary inspections showing discontinuity.

5.4.3 Supply coverage

The above approach is most appropriate to use as it provides an estimate of utilised coverage. However in some cases, an estimate of the supply capacity to meet the potential demand is also required. This requires a simple comparison of the water produced and the potential demand. A further comparison can be made to assess the degree to which the distribution system covers the population within a reasonable distance. These can then indicate where and what type of capital investment is required.

Such an approach can also be used to evaluate whether the major shortcomings in the numbers of people served relates to the production of water, the provision of infrastructure to distribute water or to uptake of available services. For instance, the volume of water produced at the works may be adequate for the estimated demand, but because the distribution infrastructure is limited, the numbers of household with access to piped water may be low because gaining access is expensive and difficult. Such problems may relate to the extent of distribution mains, but may also include the system storage capacity, which may be too small to cope with peak demands. In other cases, production and distribution may be adequate, but the degree of uptake of services limited. In this case, marketing of the water services is required, with a review of what disincentives exist to prevent uptake.

Sector performance may also be evaluated through assessment of the potential existing coverage (the total number of connections recorded) against an actual coverage (the number of active connections). The latter is effectively a measure of the number of people who have been disconnected. If the disconnected population is high (above 10%), this indicates that there are shortcomings in the supply. The monitoring of disconnection is important both from a public health and an equity aspect as disconnection represents a significant health problem as it forces use of alternative sources of often-lower quality. From an equity point of view, comparing the level of disconnection to socio-economic status will indicate whether the urban poor are being disadvantaged.

5.5 Unaccounted for water

In addition to the factors already discussed, in the case of piped water supplies the amount and nature of unaccounted for water should also be monitored. This primarily relates to supplies operated by utilities or local authorities, as this will be more difficult to monitor for community managed piped water supplies and the impact may be less critical. Unaccounted for water may have impacts on water quality, availability, reliability and cost.

Unaccounted for water is often used as a measure of operational performance as it is a measure of the efficiency of delivering services and how much water has been supplied for which costs have not been recovered. Unaccounted-for-water is a somewhat crude measure and therefore detailed monitoring of unaccounted-for-water is primarily undertaken by water suppliers who will want to obtain information regarding commercial and physical losses. For surveillance agencies, however, the principal concern will be physical losses as this may have an impact on water quality. This section discusses physical loss estimation and will briefly discuss commercial loss estimation for completeness. However, in the latter case, the principal interest for the surveillance agency is to ensure that water suppliers attempt to reduce commercial losses, rather than measure these themselves.

5.5.1 Physical losses

Physical losses derive from poorly maintained infrastructure that leads to water being lost from treatment plant, wellheads, service reservoir or distribution. Most physical loss estimates focus primarily on losses post-production within the distribution network. Physical losses are of greater concern in many ways than commercial losses for surveillance bodies. This is water for which no benefit is derived, unlike commercial losses where benefit is certainly accrued by part of the population. Physical losses are usually more expensive and difficult to reduce as often require capital-intensive investment and a commitment to more effective maintenance and rehabilitation strategies.

Physical losses largely relate to the loss of water through leaking pipes and tanks. This may have a profound impact on the reliability, costs, quality and accessibility of drinking water and may also have negative impacts on water resources as more water than required is abstracted. However, despite its great importance, leakage monitoring and control remains weak in many countries and represents a serious barrier to improving access to safe water supplies.

For surveillance agencies, detailed estimates of leakage will not be undertaken, but rather attention placed on qualitative estimates of leakage through sanitary inspection. This is usually done partly to determine likely adverse effects on water quality, but also to gain some idea of system performance. This data can be collected through interview of households in the area where the sanitary inspection is being carried out and provides a crude measure the extent of leakage occurring in the system and identification of particular problem areas.

Water suppliers should, however, be encouraged to undertake routine quantitative estimates of leakage and physical losses as a means of monitoring operation and maintenance performance. Quantifiable estimates of leakage are most reliable where systems are metered.

The use of household and bulk meters is essential to calculate losses. It is relatively simple exercise to monitor the flow between two stretches of mains pipe fitted with bulk meters between a set period of time and then take a reading of all household meters supplied by that line. The losses are then equal to the difference between the calculated flow used between the two bulk meters and the total estimate of use from household meter readings.

Leakage estimates where significant amounts of unmetered connections exist are usually very unreliable and likely to have large margins of error making decision making difficult. In unmetered supplies, monitoring of physical losses will only provide rough estimates and therefore may not be justified.

5.5.2 Commercial losses

The direct impact of commercial losses is primarily felt the utility as this represents a loss of revenue that is easily preventable. However, commercial losses may restrict the ability of the utility to undertake proper maintenance of the system and they may also restrict the extension of services to the population lacking connection to a water supply. Thus high commercial losses may indirectly lead to problems with reliability, quality and quantity of the water available and should be minimised

Commercial losses may result from a number of factors:

1. Billing inefficiency, where the number of bills produced or distributed to customers is less than the total number of customers recorded. This is a common failing in many urban utilities where customer databases are often poorly developed, although many larger utilities are now maintaining more accurate records.

2. Collection inefficiency, where the number of bills for which revenue is collected is less than the total number of bills sent out.

3. Illegal connections to the supply.

Calculating billing efficiency is relatively easy where there are reasonably reliable records of the consumers of water. Monitoring should be based on supplier records of bills sent out against recorded active accounts. This data can then be submitted to a surveillance body (usually the body that dealing with finances who then share information with other surveillance bodies) with the records open the periodic audit. This in principle can be done on a monthly basis as, unlike revenue collection, any variation in billing cycles can be pre-determined, although clearly allowance may need to be made for new accounts opened as these may not immediately show on billing cycles. In billing efficiency, the problem lies primarily with the supplier and water suppliers should be encouraged to improve billing efficiency to an acceptable level.

Calculating revenue efficiency is usually based on an assessment of how many bills have been paid to the utility. Revenue inefficiency results from a number of factors some of which are beyond the control of the supplier and the frequency of monitoring revenue collection efficiency has to take these into account. In many cases, payment may be delayed by the customer either for a short period or for an extended period where there is large debt to be paid off. It is in the best interests of the supplier, customer and surveillance agency that the system of payment is as flexible as can be realistically achieved without encouraging non-payment of bills. Where Government departments are supplied, it is common to find that very large debts build up over time and there is frequently little action that can be taken by the supplier to enforce payment and therefore this must be taken into account when assessing this component of commercial losses. In some countries, the money owed by Government is removed from estimates of revenue collection, which focus solely on collection efficiency from personal, community-managed and commercial connections.

Revenue collection efficiency may vary from significantly below 100% to significantly above 100% from month to month. This largely reflects payment patterns that may be different from billing cycles and in particular payment of large bills by Government or other organisations at one time. It is therefore better to base assessment of revenue collection efficiency on aggregated figures from a longer time period (for instance 12-month), rather then monthly figures.

Illegal connection remain a highly contentious issue in the water sector and in many developing countries, illegal connections are blamed for a great part of the problems faced in sustaining a high quality water supply. Whilst illegal connections may be a significant problem in many areas, it is often over-stated as a cause of inefficient management as clearly it is easier for utilities to blame the consumers rather than accept they can do much to improve the management of the supply. Some 'illegal' connections are not truly illegal, as often they are simply older connections for which records have not been kept or are connections for which either bills have not been produced. Assessing illegal connection is rarely easy and is only really of benefit to the supplier and financial watchdog, although high numbers of illegal connection may result in higher leakage, low pressure and deteriorating quality. It may also affect the ability of the utility to extend supplies, although this may be somewhat debatable as it is often the 'unserved' areas that have most illegal connection, thus the delivery of water has actually been achieved. Obviously the simplest way to assess illegal connection is undertake detailed surveys, although this is expensive and unlikely to be justifiable apart from a very occasional basis. An alternative way to monitor illegal connection is to calculate billing, revenue collection and physical losses and any difference left from the total production can be taken as an estimate of illegal connections.

6.

Sanitary inspection

Sanitary inspections are a key tool in the monitoring and surveillance of water supplies and are recommended by WHO and in texts such as Standard methods for water and wastewater analysis as an essential activity when samples for water quality analysis are taken. It should be stressed that sanitary inspections primarily relate to the risk of microbiological contamination and different risk assessment methodologies may be required when investigating risks related to chemical contamination.

Sanitary inspections are designed to provide an overview of the status of risk of the supply to contamination. One purpose in carrying out a sanitary inspection therefore is to identify the probable cause of failure when contamination is found. However, sanitary inspection can be used monitor the potential for contamination in the future, thus providing an important early warning function. Analysis of water quality is in itself an inherently reactive process in that identification of risk to health can only be achieved once contamination has occurred. Sanitary inspection can also be used an for monitoring operation and maintenance performance.

6.1 Systematic sanitary inspection

If the use of sanitary inspection is to be maximised, a systematic approach should be adopted. Experience from many countries has shown that unless inspections follow a standard format, comparisons between inspections done by different staff are difficult to compare. It is also difficult to quantify risks where a non-systematic approach has been adopted.

In order to provide a consistent evaluation of risks across a city or country, standard forms are used. These use a series of questions regarding principal risks to the water source or supply. The questions in a sanitary inspection are usually structured so that the answer is either 'Yes' or 'No'. A score of one point is allocated for every 'Yes' answer and zero points for every 'No' answer. On completion, a score is given based on all the 'Yes' answers, which can be converted into a percentage (to allow comparisons with operation and maintenance at different source types). Annex 3 provides examples of sanitary inspection forms. The data that can be generated through sanitary inspections is very powerful in monitoring the performance of individual supplies, as well as offering comparisons between supplies of the same type and between supplies of different types.

Sanitary inspections provide an ongoing assessment of risk and therefore can be used in a predictive manner Supplies that have high levels of sanitary risk, but no identified microbiological contamination, are not good supplies but supplies that remain at high risk of contamination in the future. When the data from sanitary inspections are used effectively actions. The presence of a risk in the water supply that would be likely to cause contamination to occur should be used as evidence for the need for action irrespective of the results of a water quality analysis.

Sanitary inspections are also powerful tools to monitor operation and maintenance as the majority questions relate to aspects that the managers of the water supply or owners of household water storage containers will need to maintain in good condition to prevent contamination of the water. Once an overall risk score exceeds 60%, the supply or storage container can be categorised as poorly maintained and likely to be contaminated at some point in the future.

As sanitary inspections are designed to provide an integrated overview of the status of the water supply, they incorporate a number of factors about a water supply that may contribute directly or indirectly to water quality failure. These can be categorised as follows:

- **Hazard factors:** these are factors from which contamination may be derived and are sources of faeces in the environment. Examples will include pit latrines, sewers, solid waste dumps, animal husbandry and stagnant surface water.

- **Pathway factors:** these are factors that allow microbiological contamination to enter the water supply, but do not provide the faecal matter directly. Pathways are often critical to whether contamination occurs, as the presence of hazard may not directly lead to contamination if no pathway exists for the contamination to reach the water supply. Examples of pathway factors include leaking pipes, eroded catchment areas or damaged protection works.

- **Indirect factors:** these are factors that enhance the development of pathway factors, but do not either directly allow water into the source nor are a source of faeces Examples include lack of fencing, faulty surface water diversion drainage or poor drainage of wastewater from the source.

Sanitary risks are often inter-dependent. A good example of this will be surface hazards such as solid waste dumps that contain faecal matter. In this case, direct microbiological contamination of the aquifer may be less likely as attenuation can be expected in the unsaturated zone (although nitrate and chloride may be problems). The importance of this hazard will be enhanced when there is a lack of surface water diversion ditches that allow direct inundation of the backfill area of a spring and this is eroded. In many cases, a series of factors such as a lack of fence, lack of diversion ditch, eroded backfill and other pollution uphill such as solid waste dumps combine to cause contamination.

Therefore, when developing sanitation inspection forms bear in mind that the indirect factors may be as important as pathways or hazards. Some example sanitary inspection forms that have been shown to be effective are provided in Annex 3 and it is recommended that these act as models, but that these are modified to ensure they are appropriate to local conditions.

6.2 Developing sanitary inspection forms

The development of sanitary inspection forms is an important component of the pilot stage of surveillance projects. Whilst the examples provided can act as the basis of a sanitary inspection forms, these should be evaluated within the national context and revised as required. Different areas will use different designs, they may have different excreta disposal methods and may have a variety of different hydrogeological regimes and risks.

The initial development of sanitary inspection forms is simple. The best approach is to visit a sample of sources to be included within the surveillance programme to assess their status and to assess factors of importance. In Uganda a sample of springs, boreholes and taps were visited and the environment and their condition of the supply were assessed and a review of designs was made. Following this, the likely major problems were identified by the project management and field staff and the forms developed. These were then piloted during training events and subsequently and revised where problems were found in identifying risks or risks were not seen to be influential. The process of revision should be ongoing to reflect increasing knowledge of the risks to water quality failure and changes in risk due to improvements.

Sanitary inspection methodology should be standardised across a country, even though different risks may be more important in different areas. If sanitary inspection forms for the same type of source vary between towns, it will be difficult to consolidate data at regional or national levels and will limit the usefulness of the data generated.

6.2.1 Risk factor weighting

In most sanitary inspections, an equal weight is given to each factor included in the sanitary inspection. This is usually done at the outset of a surveillance programme, as the most important causes of contamination may be unknown. However, certain factors may exert a greater influence than other factors on water quality and therefore it could be suggested that sanitary inspection would be more effective if the relative importance of different risks was reflected as a weighted score.

However, certain issues must be borne in mind when considering the unequal weighting of different risk factors included in a sanitary inspection. Sanitary inspection should be used not only to identify causes of contamination and the risk of future contamination, but also to an overall assessment of operation and maintenance. An unequal weighting of risk factors may produce biased results in terms of operation and maintenance assessment.

Careful consideration also needs to be given to whether the factors are weighted to reflect simple incidence (i.e. whether contamination has been found) or to the level of contamination found. For instance, in one town in Uganda, there was strong evidence that the presence of latrine uphill of the borehole was most important in there being any contamination found, but the presence of a latrine within 10m more important in determining the degree of contamination. The influence of different risk factors on the same type of water supply may vary significantly between different areas and at different times of the year. For instance, in the example from Uganda noted above, it should be pointed that it was only in this one town that significant contamination of boreholes was found.

Unequal weighting would also have to take into account relationships between different factors. This is particularly important if sanitary inspection is used as an early warning indicator as part of operation and maintenance monitoring. Indirect risks would be likely to receive a lower weighting as they will be less likely to show any association with contamination in a particular sampling round. However, it may be because that such risks exist that contamination occurs in the future as they facilitate the development of direct pollutant pathways. This has important implications in the use of sanitary inspection data in identifying remedial action. If improvements are made to reduce one particular risk without addressing the indirect factors that promote the development of that risk is unlikely to be effective.

In the case of point sources, it is not recommended that risk weighting is carried out unless there is overwhelming evidence that one or two risks, which operate independent of other risks, are the cause of water quality failure. It is more appropriate to identify the importance of individual risk factors through analysis of data and this is recommended when planning preventative and remedial action and the priority given to each intervention.

In the case of piped water supplies, there is perhaps a stronger case to be made regarding the allocation of weighted risk factors between supply and local risks. This is based on the impact on the number of users. Localised risks will affect relatively few consumers as the risks will be restricted to the immediate area around the sampling point. Supply risks, by contrast, will affect a much large number of people and the impact will be felt not only in the potential for contamination but also in supply failure leading to forced use of alternatives. Furthermore, the presence of local and supply risks represent completely different arenas for action as one entails consumer/community awareness raising whilst the other represents a field for water supplier action that may be enforced through regulation.

6.3 Frequency of sanitary inspection

A sanitary inspection should be carried out each time a sample is taken for water quality analysis by the surveillance body. However, more frequent inspections may be carried out by either the surveillance body or users of the water supply when water quality tests are not carried out in order to evaluate potential future risks or as a periodic measure of operational and maintenance.

6.4 Inspection of piped water supplies

As most sanitary inspections are based on observation of the supply, there are inherent problems with carrying them out for urban piped water systems. Leaks within deep-laid pipes are often difficult to detect through observation and given usual flow rates contamination may have occurred many metres if not kilometres from the sample site. To develop a full-scale risk assessment of an urban piped network requires collection and analysis of a range of data such as leakage rates, land-use, population density, biofilm formation potential, chlorine demand, pipe age and material and pressure data.

However, the use of simple visual and question based approaches still provide useful information regarding the major risks of the systems and the domain of principal risks – whether a general supply fault or a localised risk. This also provides a simple way to look at operation and maintenance of the supply as it will collect information on leakage and continuity as well as the degree to which pipes are properly buried and secured. Questions included on the inspection form should deal both with risks found in the immediate are of the sample point and those that relate to broader supply problems (e.g. leakage and discontinuity).

Local risks will include aspects such as development of pools of stagnant water around the joints between the riser pipe and delivery main, the leakage of the tap, exposure of the pipe and waste allowed to collect around the tap may be significant causes of failure. In Kampala, a total of 37 samples out of 1459 samples taken from the piped network had microbiological contamination. In all cases, localised risks were identified as potential sources of pollution and in roughly half, localised risks were concluded as the direct cause of failures based on absence of supply risks.

An example of a simple inspection form for an urban supply is shown in Annex 3 and this illustrates the combination of localised and supply related risks. In this form, the first six questions specifically relate to the immediate environment surrounding the sampling point. Questions 7-10 relate to major supply faults for which data can be obtained through visual assessment or questions asked of community members.

Inspections are required at service reservoirs as these represent a critical point for widespread contamination. This should be done by the water supplier and where possible, by the surveillance agency. However, access to such facilities may not always be easy to gain for non-staff members of the water supply body and that furthermore, independent inspection may not be required if there is collaboration between the supplier and surveillance body.

Given the difficulty in trying to provide a sanitary inspection of an entire urban piped water system in one day, a decision will have to be made regarding the scope of the sanitary inspection on any single day of sampling. The area to be covered by a sanitary inspection carried out by field staff should be set so that it can be easily covered within one day and can be easily related to sample points for water quality analysis. For surveillance agencies, this may done in relation to administrative boundaries (as was the case in work done in Ghana and Uganda) or in relation to known supply zones (as was the case in Bangladesh). For water suppliers, sanitary inspection should cover a piped water zone as discussed in Chapter 8. Where this is covers a large area then the zone can be sub-divided and inspection carried out progressively.

6.5 Treatment plants

Routine inspections should also be carried out at treatment plants, although this would typically be the responsibility of the water supplier rather than the surveillance agency unless community-managed treatment plants exist. In the latter case, the surveillance agency should include routine inspection of such plants, as this may be critical to ensuring safe water supplies. Inspection of treatment plants requires a reasonable knowledge of how treatment processes work and therefore if this is to be included in surveillance activities additional training may be required.

When assessing treatment plants, the operational requirements of different processes should be understood. In some cases, a review of records on plant performance can then suffice to review performance, provided these are kept up to date. However, records are sometimes misleading and inspections of routine cleaning practices is highly recommended. For instance, in a small town supply in Zimbabwe, the records showed that backwashing of the filters was carried out at the specified design intervals. However, a site inspection showed that this was done ineffectively as the bed was not fully disturbed, leading to a build up of mud balls within the filter.

An example of a sanitary inspection form for treatment plants is shown in Annex 3 and can be used as a basis for development of forms at a national level.

6.6 Point sources

In sanitary inspections of point sources a visual assessment of the major risk factors is usually possible. However, in some circumstances, the nature of the groundwater regime may change the influence of different hazards. For instance, the presence of fracture flow aquifers will allow microbiological contaminants to travel significant distances with little or no attenuation and this may need to be considered in the sanitary inspection. It is therefore important to have some knowledge of the nature of groundwater flow when developing sanitary inspection forms.

The hazards for point sources relate to those that allow the accumulation of faecal material and therefore when developing sanitary inspection tools, it is important that the excreta disposal methods in the area are known. Faecal material may be derived from a variety of on-site sanitation systems (including pit latrines and septic tanks) as well as leaking sewers. In addition, where excreta disposal facilities are limited, faeces may be disposed of in bags or other containers on the ground surface in waste dumps or drainage channels. The forms provided as examples in Annex 3 were developed in a context where urban excreta disposal methods were poorly developed and the surface disposal of faeces was common. In other areas, this will not be case and therefore other factors (such as sewers uphill of a point source) may be included.

The presence of latrines or on-site sanitation should always be included because these are hazard with potentially highly concentrated faecal matter. Furthermore, the faecal matter may be released into the environment below the most significant attenuating layer (the soil) or may place a high hydraulic loading of contaminants into the sub-surface which may limit the potential for attenuation. This may be further exacerbated by high water tables that allow contaminants to reach the groundwater without sufficient time for attenuation of microbes. Other hazards include solid waste dumps, particularly in areas where sanitation is poor as this may contain significant amounts of faeces. Surface water that is allowed to form polls uphill of a source may also be a risk, particularly where sanitation is poor as faecal matter is often disposed of into drains and pools of water is such circumstances. The access of animals within 10m of a water source represents a factor representing a potential hazard as animal faeces can then potentially enter into the water source.

The pathways that would usually be assessed in a sanitary inspection of a point source usually relate to the immediate sanitary protection or completion measures around the source itself. These will include factors such as the erosion of the immediate area behind the retaining wall or spring box in the case of protected springs or a cracked apron in the case of boreholes. For boreholes, factors such as inadequate size of apron reflect a pathway (as wastewater is not properly removed from the area around the riser pipe) and also a major design flaw.

Indirect factors will be those that enhance the possibility of development of a pathway for contaminants to enter the source. Such factors include lack of fences and surface water diversion ditches. These are factors that for instance allow inundation of the backfill area of a protected spring allowing both erosion of the cover and direct ingress of contaminated surface water once a pathway has developed. Where fences are absent, both people and animals can gain access to the backfill area and cause erosion (for instance through the development of a footpath through the backfill area) and for faeces to accumulate on top of the backfill area. Flooding of a collection area is also an indirect mechanism as this relates to the increased likelihood of collection of contaminated surface water by users.

6.7 Household water

In many cases, routine inspection of household facilities is not undertaken because the presence of contamination may relate to other factors, such as whether the water is boiled, rather than observable factors. However, inspection can be carried out and an example form is shown in Annex 3. Where water is stored in tanks within the home, additional forms may need to be developed which should look at the cleanliness of the inside of the tank, whether the tank is covered and whether the tank is located away from potential sources of contamination such as birds or rodents.

6.8 Community monitoring and sanitary inspection

As discussed in Chapter 4, community participation in surveillance is important and requires good planning. The ways in which this can be achieved is outlined in Chapter 4, thus here only possible tools are reviewed.

It is desirable that communities also monitor their water supplies and identify any changes in quality (often through simple observation of colour changes) and increased risks. The advantage of sanitary inspection is that it allows simple assessments of the water supply to be done and can be translated into a community tool. One approach is to use a visual rather than written form of sanitary inspection, although in many urban communities literacy rates are high and therefore simple checklists may be adequate.

Communities may have different priorities to health bodies and water suppliers in what is important about the quality of their water supply and issues such as costs, continuity and financial sustainability may be more important that possible deterioration within the source. It is important therefore to ensure that where communities undertake inspections that the information collected is meaningful both to themselves and can be linked to surveillance data. An example is provided below in Figure 6.1.

This checklist allows simple information collection by community members and as it has an action list, it allows the committee and community to monitor whether the action is taken by the caretaker to reduce the risk. This allows both monitoring of the sanitary risk of the water supply and operational performance. Such checklists should be translated into the local language to ensure their effectiveness and this was carried out in Uganda.

Checklist	No	Yes	Action
Does the water in the spring change colour after heavy rain?			
Have the public health department tested your spring recently?			
Were you told the result and given any advice?			
Did you act on the advice?			
Is the retaining wall showing any signs of damage?			
Does the retaining wall need repair – what is this and can you do it yourself?			
If you cannot do it, is there anyone in your community who can do this repair?			
How much will the repair cost? (think about labour as well as material)			
Does the uphill diversion ditch need cleaning?			
When was it last cleaned?			
Is the drainage ditch below the spring blocked or need clearing?			
Does the fence need any repairs?			
If repairs are need, what is required and can you do it yourself?			
If you cannot do it, is there anyone in your community who can do this repair?			
How much will the repair cost? (think about labour as well as material)			
Do the steps need cleaning?			
Do the steps need any repair?			
If repairs are need, what is required and can you do it yourself?			
If you cannot do it, is there anyone in your community who can do this repair?			
If there is a hedge, does this need trimming?			
When was the hedge last trimmed?			
Does the grass within the fence need slashing?			
When did you last slash the grass?			
Are the outlets from the retaining wall showing any leaks?			
Are there any other problems with your spring that need attention?			
What are these?			

Figure 6.1: Community sanitary risk checklist

6.9 Linkages to other risk assessment tools

Whilst sanitary inspection is an extremely useful tool in assessing the likely causes of contamination and the risk of contamination in the future, there is sometimes a need to link this to other risk assessment tools. Sanitary inspections tend to be focused on limited areas and this is in general justified as a great deal of the microbiological contamination found in water supplies is caused by local problems. However, in some situations the cause of contamination may be beyond the normal scope of a sanitary inspection. Furthermore, there is also a need to look at broader issues relating to catchments and source/resource sustainability both in the context of an overall management approach and to take into account pollutants not routinely tested in surveillance programmes. The latter will include chemicals and pathogens.

Below is briefly discussed the need and methods for carrying out environmental risk appraisals on groundwater and surface water catchments. However, the techniques discussed here are for brief appraisals. For more in-depth environmental impact assessment, appropriate texts should be consulted.

6.9.1 Environmental risk appraisal/pollution risk appraisal

There is a number of other risk assessments methodologies that address potential risks to water quality beyond the factors typically included within a sanitary inspection. In particular, there may be a need to broaden the scope of risk assessment for groundwaters if the hydrogeological conditions are such as to make more distant sources of pollution important. A good example of this would be where fracture aquifers are exploited. Such aquifers may have flow rates of many 100 of meters per day and therefore a source of contamination in a recharge area may be distant from the source being exploited for drinking water supply, but able to deliver substantial numbers of microbes.

Such a risk assessment would not be routinely undertaken by surveillance staff as it will require a more detailed knowledge of groundwater conditions in the area than would typically be found in non-specialist staff. An investigation of this kind would require a hydrogeologist or hydrologist and would be required as a one-off assessment rather than a routine evaluation. This kind of investigation is likely to be expensive and would be justified only where sustained high contamination was found when no local sources of pollution or pathways were identified from sanitary inspection.

Sanitary inspections are primarily designed to assess the risk related to microbiological contamination and therefore may not provide the information required when looking at the potential for chemical contamination of water supplies, particularly in relation to increased chemical contamination of water sources. In order to assess such risk other forms of simple pollution risk appraisal may be required that look at the activities within the catchment, the likely pollutants that will be discharged into the source and the capacity of the source to reduce the pollutant load through dilution. However, such activities would normally be carried out by water suppliers and environmental agencies rather than surveillance bodies, although there may be a requirement for these to be periodically carried out and reports supplied to the surveillance agency. Some simple pollution risk assessment forms are shown in Annex 3.

The other form of risk assessment that is likely to be periodically required in the water sector is an environmental impact assessment or EIA. These would typically be done when a new source is being developed or a new activity that potentially may pollute the source of water is proposed within a catchment area. This again would usually be done by a water supplier or environmental agency and a detailed discussion is beyond the scope of this text. Annex 6 provides information of suitable further reading on EIAs.

7.

Analytical ranges in water quality surveillance

There are many different micro-organisms and chemical substances as well as physical characteristics of water which define its quality. Some substances and organisms exert a profound impact on health, other substances may cause rejection of water by consumers, whilst other substances may affect the operational efficiency of the supply. Some parameters will require frequent regular testing throughout the water supply system, whilst others may be restricted to headworks analysis and done either through regular monitoring or periodic analysis. In the WHO Guidelines for Drinking-water Quality, a total of 128 chemicals as well as key microbiological and physico-chemical parameters are included that have a direct impact on health or acceptability of water.

Given the wide range of potential contaminants, priories must be set. The overwhelming priority is the microbiological quality of drinking-water as it is the contamination of drinking water with pathogenic organisms that contributes the greatest health burden and that leads to outbreaks of infectious disease. In addition, physico-chemical parameters that cause rejection of water supply such as colour or taste are also a high priority. Other chemical contamination is always of lower priority.

If monitoring of water quality is to be driven by management needs, the use of different data should be carefully considered at the outset of the programme. For instance, microbiological testing results can be used to make improvements in systems operation and maintenance, improved design and in health education. However, monitoring of organic chemicals may lead to less tangible uses unless there is a commitment to implementing costly improvements in treatment. The link between environmental legislation and drinking water quality is profound and the routine assessment of land use in catchment areas may be more appropriate than analysis of water quality in some circumstances.

7.1 Selection of parameters

The selection of parameters included in a programme of water quality analysis is likely to country (and possibly region) specific and may also be specific to certain types of water. Furthermore, the range of analysis and frequency of testing will be constrained by the resources available for water quality analysis and whilst it may be desirable that a great number of parameters are analysed frequently, budget limitations may constrain how much testing and which parameters are analysed. However, in general, there are some basic rules that should guide the development of water quality analysis programmes.

The first step in deciding whether a particular parameters should be included in a monitoring programme is to ascertain whether the substance exists in the waters of the country and whether it is in all waters or only in restricted areas or types of water (e.g. groundwater below 40m etc). This can usually be assessed by reviewing existing data, if this does not exist then a brief assessment could be made of waters in the country to evaluate whether:

1. the substance is present;

2. if so, at what levels does it exist and do these approach or reach levels which are of concern;

3.   the extent of the presence of the parameters;

4.   whether any activities currently exist or are proposed in catchment areas that may cause the substance to become present in water or for levels to increase.

In terms of priority the parameters to be included in surveillance programmes can be summarised as follows:

1.   Microbiological quality and those parameters that control microbiological quality (disinfectant residuals, pH and turbidity)

2.   Parameters which cause rejection of water (these include turbidity, taste, colour and odour of water);

3.   Chemicals of known health risk;

In addition, water suppliers should prioritise parameters that control operational efficiency such a corrosivity and hardness.

Microbiological quality is the principal health concern and therefore routine monitoring of microbiological parameter is the first priority in a water quality surveillance programmes. This should be combined with parameters that may cause rejection of an otherwise good quality water supply. As routine monitoring of these parameters is successfully implemented and the results used to improve water supplies, then other parameters of concern can be included. There will at times be exceptions to this general rule, such as when severe chemical contamination is known to exist at levels that cause elevated risks of poisoning. However, in general the above rules of thumb are valid.

Unfortunately, there is a tendency in some countries to place undue emphasis on substances that are of limited or unproven risk to health and for which analysis is expensive and complicated. This may lead to reduced effectiveness of monitoring of key parameters relating to microbiological quality and can be counter-productive in terms of reducing the risk to health. Very often such approaches are primarily driven by the demands of the rich to the detriment of the poor.

The costs of analysis in most cases will ultimately be carried by the consumer and an over-emphasis on parameters of interest to the rich may increase costs that make safe water supply more unaffordable to the poor. As surveillance should be driven in part by equity, the impact of any expansion in analytical range on costs should be carefully considered. These impacts need to be considered not only in terms of paying for analysis, but also likely changes in water supply requiring large-scale upgrading. In Ghana, when work was carried out to advise on drinking-water quality standards, an explicit objective was to review the likely impact on any changes recommended in water supplies to meet water quality criteria. In particular, there were concerns that the setting of standards for some substances would substantially increase the costs of water to the urban poor and as a result lead to increased inequity in access to water supplies.

There are some key points about water quality monitoring, whether carried out by suppliers or surveillance agencies, which must be borne in mind when carrying out monitoring programmes.

1. Water quality is only aspect of water supply of relevance to health. Over-emphasis on water quality may lead to neglect of other issues of equal importance and water quality analysis should be seen within the context of the broader impacts of health. For instance, setting water quality standards without complementary targets on cost, access and continuity may be counter-productive.

2. Water quality analysis alone is very unreliable measure of system performance and provides little or no information about risks in the long and short term and provides limited information about causes of water quality failures and sources of pollution. Furthermore, water quality analysis are inherently temporally and spatially constrained and, whilst results from small samples are used to predict quality for larger volumes, this entails a certain degree of inaccuracy ad unreliability.

3. Risk assessments are essential to complement water quality analysis in order to determine risks of contamination and sources of pollution. Risk assessments should encompass both localised and broader evaluations of risk to be useful.

4. Process control during treatment and source protection are essential complements to water quality analysis. By ensuring adequate performance and protection, the risks of contamination are greatly reduced.

5. In terms of health risks from contaminated drinking water, microbiological parameters are the priority because of their link to infectious diarrhoeal disease. Chemicals of health concern do exist and should be monitored but the relative importance of these must be careful evaluated against occurrence, the numbers of people likely to be affected, control of microbiological contaminants and the life expectancy and immune status of the consumers.

7.2 Microbiological quality and indicators

As noted above, microbiological quality is the priority area for water quality analysis because of its relation to the spread of the infectious diarrhoeal diseases discussed in Chapter 1. There are numerous micro-organisms that are pathogenic to humans that include viruses, bacteria, cysts and helminths. Infective doses of such pathogens vary enormously from very few or single organisms (in the case of cryptosporidium and viruses) to many tens of thousands per milligram in the case of many bacteria. Infective doses will also be expected to vary between age groups and between groups of different immunity (determined by nutritional status, existing burden of disease, previous exposure and immune system status).

Testing of pathogens is not feasible for routine monitoring as the number of different pathogens is large and their analysis is often difficult and expensive. Pathogens that cause diarrhoeal disease share a similar faecal source and therefore microbiological quality is assessed using bacteria that indicate faecal contamination occurs.

It is presumed most readers of this manual will be aware of the principal indicator bacteria and the reasons for their selection. For more detail on the nature of indicators and the characteristics of the ideal indicator, readers are referred to Volumes 1 and 2 of the WHO Guidelines for Drinking-water Quality.

7.2.1 *E.coli* and thermotolerant coliforms

The principal standard indicator for microbiological contamination is *Escherichia coli* (*E.coli*), or thermotolerant coliforms as a surrogate. Whilst *E.coli* is not a perfect indicator, the evidence suggests that it remains the best available option. *E.coli* is derived from the faeces of warm-blooded animals, including humans. It has reasonable environmental resistance in surface and groundwater supplies and is abundant in fresh faeces. However, *E.coli* is more susceptible to chlorination than some other organisms and therefore a certain degree of caution is applied when interpreting data based the absence of these bacteria. In addition to measurements of indicator bacteria, a set of other key parameters will also be analysed to determine the risk of microbiological contamination. These are:

1. **Turbidity:** this is measured as many bacteria adsorb onto suspended solids and enhance survival of bacteria in water and may protect bacteria from the action of disinfectants

2. **Disinfectant residuals:** this will usually be chorine and critical will be the free chlorine residual

3. **pH:** this is critical in chlorination efficiency.

These parameters with analysis of *E.coli* or thermotolerant coliform constitute the WHO *critical parameters* that are the priority parameters to be tested in all water supplies, supported by a sanitary inspection.

Direct measurement of thermotolerant coliforms is possible by membrane filtration and this is the recommended approach for surveillance bodies as results can be obtained rapidly and the calculation of the number of bacteria in 100ml (the standard volume for indicator results) is simple. Results from membrane filtration can be gained within 18-24 hours.

The multiple tube method may also be used, but this technique is more time-consuming and requires greater labour and consumable inputs than membrane filtration. It may provide greater sensitivity in analysis of thermotolerant coliforms, particularly where these are injured or stressed. In very turbid waters, for instance in raw surface waters, the multiple tube method may have to be used as the suspended solids may clog the membrane filters and interfere with counts. Other rapid techniques exist, such as colilert (a modified version of the multiple tube method) but these are generally more expensive and would be less appropriate low and middle-income countries. In all cases, *E.coli* is identified through confirmatory tests on thermotolerant coliforms and typically samples require an additional 24 hours incubation at 44°C before a result is obtained.

7.2.2 Other indicator bacteria

In addition to thermotolerant (faecal) coliforms, a number of other indicator bacteria are available and for more details on the potential uses of such indicators, readers are referred to the WHO Guidelines for Drinking-Water Quality Volumes 1 and 2 for further information. However, below is a brief review of the indicators that are available and the how these may be used.

Total coliforms

The total coliform group of bacteria includes *E.coli*, but include other bacteria that are not faecal in origin but derived from environmental sources. As a result, these bacteria are unreliable as an indicator of faecal contamination. Total coliforms in distribution systems may come from biofilms and therefore their presence even in chlorinated piped water supplies is not conclusive evidence that there has been ingress of contaminated water. The majority of organisms in biofilm will be environmental in nature of little relevance to public health, although pathogen survival may be extended. Therefore total coliform analysis even in chlorinated piped supplies is of questionable value.

In point supplies and rainwater collection there is little value in total coliform analysis. In such systems, where no treatment has been applied, the presence of total coliform would generally be expected and thus their analysis would yield little useful information.

Faecal streptococci
Faecal streptococci are useful indicators of faecal contamination as they have greater environmental resistance than faecal coliforms and rarely multiply in polluted water. They are also resistant to drying and have value for routine monitoring after laying of new mains or repairs of distribution systems and for detecting pollution by surface run-off into groundwater.

Statistically significant associations have been noted between faecal streptococci and diarrhoeal disease and therefore their use has particular for public health bodies. However, analysis of faecal streptococci typically takes 48 hours although direct counts are possible using membrane filtration. Their use tends to be more limited because of the time of analysis and therefore would more commonly be used as an assessment tool rather than for routine monitoring.

Clostridia perfringens
Clostridia perfringens, an anaerobic spore forming organism, can also be used for water quality monitoring and may be useful in detecting biofilm sloughing. However, they are not exclusively faecal in origin and therefore may be best used to assess treatment efficiency, particularly filtration. Their presence in disinfected water may provide evidence of chlorine-resistant pathogen survival. Their use in routine monitoring is not recommended.

Heterotrophic plate counts
Heterotrophic plate counts at 22 and 37°C are also sometimes employed in analysis of the microbiological quality of piped water. These are not all the bacteria in water, but those that will produce visible colonies on the media used and under prescribed conditions of temperature and incubation. Heterotrophic plate counts are of limited sanitary value, but can be used to monitor the effectiveness of treatment and at 22°C the cleanliness and integrity of the distribution systems. However, the principal approach is to limit the numbers of colonies rather than complete absence. Complete absence is unlikely to be achieved as treatment processes are designed to disinfect (i.e. remove pathogens and indicators of their presence) rather than sterilise water. Thus, heterotrophic plate counts are primarily used to assess whether treatment processes have reduced the microbial load and to monitor increases in distribution that may provide an early warning of potential pollution.

Bacteriophages
There is increasing goof evidence that bacteriophages can be used as indicators of microbiological quality and in particular for virus survival. However, their use in routine

monitoring remains limited, although this may become more common as the evidence of their usefulness increases.

Sorbitol fermenting bifidobacteria and *Rhodococcus coprophilus*
There are indicator bacteria that are more specific to human and animal faeces. Sorbitol fermenting bifidobacteria are specific to human faeces. The use of these bacteria has been demonstrated in both surface waters and shallow groundwaters in urban areas. The use of such bacteria can therefore be useful in identifying whether animal and human faeces are present.

However, there are certain limitations of the use of these bacteria. Sorbitol fermenting bifidobacteria are more environmentally sensitive than thermotolerant coliforms or faecal streptococci and are present in lower quantities in raw faeces. Therefore, whilst the presence of sorbitol fermenting bifidobacteria confirms the presence of human faecal contamination, their absence cannot necessarily be taken to indicate that human contamination has not occurred. However, the use of such bacteria can be useful under certain conditions. For instance, in an outbreak of infectious disease the role of water as a transmission route may not be known. Analysis of sorbitol fermenting bacteria can be done using membrane filtration and provides results within 48 hours. However, the difficulties in relating the results to standard indicators makes their use in assessments rather than routine monitoring more appropriate.

Rhodococcus coprophilus are specific to animal faeces (except domestic animals) and are more environmentally robust than the sorbitol fermenting bifidobacteria and therefore their presence is useful in indicating long-term contamination from animal faeces within water. However, as the analysis of these bacteria takes between 7 and 22 days, their use tends to be restricted to assessments rather than routine monitoring as the time taken for adequate information to be generated and acted upon is longer than would usually be desired.

7.2.3 Weaknesses of the current indicators

There has been much debate over the value of microbiological indicators over recent years. Whilst this text is not designed to discuss these in detail, a brief review is provided below which may allow the reader to understand why existing indicators remain those of choice, but highlights their weaknesses and the emphasises the need for non-analytical approaches to monitoring.

Essentially, the criticism of thermotolerant coliforms and *E.coli* can be summarised as follows:

1. Environmental resistance may be significantly lower than many pathogens (particularly viruses and protozoa) and therefore, whilst providing an indication of the risk of pathogen presence, the absence of indicators cannot be taken as confirmation that pathogens are absent

2. Thermotolerant coliforms are more sensitive to chlorination than many pathogens, especially cryptosporidium but also some viruses and pathogenic bacteria.

3. In tropical or semi-tropical climates, there is some evidence that E.coli can multiply in the and therefore its presence may be unreliable in terms of indicating faecal contamination.

However, the routine testing of pathogens remains less desirable than the use of indicator bacteria. The wide range of pathogens that potentially can be transmitted through water means that the selection of pathogens for analysis is difficult. The most resistant pathogen could be selected, but the absence of the pathogen may be due to the fact that has not been introduced into the water being tested and therefore this is not a reliable guide for other pathogens. Analytical methods are still lacking for some pathogens and where they exist are often expensive and time-consuming to perform.

Whilst the weakness of the current set of indicators is well known, at present they still offer the best option for microbiological testing, provided this is supported by sanitary inspection and other critical parameters. Greater emphasis should be placed on the use of risk assessments and a move towards a HACCP approach is certainly required. For local level surveillance, emphasis should remain on the testing for thermotolerant coliforms or *E.coli*, with periodic assessment of faecal streptococci. Water suppliers where they have capacity should broaden the range of analysis to include other bacteria such spores and clostridia.

7.3 Physico-chemical parameters

In addition to microbiological quality, there are also a set of physico-chemical parameters that either influence the microbiological quality or cause rejection of water on acceptability grounds. The key physico-chemical parameters of importance for surveillance are as follows:

- Turbidity or suspended solids

- Disinfectant residuals

- The pH of water

- Colour

- Odour and taste

7.3.1 Turbidity

turbidity is a measure of the 'cloudiness' of the water and is often used as a simple surrogate for suspended solids. Turbidity may cause rejection of water by consumers, but is also associated with bacterial survival, as adsorption onto suspended solids by micro-organisms is common. Turbidity should always be tested whenever a sample is taken for water quality testing and should be tested on-site as transport may cause erroneous results to be obtained.

Turbidity control during water treatment is important for disinfection as raised turbidities will affect disinfection efficiency. An increase in turbidity during distribution may indicate the ingress of surface water into the piped system and therefore an increased likelihood of microbiological contamination. Turbidity above 1 TU has been associated with cryptosporidium in water, in particular surface waters that pass through treatment plants. The WHO Guideline Value for turbidity is below 1TU, although previous GVs have been set at 5 TU. In practice, monitoring of compliance with 1TU is unlikely to be carried out by surveillance bodies, as this requires relatively expensive equipment, although at water treatment works it is preferable that this level can be tested.

71

7.3.2 Disinfectant residuals

Disinfectant residuals are designed to provide ongoing protection against microbiological contamination during distribution of water. Where chlorine is used, which in general is the case, the residual will be composed of free chlorine residual and a combined chlorine residual. Free chlorine is able to inactivate microbes that enter the water either through leaking pipes or from biofilm developed on the piped wall, whereas combined chlorine is the chlorine that has already reacted with substances in the water and has much lower disinfectant properties.

Monitoring chlorine is also a useful way in identifying vulnerable parts of the supply. Chlorine is a volatile substance and residual loss in distribution is a significant problem in many parts of the world and in particular in countries where the ambient temperature is high. Particular problems are found with service reservoirs as these are usually on hills and are not shaded to avoid unwanted bird and animal contamination. A further problem in chlorine loss is that flushing and cleaning of service reservoirs and distribution mains is not carried out as frequently as required and are often allowed to become dirty, which promotes chlorine reactions. The materials of pipe walls may also be particularly significant in promoting chlorine decay.

Where chlorine residuals are lost in particular parts of the system, this indicates that there is a need for cleaning and maintenance work. Free chlorine residual should be tested at every site where a sample of water is taken for microbiological analysis and in some circumstances may be tested more frequently or at more sites. The testing of total chlorine residuals is usually much lower intensity, with a smaller number of samples taken to check the amount of chlorine being dosed. However, total chlorine analysis is also important where chlorine loss is suspected in service reservoirs as the loss of total as well as free chlorine (as has been observed in several African countries where dosing at the plant was known to be adequate) indicates that it is unlikely that chlorine can be maintained throughout the system without booster disinfection.

7.3.3 pH

The pH of water is important primarily because this is a controlling factor on chlorination efficiency. Where the pH is above 8.5, chlorination efficiency becomes impaired as much of the chlorine is used up in acid-akali reactions. The optimum pH for chlorination is between 6.5 and 8.5. The pH of water should be tested whenever a free chlorine residual test is taken.

7.3.4 Colour

The monitoring of colour is also important as highly coloured waters will be likely to lead to consumer complaints and rejection. Colour may be derived from suspended solids, organic material in the water, dissolution of dyes and cements or corrosion of iron pipes. Surveillance bodies may only monitor colour in terms of observable colour or appearance, however, water suppliers should carry out colour testing following standard methods. In boreholes, changes in colour over a period of time indicates corrosion of the rising main whilst short-term changes in response to rainfall in point sources indicates that sanitary integrity has been compromised and there is a need for remedial action.

7.3.5 Taste and odour

Taste and odour problems will also lead to consumer complaints and possibly rejection of the water in favour of alternative, possibly more microbiologically contaminated water sources. For both taste and odour, the best way to monitor this is to ask the users whether they have noted any changes in smell or taste since the last visit. Clearly, tasting water that you do not know is of good microbiological quality is unwise.

7.3.6 Other physico-chemical parameters

Hardness is often considered a major problem. For instance in some countries water sources may be rejected because the water is hard. However, there is no evidence of any health-related problems derived from hardness although there is some evidence that hard waters may lead to a lower risk of cardio-vascular disease. Hardness is primarily related to acceptability of the water and operational efficiency as very hard water may interfere with filtration and cause deposits to build up pipes reducing their internal diameter. In Zimbabwe, one water supply that took its water from an abandoned gold mine shaft had water that was so hard it formed calcretes (a carbonate rock) in the sand filter beds. Thus whilst the control of hardness is important for the supplier it is not routinely monitored by surveillance bodies, analysis being more likely in response to consumer complaints. Corrosivity is also important for water supplies to monitor as this may cause deterioration in the distribution network and lead to greater leakage problems. It is not, however, of importance for the surveillance agency to monitor.

7.4 Chemical parameters

As noted at the start of this chapter, in general chemical substances are treated as a lower priority unless they contribute to rejection of water by consumers or there is risk to health in the short-term. Chemical contamination is often restricted to certain areas or water source types, for instance fluoride is most commonly associated with groundwater derived from acidic igneous complexes. Arsenic has become of increasing concern, particularly in Bangladesh and India, but also increasingly elsewhere where groundwater development has been the driving force of water supply improvement or where mining activities pollute surface or groundwaters used for drinking water supplies.

When a source is being developed, it is essential that a full suite of chemical analyses are undertaken combined with a pollution risk assessment in order to evaluate whether the source should used and whether additional treatment may be required. Few chemical parameters may be included in routine surveillance programmes in low and middle-income countries, unless there is good reason to suspect that there is a problem with that parameter. In general, where chemical parameters are routinely tested this is done at lower frequencies than the critical parameters as changes are likely to be longer-term. The role of regular and systematic pollution risk assessments in the catchments of water sources that are used for drinking is important in determining whether additional chemical parameters need to be included in monitoring programmes. Changes in land-use, new industrial developments and urban growth within the catchment should be carefully evaluated in the light of potential pollutants that may be produced.

Selection of chemical parameters to be included in monitoring programmes at any given time should be based on the known level of health risk, known impact on acceptability, presence in the waters of the country, analytical capacity and the ability to remove the substance through treatment or source protection measures. In general, priority should be given to those chemicals that will lead to rejection of water supplies or that have known toxic effects and which are persistent in water.

The most common chemicals to be included in routine monitoring are:

- Nitrate

- Arsenic

- Fluoride

- Iron

- Manganese

- Aluminium

7.4.1 Nitrate

Nitrate is one of the most ubiquitous chemical contaminants of water bodies world-wide as it is derived from human activities and in particular from the disposal of human wastes and the use of inorganic fertilisers in agriculture. Nitrate is of concern because of its link to methaemoglobinaemia or 'blue-baby' syndrome. Although the actual health burden from nitrate may not actually be significant (because of breast-feeding practices etc), nitrate is of particular concern because of its conservative nature in water that is oxidising. Once nitrate has entered a water body that is oxidising, only the processes of dilution are likely to cause significant reductions in concentrations until the input load is reduced. Thus if nitrate is allowed to increase in source waters, then long-term resource problems may result leading to costly investments later. As nitrate is extremely expensive and difficult to remove during treatment, blending nitrate-rich waters with low nitrate waters may be the only viable option.

Nitrate should be monitored at headworks and source water bodies on a regular basis and strong links made with environmental monitoring and regulatory bodies. The frequency of testing is likely to vary with country and water type. Surface waters are likely to show pronounced variation depending on rainfall and, where the nitrate load primarily derives from agriculture, application of fertilisers. In shallow groundwaters the level of nitrate is likely to be highly season dependent, in Uganda for instance nitrate in protected springs show significant seasonal variation. In deep aquifers, relatively stable or steadily increasing nitrate trends may be seen, but it is unlikely that seasonal peaks will be found.

7.4.2 Arsenic

Arsenic should be included where there is a known or suspected problem. Arsenic has become one of the principal water quality issues over recent years as evidence has emerged that water supplies using shallow groundwaters contain toxic levels of arsenic and associated skin and other cancers that have resulted. Arsenic may be derived from the dissolution of arsenic-bearing minerals associated with volcanic activity or may be released by industries. There is often limited information regarding the presence of arsenic, but if there is any concern regarding the presence of arsenic in the water, it is wise for testing to be undertaken at the source selection stage and periodically after this.

7.4.3 Fluoride

Excess fluoride is associated with dental and skeletal fluorosis that may cause severe deformation and disability in susceptible individuals. However, a lack fluoride is also associated with dental caries and therefore in some countries fluoride is added to drinking water to improve dental health. This remains a controversial issue and may not be the most effective mechanism to reduce the incidence of dental caries. Although fluoride may be released by industrial pollution, the majority of fluoride found in drinking-water supplies at levels of health concern is derived from natural sources.

Fluoride should always be analysed during source development, in particular for groundwater. After initial source selection, the frequency of analysis will depend on the nature of the source and initial assessments, but is unlikely to exceed quarterly testing and may be substantially less frequent. Analysis of fluoride will remain focused on raw water and where treatment is applied to final treated waters.

7.4.4 Iron and manganese

Iron and manganese may both cause rejection of water by consumers because of the colour that develops when iron oxidises into the ferric state. Iron and manganese cause colouring of clothes and sanitary ware. Iron contamination is a particular problem with groundwater supplies usually due to the oxidation of ferrous iron in the water itself, because of corrosion of galvanised iron riser pipes and in some cases from iron bacteria. Some surface waters also have iron problems, particularly related to colloidal iron.

Manganese is most commonly associated with surface water sources where water is pumped from lower levels and the bottom sediment is disturbed. The analysis of iron and manganese is best carried at the treatment works or wellhead. Testing of distributed waters is likely only to be done in response to complaints.

7.4.5 Aluminium and other metals

Aluminium in drinking water is usually derived from poor operation of coagulation-flocculation-settling steps in water treatment leading to carry-over of micro-floc into final waters. Routine testing of aluminium in drinking water is primarily justified in terms of treatment efficiency monitoring and therefore is of greater interest to the water supplier than the surveillance body.

Other metals will usually only require testing at source selection and infrequent periodic assessment after that, unless changes in land-use indicate that the release of heavy metals into the environment is likely. In areas where there is much industrial development within the catchment, heavy metals may be released into the source water and become adsorbed onto sediment. Where significant amounts of these substances are released into the source water body, periodic assessment may be required, including sediment analysis as well as water quality analysis. In these circumstances, however, it is better to focus attention on pollution prevention than water treatment.

7.4.6 Organics and pesticides

A great deal of attention is focused in many parts of the world on the monitoring of organic chemicals and pesticides in water bodies. Much of this concern has been driven by concerns in Europe and North America, but is also increasingly being considered in many low and middle-income countries. Whilst many of these products are of concern to health, the true nature and severity of their impacts often remains uncertain.

Analysis of organics and pesticides is expensive and requires large capital investment in analytical equipment and training if it is to be effective. Before embarking on any programme of routine monitoring of these substances, it is essential that proper consideration is given to a number of key factors:

- What is the extent of the problem likely to be – is there is strong evidence of the likely presence of organics and pesticides in water sources at present or in the near future?

- What contribution will be expected to be derived from drinking water and how much from, for instance, food products?

- How severe a health problem is likely to result – are infant mortality rates and diarrhoeal disease high and life expectancy low?

Unless there is good evidence that organic substances are currently found or will be found in the near future at levels that may compromise the health of a large proportion of the population, the inclusion of such substances in *drinking* water monitoring programmes is not justified where resources are limited. However, there is a value in the monitoring of such substances within a water resource monitoring programme and these results should be shared with both water suppliers and surveillance bodies to allow them to make informed decisions about the need for monitoring in drinking water supply.

In terms of drinking water it may be more effective to maintain an ongoing programme of pollution risk assessment of source catchments in order to monitor the risk of increased contamination. Once this is perceived as being sufficiently raised, then a programme of routine sampling could be initiated.

If organics are to be included within routine monitoring consideration should be given to which organisation would be best placed to undertake such testing and which organic substances would be included. In general, most organics are found in source waters rather than subsequent entry into distribution systems and thus is it will be more effective for water resource and water supply agencies to undertake routine monitoring, with the surveillance body retaining a right to assess data as appropriate. In terms of the substances to be included, this should be based upon assessments of the types of substances being released into the aquatic environment.

7.5 Analytical methods and quality control

At the outset of the development of surveillance, a decision should be made regarding the methods used for data collection and in particular with regard to water quality data. The collection of water quality data can be laboratory based or field based. In the first case, samples are taken and transported to a laboratory for analysis. In the second, the sample can be taken, analysed and read in the field.

Laboratory based approaches have a number of drawbacks. They limit the potential for community participation, lead to delays in reporting of results, experience common problems with sample deterioration and provide limited interaction between analysts and staff utilising results in the field. Laboratories may provide better analytical environments, although in practice poor quality control remains a major problem in many laboratories.

For microbiological water quality testing, there appears to be little difference in the reliability of the results obtained, provided aseptic techniques are followed. The use of field-based approaches offers significant added benefits when working with low-income urban communities. Firstly, it usually greatly reduces the time required for reporting of results to staff and users, thus enhancing the rapid use of the data. Secondly, as the process is usually carried out within the community, it facilitates the process of community participation in surveillance, as community members can become active participants in the process. Thirdly, the surveillance data can be used as a direct health education tool by reading results with community members in the field. In most urban areas in developing countries, community participation in the delivery of services is essential and field-based surveillance can play an important role in promoting and enhancing community participation.

Field equipment for microbiological analysis is widely available and generally if used correctly provide the same level of reliability as laboratory methods. Some physico-chemical parameters are best analysed on-site given the high likelihood of changes induced during transport. In general, meters and probes for such parameters provide reliable results.

Chemical field testing equipment can be more variable, although there are relatively inexpensive spectrophotometers that have been shown for heavy metals to have the same degree of accuracy as laboratory methods. Other field equipment for chemical analysis, such as portable photometers or probes may only give results that are accurate to one order of magnitude. Such equipment is best used when trend analysis is being carried out rather than precise measurements of concentration. Laboratory testing may therefore be necessary for chemical analysis.

7.5.1 Analytical quality assurance

Quality assurance is increasingly demanded by users of water quality results to ensure that decisions are based on reliable and accurate data. Standard operating procedures for all tests performed, including those using field tests kits should be developed and followed and that quality assurance is undertaken.

Whilst many quality control procedures can form the basis of quality assurance, these alone are insufficient to provide quality assurance – for instance systematic errors during handling may produce results within quality control boundaries but are still incorrect. The development of good practice and periodic assessment is critical to quality assurance. This includes aspects such as aseptic technique evaluation, inspections of equipment, good record keeping, sample tracking and general analyst hygiene.

Quality control procedures have been widely developed for chemical parameters and systems for determining the reliability of the results, based on accuracy and precision are available. Most chemicals in a sample are effectively randomly distributed, as any non-random distribution tends to occur at the molecular level, which is generally below the level of routine detection. Thus, it is generally fairly simple to ensure that results from samples are reliable through duplicate testing and statistic analysis of the results.

Quality control of microbiological parameters is more problematic, largely because of their discrete nature in water as opposed to solute nature of chemicals. This means that is it more difficult to apply the procedures used in quality assurance in chemical analysis. However, microbiological quality control procedures do exist and this can be exercised through two key ways:

1. The use of split samples

2. Analysis of pre-prepared vials containing bacteria

Both these approaches have drawbacks. In the first case, a range of acceptable values can be calculated from the results of an analysis based upon the likely distribution of microbes in the sample (usually taken as being a Poisson distribution). However, this is not an entirely fool-proof system and results that are outside the calculated range may still be valid. However, this approach provides some degree of quality assurance and can be translated into a field-testing programme relatively simply. If this is done, a process of aseptic technique evaluation should also be followed. In this case, the analyst is assessed on the degree of successful completion of the tasks involved in water quality testing and sanitary inspection and in particular whether equipment has been kept sterile at critical points. An example form is shown in Annex 4.

The second approach to quality assurance involves the preparation and distribution of vials with known numbers of bacteria. This is then made up with a prescribed volume of sterile water and an analysis performed. Again, a range of results can be calculated based on the likely distribution of bacteria in the water. This technique is expensive and may not necessarily provide any greater confidence in the performance of the analyst.

Whilst quality assurance and quality control is extremely important to ensure the reliability of the results obtained, it is important to bear in mind how the results from quality assurance should be used. One response that some monitoring bodies have had to poor quality control and assurance is to remove all data that is not within the prescribed quality control criteria. Whilst this may be necessary in the case of programmes geared towards proving compliance with standards and where the vast majority of samples would meet quality control criteria, it may not be the most appropriate response in other cases.

Discarding all data that cannot be shown to have met quality control and assurance criteria (including historical data) is inadvisable as this may result in a very limited database. It is better to recognise the weaknesses indicated by poor quality control practices and to resolve these through training, investment and better management, than to throw away what may be a reasonable historical record. For more detail on quality control and assurance please refer to the WHO manual on QC/QA listed in Annex 6 or relevant ISO and national documents.

8.

Routine water quality sampling network design

The design of sampling networks is crucial to the process of monitoring water quality. Key to sample network design is to set clear objectives to the sampling programme and to ensure that factors that influence water quality are taken into account when designing monitoring programmes. Critical to any water quality surveillance programme is to determine how many samples should be taken and where sample points should be located. At the outset of determining sampling frequencies and sample point locations, it is essential to recognise that the needs for assessment are different to routine monitoring. Therefore, the objective of the sampling programme must be clearly defined before sample sites and frequencies are determined. However, in both cases it is important to ensure that the data generated is reliable and provides a reasonable estimation of real-life conditions.

The sampling network should provide data which is representative of the water supply within an urban area and thus needs to take into account the water supply characteristics (sources, distribution etc), known or suspected water quality variation and the populations of different areas. Different approaches may be needed by different agencies in developing sampling networks. For instance, the utility operating the piped water supply will not be interested in the quality of alternative sources nor are they likely to undertake any routine monitoring of the quality of water stored in the home. They will focus on ensuring water quality in their distribution mains remains of an adequate quality up to the limit of their responsibility. Sample numbers and locations will be likely to be determined by numbers of users or volume of water and in some cases known problem areas.

By contrast the surveillance agency will need to take samples from piped networks, and other available water sources and from water quality stored in the home. As surveillance should be focused on the urban poor, the number of samples taken from the piped network may be relatively limited. The sample numbers and frequencies for all available sources should reflect their importance as determined by zoning of the urban area. In addition, where samples are taken from the piped water system, at certain times unflamed samples may be taken by surveillance staff as it is the actual quality of water consumed or collected that is of interest. Thus if contamination is introduced through the use of dirty pipe or contamination of the spigot, it is important to identify this.

8.1 Sampling strategies

In a piped water system, a purely random approach could be adopted with samples taken throughout the system with numbers of samples based on population served with sample points selected based on random tables as discussed later. However, a purely random approach to collection of samples from a piped network is probably only of value in small systems where there is a single source and service reservoir and there are no connections direct onto the transmission main. In general the urban water sector is more complex and therefore different sampling approaches are required.

The basis of simple random sampling is that all parts of the distribution system have an equal chance of showing contamination. However, this is unlikely to be the case for piped water networks where there is more than one service reservoir or source as the different sources or service reservoirs may exert a significant influence on quality. Thus lines supplied by one reservoir or source may show a consistent difference in quality than another part of the system and it is therefore more effective to divide the system up into discrete areas all served by single reservoirs or sources.

Point source sampling would usually be carried out on a rolling basis, however this may not be truly random as there may be temporal (e.g. seasonal) stratification. If a specific study is being undertaken to look at seasonal variation, a cluster sampling approach may be followed based on the population densities, initial water quality results from assessment or on the basis of identified risks.

The urban zoning approach outlined in Chapter 2 provides a systematic approach to stratified random sampling design for surveillance activities as it covers all types of water supply and defines priority areas. For surveillance agencies this approach allows activities to be targeted on the most vulnerable areas and allows the types of sources to be sampled and the frequency of analysis. As discussed in Chapter 4, unprotected sources would not commonly be tested, as they are open to contamination and the action that is required is known prior to any sampling and inspection – that if used for drinking the source needs to be protected. Testing may therefore only be done in response to a particular outbreak of disease.

The following section discusses sampling approaches and how these may be defined for piped, point and household water quality programmes.

8.2 Piped water supplies

Sampling of piped water supplies often entails another form of zoning that is solely based on the water supply system itself. Zoning of piped water supplies is a well-developed technique which is widely used in more industrialised countries and forms an integral part of the EC Directives on water quality, for instance, with the number of samples to be analysed by water suppliers or surveillance agencies defined on a zone basis.

The purpose of zoning is to ensure that different parts of the water supply system that may have different levels of risk are adequately covered. They can also be used to focus monitoring on areas where problems are known or are more likely to occur and to ensure that suppliers and surveillance agencies take into these into account to ensure that sampling is focused on priorities and problems. The use of zoning is particularly useful where the water supply multiple sources or where different service reservoirs supply different parts of the system. It may also be used when different parts of the distribution system operate at different pressures and elevations or where leakage or reliability varies across the system.

For routine monitoring, zoning is limited usually to definition of zones based on source and service reservoir. Areas with direct connections onto the transmission or pumping main should always be treated as a separate zone. Such areas may be more prone to discontinuity given that no demand balancing is available from service reservoirs and because it can be expected that disinfectant residuals will be higher as there has been limited opportunity for free residual loss during bulk storage.

An example of a zoned piped water system from Uganda in given in Box 8.1. The benefit of zoning in ensuring that monitoring information becomes targeted on management decision is great. In the case of Kampala, a key reason to zone the piped water system was that certain areas of the City were reporting consistent lack of residual chlorine as well as other water quality problems. However, until the system was zoned, it was difficult for the problems to be tracked back to a particular main coming from a service reservoir. The original sample site selection had not been related to distribution mains, leading to the sampling programme being not fully representative of the system and its components.

Box 8.1: Zoning of the Kampala piped water system

The Kampala water supply operated by National Water and Sewerage Corporation draws water from Lake Victoria in Murchison Bay, which is treated through two conventional types plants: Gaba I and Gaba II. Gaba I (the older plant) does not include coagulation and primarily serves low-level mains without passing through an distribution service reservoir. Gaba II serves much of the high-level mains and feeds the main balancing tanks in Muyenga (Tank Hill) with no direct connections onto the transmission main. There are 5 other, smaller service reservoirs in the system. The balancing tanks in Muyenga feed high level mains that flow up to the furthest reaches of the system. The remaining reservoirs serve a variety of principally low-level mains. There are four booster stations in the system to cope with the pronounced topography. The supply network can be broken down into the following zones:

Zone 1: Gaba low-level

Zone 2: Muyenga zone

Zone 3: Gun hill zone

Zone 4: Naguru zone

Zone 5: Rubaga zone

Zone 6: Mutungo booster and high-level zone

In addition a number of smaller zones can be defined as follows:

Zone 7: Buziga low-level booster

Zone 8: Makindye booster

Zone 9: Kololo tanks zone

Zone 10: Namirembe booster

In some approaches to zoning, the size of a zone is limited by the population served in the zone. For instance, UK practice has been that no zone is allowed to exceed 50,000 population, irrespective of the total population served by a single reservoir. The purpose of population limits on zones is to ensure that the numbers of samples taken in each zone provide an adequate safeguard for public health. This is particularly important where regulations define the number of samples to be taken in a zone.

Whilst the basic underlying concept of zoning of piped water systems is simple, it should be emphasised that the actual process is time consuming and requires a thorough understanding of the system. Unless it is known which pipes are supplied from different service reservoirs and the pressure or elevation differences of different pipes, zoning is difficult. It is therefore essential for engineers operating the system and water quality staff to work closely together to avoid mistakes. Particular care should be taken when rationing of water occurs and where transfers of water between different pipelines served by different service reservoirs is practised. This can easily be incorporated into a zoning process where there is the practice of rationing or transfer is regular. Where such practices are more ad hoc, it is essential that when samples are taken, the supply operators are consulted concerning where water came from at the time of sampling.

8.2.1 Sampling frequency and numbers

Sampling and inspection of piped water supplies should be carried out frequently as failures are unlikely to be as seasonal-dependent as for point sources. Contamination will typically result from failures in treatment or distribution and whilst the risk of contamination may increase with heavy rainfall, failure may occur at any time. In addition to failure in operation or physical failure in infrastructure, the growth of biofilm in the distribution system may cause contamination because of sloughing or localised contamination may result from poor maintenance of the environment around taps and pipes.

Samples should be taken throughout the distribution systems at least every month, with samples spread over the month. If possible, more frequent sampling will be carried out and water suppliers should have a programme of daily or weekly sampling depending the numbers of people served. Where community-managed piped water supplies are used, less frequent (monthly) samples may suffice particularly where there is no treatment or disinfection.

The numbers of samples to be collected during monitoring or assessment can be calculated to provide statistical validity, although this entails either existing information regarding the distribution of the bacteria or assumptions that can be made about the likelihood of presence. However, the numbers of samples that can be collected routinely or on any single sampling round will usually be determined by the availability of funds and time to carry out sampling and analysis. Other factors may also limit the numbers of samples that can be taken. The use of portable on-site microbiological testing kits may limit the number of samples that can be collected to a total of 16, all of which must be collected and processed within a 3-hour period from the processing of the first sample. This time allowance is required to allow an adequate resuscitation time for bacteria in the last sample.

There are two approaches to sample number calculation. These can be based on the population served, which is the approach used, by WHO in the *Guidelines for Drinking-Water Quality*. Such approaches are based on the assumption that more samples should be taken where more people utilise the supply, as there is a greater potential for contamination to lead to a disease outbreak that affects many people. Where more people use the supply, there will also be a higher volume of flow and therefore more samples may be required to ensure that there is adequate quality control of water.

If a population approach is adopted, then the number of samples should be based on the number of people using the piped water supply and not the number of people residing in an area. This is important, as where resources are limited, an undue emphasis may be given to analysis of samples taken from the piped water system whilst failing to monitor the quality of water from alternative sources widely used by the low-income population. The population served will be all those with a direct connection, all areas with no alternative supplies with the remaining population estimated by using a discount factor to take into multiple source use.

An alternative approach to calculating sampling numbers is to look at previous results to identify whether there are any areas that consistently fail on microbiological quality or other parameters such chlorine residual. Other factors may include the density of population and typical level of service. These should form part of the zoning process, with a greater number of samples taken from higher-priority areas (i.e. low-income, high density and where direct connection rates are low).

Table 8.1 below shows examples of population based sampling numbers and frequencies for microbiological parameters drawn from WHO and the EU.

WHO		EU (minimum = C1)	
Population	*Samples/month*	*Population*	*Samples/year*
Less than 5000	1	Less than 5000	Discretionary
5000-100,000	1 sample per 5000 population	10,000	12
Above 100,000	1 sample per 10,000 plus 10 samples	50,000	60
		100,000	120
		150,000	180
		300,000 and above	360

Table 8.1: Examples of sampling frequencies

8.2.2 Sample locations

When the sample numbers and frequencies of sampling visits have been calculated, the final stage is the selection of sampling sites. Sample sites will usually be taken as being representative of a wider area. Samples sites can be either fixed (every time sampling is carried out in the area, a sample is always picked from the same point) or random (the exact location of the sample point in any zone or area varying between sample rounds).

Fixed sample points are often used by water suppliers. Fixed sample points should be kept to an absolute minimum in any monitoring programmes. The points where a fixed sample point would be justified are the point where water leaves the treatment works (usually the first tap, but sometimes the clearwell outlet) and the inlets and outlets of service reservoirs. There may also be particular taps where contamination would represent a particularly elevated risk, such as public taps in a market that may also become fixed sampling points. However, in general within distribution systems, the reliance on fixed sampling points means that there the probability of detecting a failure when it occurs is reduced and misleading results in terms of system performance may be produced.

It is preferred that random sampling is followed within the distribution system, although this may be stratified as discussed in the previous section. The selection of random sampling sites can be done using random numbers tables, or by an ad-hoc approach. The approach used is highly dependent on the degree of detailed information is available regarding connections and the degree to which local staff have access to reliable maps. Selecting sample site selection using random numbers involves first dividing the zone or area into a grid with all available connections from which a sample can be taken marked and allocated a number. The sample site for each sampling round are then done from a table of random numbers. Whilst this maximises the random nature of the sample to be taken, it is reliant on there being adequate detailed information available on the system. Commonly this may be held by water suppliers (although frequently it is not) but it is not always possible for surveillance bodies to gain access to this information. Furthermore, this process will only work where surveillance or water supply staff have access to reliable maps so that the sample point can be exactly located in the field.

Other further key decision will be whether the selection of a particular sample point used in a sample round excludes it from the list of possible sites that can be selected in the next round. This may be done to prevent frequent repeat samples from the same point, a process that clearly limits randomness. If the site is not to be included in the next sample round, a decision will have to be made regarding when the sample point can be re-introduced.

The ad-hoc approach to random sampling is often used by surveillance bodies or water suppliers where there is low availability of detailed information on exact locations of connections and where maps of the area are inadequate to ensure that field staff can find selected sites. It is also a much quicker and cheaper method of random sampling. In this approach, a broad area will be defined from which a certain number of samples will be taken. The exact location of each site is then selected by the sampler whilst in the field. This approach can be as effective as more systematic approaches in ensuring that samples are taken in entirely random nature and is the approach used by public health staff in Uganda where access to the detailed information required for a more systematic approach is very limited. However, care must be taken that field staff avoid an over-concentration of samples being taken in one part of the sampling area if this approach is adopted. If staff allow too many samples to be taken within a restricted part of the sampling area, true randomness may be lost.

When sampling from piped water supplies, the issues of flaming taps will arise. Flaming is often carried out to ensure that contamination that may have been transferred to a tap by people hands does not contaminate the water sample. The same approach may also be used for boreholes. Taps may also have a rubber hose attached to the tap to direct water into collection vessels efficiently in order to reduce wastage.

For water suppliers, flaming should be carried out as it is the quality of water that they are supplying that they wish to test. However, for surveillance bodies, choosing to flame a tap requires decisions to be made as to whether what is important is to test the water in the supply or the quality of water actually collected by the users. Where samples are taken for regulatory purposes, the actual water in supply is most important. However, in many cases water quality may deteriorate because a fixture is added to the tap and this may be important to know for health education programmes. Therefore in surveillance programmes it is recommended that both flamed and unflamed samples are taken. As taking both unflamed and flamed samples at each site may limit the number of site that can be visited in one day, one approach to reduce the time required is to take unflamed samples on most taps, with a smaller number of samples also tested when they have been flamed.

8.2.3 other water quality parameters in piped water surveillance

Other water quality parameters will include those affecting aesthetic qualities such as colour and iron as well as chemicals of known health concern, particularly nitrate and arsenic.

Colour should be routinely monitored in distribution with analysis at least quarterly and preferably more frequently. Colour analysis at the treatment or headworks should be undertaken on a daily basis by the water supplier. Where equipment is not available for measurement of colour in terms of true colour units, then the appearance of the water can be assessed instead,

Iron contamination is likely to be primarily due to poor source water quality and thus the major focus on analysis should be at headworks and carried out on a quarterly basis. However, as iron contamination may also result from corrosion of galvanised iron pipes, quarterly samples should be taken from distribution systems where this has been identified as a problem.

Nitrate, arsenic and other chemical contaminants will be expected to largely derive from source waters and it is not expected that contamination during distribution will be a major problem. Thus these parameters are best tested for and controlled during water production. Occasional samples may be taken from the distribution system to detect breakthrough from headworks. In addition to analysis of chemicals, it is important that operators carry out routine jar testing on raw waters to calculate coagulant dosages required.

Suggested frequencies for sampling from both headworks and in distribution are given in Table 8.2 below.

Parameters	Headworks	Distribution
Turbidity & free chlorine residual, pH	Preferred: hourly Minimum: twice daily	Preferred: daily Minimum: monthly
Thermotolerant (faecal) coliforms	Preferred: daily Minimum: weekly	Monthly as per table 1.
Jar tests	Preferred: daily Minimum: weekly	
Total coliforms	Preferred: daily Minimum: weekly	Monthly
Colour	Preferred: daily Minimum: weekly	Preferred: monthly Minimum: quarterly
Iron	Preferred: monthly Minimum: quarterly	Occasional
Other inorganics	Preferred: monthly Minimum: quarterly	Occasional

Table 8.2: Recommended sampling frequencies

8.3 Point sources

Samples should be taken from point sources from the principal outlet – handpump, spring outlet or bucket used to take water from a well. As discussed in chapter 4, an initial assessment should be carried out of all point sources and subsequent routine monitoring programmes based upon the results of the assessment and likely variations in relation to season.

As a minimum, point sources should be tested for microbiological quality and turbidity with a sanitary inspection undertaken at least once per year during periods when failure is most likely. This will usually coincide with wet seasons. However, the sanitary risks should be carefully considered. Where contamination is most likely to result from a combination of surface pollution sources and direct pathways as opposed to direct aquifer contamination, more frequent testing may be warranted in an urban area where the source of contaminated surface water will be more common.

In some cases it may be necessary to undertake an extended assessment of point source quality in order to develop an understanding of the processes causing water quality failure and thus the appropriate interventions required to improve the water source. This may be due to a general lack of information about the quality of sources or because the conditions when the assessment occurred were perceived as abnormal, such as excessive rains as was the case in Kampala in 1997 when the El Nino climatic disruption affected rainfall patterns.

When analysing data on the causes of water quality failure, it is preferable to base these on an extended dataset of repeat sampling. One-off sampling rounds may provide limited information, as they do not take into account seasonal influences. Such extended assessments need not be done in all towns nor include all water sources, provided there are several study sites and a representative sample of point sources. In Uganda, these assessments were done in 3 towns and covered both springs in areas of different population density and initial quality as well as boreholes. The assessments ran for 12 months after which time, routine testing involving twice yearly sampling (to reflect both wet seasons) were initiated. However, the main output of the assessments was a clear understanding of the causes of water quality failure, which related to poor sanitary maintenance and design and a model of failure was developed that linked surface pollutant sources and key sanitary protection failures. The influence of latrines was also assessed and was found to be limited at most springs. This led to the development of improved designs and the re-protection of some springs.

In routine monitoring, boreholes will generally require less frequent sampling as they are usually of better quality than shallow groundwater systems such as springs and dug wells given the greater depth of water abstraction. However, extended assessment data should be used to define water quality changes in boreholes to identify areas where borehole performance is weak and define the major factors relating to failure.

Chemical testing would generally be of far lower frequency and may only be carried out as part of a specific study. The selection of parameters is discussed in the previous Chapter. In general, sampling will only be carried out annually or possibly less frequently depending on the severity of any problems found during assessment or perceived likely rapid change. In the case of some chemicals, notably nitrate and chloride, testing should take into account pollutant recharge and dilution. In shallow groundwater, both may vary significantly with season. For instance in Uganda, nitrate showed a drop during the onset of rains, with subsequent increases as the rains continued and then reducing in drier periods. By contrast, chloride showed a marked peak at the onset of rains (which was co-incident with a microbiological contamination peak) with subsequent decrease during the wet period.

8.4 Household water

Household samples should be take from the drinking-water storage vessel used by the family and containers used for collecting and transporting the water. A water chain can be tracked from source to storage with samples taken from source, collection vessel and water storage container.

The type of household testing undertaken will be determined by the nature of water supply and strategies that must followed by low-income houses in storing water. Collection of water from communal sources and storage of drinking water within the home is commonly associated with deterioration in quality due to poor handling and storage practices. The re-contamination of water represents a major risk to health and both surveillance and improvement are required. Where access at higher service levels is low then the majority of the population is likely to use communal sources and store water within the home. Where access to direct connections are high, but continuity in supply is poor, water must still be stored within the home and therefore again deterioration may occur.

The numbers of samples and the selection of households will depend largely on what the principal objective for the testing of household water. If the major purpose is to simply undertake random sampling of household water (which is an important part of surveillance) then a stratified random sampling approach can be adopted. In this case, no specific intervention is being evaluated although the collection of information about sources and the type and cleanliness of the storage container may indicate where major problems lie. This data can also be used to check on the use of feedback of surveillance results on household water quality. For instance in Uganda, the simple process of feedback of information and routine testing led to observable improvements in water quality stored within the home.

In this situation the zoning process will identify areas where there is high use of communal sources and household storage is common due to low connection rates and this may be used to develop a rolling programme of testing in such areas. When such programmes are initiated it is important that different households are visited in each sampling period to prevent a bias developing due to repeated visits by surveillance staff. However, a cluster sampling approach may be adopted by identifying sentinel communities believed to be at greater risk because they have least access to direct connection or because they are more affected by interruption in supply.

However, in some cases there may be other specific objectives for testing water in the home. These may include evaluating the impact of particular health education programme or household water storage and treatment interventions. In this case, a study would be designed to measure the impact between an intervention group and a control group thus allowing an evaluation of the impact of the intervention. Alternatively, the influence of the type of source, frequency and duration of discontinuity, or type of storage vessel on water quality on household water quality may be assessed in a community. In this case, a cluster sampling approach would typically be used to keep the number of households included to a reasonable number that allows intensive investigation.

9.

Water Usage Studies

Water usage studies are an integral part of surveillance activities. In order to develop routine water quality surveillance programmes, it is important to understand where people collect water used for drinking or food preparation. In order to develop appropriate interventions to improve water supply, it is also important to understand why different sources are used and how quantities of water collected vary between different source types and service levels.

The use of socio-economic and demographic data in targeting surveillance has already been discussed. Water usage studies are often critical within this process to ensure that resources are targeted on the most needy population and on sources of water used for drinking. Such studies provide more detailed knowledge about the water supply situation amongst the urban poor and can be used to refine surveillance programmes, to develop programmes to improve water supply and to facilitate greater community involvement in decision making.

In water usage studies, as in all social surveys, it is essential to be clear about:

- What type of information you wish to collect

- Why such information is important

- Who you need to collect the information from

- Where can you find these people

- What is the most appropriate method of collecting the information

- When is the most appropriate time for data collection

Furthermore, you should always assess whether the information you want can be gathered from elsewhere using less time-intensive methods, for instance by reviewing similar studies or data that is available in other agencies. Water usage studies should be carried out when the information required is not available or is very out-of-date.

9.1 The purpose of water usage studies

Water usage studies are primarily studies that explore which water sources the population commonly use and their relative importance, what these sources are used for and reasons influencing these decisions. They also look at collection, storage and treatment of the water collected.

The use of water usage studies is highly recommended in refining urban water monitoring and surveillance programmes where the water supply situation is complex with a variety of alternative sources available for use. Monitoring and surveillance programmes focus on sources that are used for drinking and food preparation/cooking and therefore it is important to understand what the different types of water sources accessed by the population are used for. In addition, it is useful to find out how many sources are used, how often are sources are visited and typically how much water is collected as this will determine the relative importance of different source types and thus their importance for the surveillance programme.

An indication of availability of sources can be determined from the inventory. However, the simple presence of infrastructure is not necessarily a good indicator of which water sources are used by all or even most of the population or whether they use several sources. In other situations, piped water sources may be present in an area, but due to the cost of the water, few people may use taps preferring protected springs that bear no cost.

Point sources and unprotected water may be available in a community but may only be used for specific activities and not for drinking or food preparation. It has been noted in some communities that a 'rationality' factor comes into play with water sources and that known high quality sources may be used for drinking and food preparation with less secure supplies only used for non-consumptive use. Information regarding which particular sources (or source types) are used by a sub-population and whether these sources supply water that is used for consumption can be gained from carrying out a shorter water usage study (see Annex 5 - short form of questionnaire)

A second objective of undertaking a water usage study is gather information which will help in the process of developing or focusing intervention strategies (such as infrastructure improvements, health education, policy). In this case the study would be more comprehensive than that used for surveillance and would, for example, collect data concerning factors which influence the decisions households make regarding where they access their water and what they use it for. The reasons for choosing a particular source, reasons for using multiple sources, the influence of cost or proximity should all be included when planning improvements in the water supply of an area. Whilst information regarding factors such as cost can be gained from the inventory, a water usage study may provide a check on cost data and this may be particularly useful if the inventory had been undertaken some years previously. Additionally a water usage study may include collecting information about collection, storage and treatment of water collected. This information can potentially inform the focus of health education interventions (see Annex 5 - long form of questionnaire).

Water usage studies can also be used to assess the impact of an hygiene education intervention on water usage behaviour, for instance the promotion of low-risk sources for drinking water collection. By undertaking an initial water use study, baseline data can be established from which an intervention can be designed. Following the intervention, a second study using the same procedure could be used to measure any changes in water use behaviour that have been achieved.

Thus the information required for simply refining surveillance programmes and that required for developing an improvement strategy are different as noted in Table 9.1 below. These differences in turn will influence the costs of data collection and analysis.

Information for improving surveillance	Information for focusing intervention
Sources types used	Personal reasons for use
Multiple source use	Cost
Rationality factor	Proximity
	Collection storage and treatment
	Water use behaviour

Table 9.1: Water usage information needs for surveillance and intervention

However, whilst water usage studies are useful tools in collecting data for developing surveillance and intervention strategies, their use is dependent on the water source infrastructure in urban areas and the objectives of the study intended to be carried out. Thus water usage studies are not required in all situations or necessarily for all towns. In urban areas where one type of water source predominates there is little point in undertaking a water usage study looking at water source use. For example in Uganda, the towns of Jinja (all piped sources) and Mukono (all point sources) were not considered appropriate for water usage studies.

Three towns were selected for studies since they represented the three different supply patterns in Uganda and information gained could broadly be applied to the remaining towns in Uganda. These were Kampala a large city with complex water availability characteristics; Soroti a town with access to multiple sources where the piped water is managed by the Municipality; and, Masaka a smaller town with access to multiple sources where the piped water is a parastatal supply.

9.2 Approaches to water usage studies

Water usage studies can be undertaken using a variety of techniques. They can be broad-spectrum surveys that are questionnaire based and provide quantitative data or they can incorporate components of more participatory approaches to data collection, which provide more qualitative data.

Broad-spectrum surveys can provide information about a larger number of people and therefore usually collect data on a wide range of variables. However, this approach does not allow for much discussion around a subject with a respondent, as the data to be collected is pre-determined. This type of approach is most appropriate where the principal purpose of the study is to gain an urban wide assessment of water collection behaviour, as this is more cost-effective than other approaches.

Participatory approaches to data collection are methods where there is much greater direct involvement by communities in the definition of data to be collected and the type of information that is generated. These include methods such as focus-group discussion. In general, participatory methods are more time intensive than questionnaires but allow discussion of the issues and do not pre-determine the data to be collected beforehand. Given the time and funds required to carry out such studies, they are more appropriate for gaining detailed information about a particular issue. They are usually too time consuming and expensive to be utilised on a large scale and as such are less appropriate when trying to build a picture of the whole city.

As participatory techniques demand a significant amount of time from the members of the communities in which they are undertaken, and engage members in dialogue, these are effective where a key objective is to initiate action within the communities where the study is being carried out. Such approaches may also be of value when a triangulated study is being undertaken as the data collected from one method can be validated against data collected using another method.

The data collection approach adopted will depend in part on the resources available and the objectives of the study. It is essential that the objectives of the intended study, the type of data that is desired, the target group and the use of the data are all clearly established during the planning of the study. This will help determine whether a broad-spectrum survey or a participatory approach is to be used. It is important that studies undertaken always follow ethical principles with written or verbal consent obtained from participants and where required, approval should be sought from appropriate national research ethics boards.

9.2.1 Broad spectrum surveys

Broad-spectrum surveys tend to be undertaken through using questionnaires or structured interviews. However, reliance on questionnaires or structured interviews has some drawbacks, not least of which is that the data to be collected is pre-defined and therefore potentially useful information may be missed. Furthermore, there may be problems with obtaining socially desirable responses – for instance about boiling of water in the home – in an approach where there is little opportunity for exploring responses to questions in greater depth. This makes careful questionnaire design and pre-testing vital if such an approach is to be followed.

Questionnaires

The type of questionnaire used in the study will be determined by the objectives of the study. An established questionnaire may be appropriate for your purposes, alternatively selected items from an established questionnaire can be used. The questionnaires developed in Uganda may be used, although this should be reviewed within the context of each country. If a new questionnaire is to be developed, this should be done in conjunction with someone who has knowledge of questionnaire design. Whether designing a questionnaire or using a pre-existing questionnaire, it is important that the items (questions) on the questionnaire yield information relevant to the objectives of the study.

The way in which questions are asked in a questionnaire will dictate the way the respondent answers and in turn the data will be analysed. In many questionnaires, the available answers to a question may be pre-defined, for instance, presence or absence of a fact, a sliding scale or categorised. The latter can be a forced choice (i.e. chose only one) or multiple responses (i.e. chose more than one). Some question may allow for free response, although this will mean that such data is analysed using qualitative rather than quantitative techniques see Box 9.1 below for examples of questions.

		Type of response
Q1.	Do you use a vendor? Yes/No	**Presence/Absence**
Q2.	How often do you go to this source? Daily Once a week Once a month Occasionally	**Sliding scale**
Q3.	What are your reasons for using source 1? Cost Distance Quality Reliability	**Categorical** **Multiple response**
Q4.	What is the main reason for using source 1? Cost Distance Quality Reliability	**Categorical** **Single response**
Q5.	What do you use the water for? Drinking Cooking Bathing Washing	**Categorical** **Multiple response**
Q6.	How many 20L Jerrycans of water do you collect from this source on each occasion	**Free answer**

Box 9.1 Examples of questions and types of responses (Full questionnaire in appendix)

The nature of the questions will influence the amount of training enumerators need in order to successfully use the questionnaire. For example when using categorical answers there are two ways in which this can be done. In Q3 and Q4 in Box 9.1, reasons for use are categorised into 'distance', 'quality', 'cost' etc. One approach is to read out the categories and ask the respondent to chose. Alternatively the question can be presented as a free question and the responses are categorised by the enumerator. In the latter case the response to questions may not come directly in this form, but as 'near', 'close', 'water is good', 'clean', 'free' and so on. This means that the enumerator should classify the answer given and this provides a way of incorporating the broader meaning of concepts in some countries. It may be preferable to allow respondents to answer freely with enumerator classifying response as the reading of a simple list may lead to bias. However this implies that the pre-defined categories are based on reliable assessments. Thus a pilot study may allow completely free text answers which the project team then analyse in terms of category of answers. This can then be used in a larger study where free answers to questions are classified by the enumerators. Clearly, the enumerators must be trained to ensure that they can categorise free responses appropriately.

The questionnaire should be in the local language of the study site. In this case, either all questionnaires will be filled out in the local language, or the questionnaires filled in English, with a copy of the translation given to each enumerator for reference. If the questionnaire is developed in one language and needs to be translated, then a process of translation/back-translation should be used. The questionnaire should be translated by one person and then back translated by a second person. The two translations can then be compared and significant changes in meaning identified. However, bear in mind that different languages express particular concepts in differing degrees of detail and therefore a phrase that may appear to have changed meaning during back-translation, in reality may not have done because the meaning in the local language is broad. Once the back-translation is received, the project team should review the original and back-translated versions and discuss where there have been changes in meaning, establish to what degree and how important such changes in meaning are and then revise the questionnaire as appropriate.

Piloting

It is always preferable that a pilot study of the questionnaire has been undertaken somewhere in the country using the questionnaire to be used before embarking on a larger study. Pilot studies can have a number of purposes however two will be discussed here. A pilot study can be used to ensure that you are collecting reliable date. This is particularly important if you have designed a new questionnaire. One way to do this is to pilot the questionnaire in conjunction with other tools and compare responses obtained from each tool to see if they are similar and to identify any major discrepancies. This may be done in the form of a triangulated approach, for example using the questionnaire and also focus group discussion and observations. If discrepancies are found, a process of reviewing the questionnaire should be undertaken and amendments made. If significant changes are made to the questionnaire, it should be piloted again in conjunction with the other data collection techniques. This process gives some confidence that the final questionnaire is giving reliable information.

A pilot study should also ensure that the questionnaire is understandable and makes sense to the respondents. It is particularly important to ensure that the questionnaire is culturally sensitive and appropriately translated. One way to do this is for pre-testing to be carried out by field staff to identify any potentially confusing or problematic questions. Where these are identified, the nature of questions and the structure of the questionnaire can be altered where required.

Target population for the study

When undertaking a broad-spectrum study, it is critical to define the study target group, which is unlikely to be the whole population in an urban area. A target group is the pre-defined sub-population that you are interested in learning about. Water usage studies undertaken to inform surveillance programmes should target the low income population who live in areas where it is not clear from the inventory which sources they are likely to use.

If the study is primarily to guide intervention approaches, the target population may be more specific. This could be a particular community where infrastructure improvements are planned or where a health education programme is going to be initiated. Clear criteria for the target population should be drawn up during the planning stage to ensure that an appropriate sampling strategy is developed.

In Kampala, Uganda a broad-spectrum water usage study was designed to refine the surveillance programme and the target population was defined as those people who:

- lived in parishes of low socio-economic status

- lived in parishes were there was a choice of water source type

- were women, men and children over 14 years of age

Sampling strategy

A sampling strategy is a means of accessing a representative sample of the population. When undertaking a broad-spectrum survey, a simple random sampling procedure is often not appropriate or practical because this can potentially involve a highly dispersed population which causes logistical problems and increased costs. In addition, given that the available water infrastructure policy influencing this may vary across the municipality it is important to access the target population throughout the municipality.

In order to address these problems, single or multi-stage sampling using stratification can be adopted. Stratification is a process whereby the target population is divided into sub populations from which a random sample can be taken. These are known as the primary sampling units (PSU). This can be done on the basis of administrative units in the municipality and in Uganda these were Divisions. A single stage design would then involve random sampling of household from each primary sampling unit.

However, in a large municipality a single stage stratified random sampling approach may still result in too large a dispersion for practical purposes and thus multi-stage sampling can be adopted. A multi-stage approach involves defining a set of secondary sampling units that are common within all PSUs, such as a lower level of administrative unit- for instance in Uganda secondary sampling units were Parishes. A random sample of secondary sampling units from is taken using a random numbers table. Following this, a random sample of households is taken from each of the small administrative units selected. This can be done in a number of ways. Where existing frames of sampling are found (for instance relating to political constituencies), a systematic procedure can be used. However, there are a number of problems of using this approach in low-income areas of developing countries. Often no existing frames of sampling are available and where they are available, they often do not include substantial proportions of the target group who may be illegal or unregistered occupants. Furthermore, a lack of detailed maps may make identification of houses difficult.

An alternative approach is to take more practical approach based on a systematic procedure. For example enumerators may select every 5th house on the right. An example of the procedure adopted in Kampala is given in Box 9.2.

Aim:

To assess the level of use of protected point sources in low-income households for consumption, where there is access to multiple source types including piped sources.

Target Population

Low-income & access to both piped and protected point sources

Sample Design: Stratified, two-stage sample design.

- Stratification by division

- Proportional sample of administrative parishes in each division.

- Systematic random sampling of households from each parish.

- Sample size 1000 households

Stratification

Kampala is divided into five divisions, each represents varying populations, in terms of size, density and socio-economic level. A representative sample of low-income communities was obtained by stratification on the basis of division. This was deemed useful as:

- There is a differing distribution of source types across the divisions

- Public health department staff undertaking the study are organised on a Divisional basis

Proportional sampling of parishes

Estimates of target household population within each division was determined by identifying the parishes meeting the criteria above and totalling the number of people in parishes. This was based on census data and projected population using urban growth rate and average household size in each parish. Each Division was allocated appropriate numbers of interviews on the basis of the proportion of the target population, as households, residing within that Division.

The city of Kampala is divided into 100 Parishes, which provided a good sampling unit. Of these, 45 Parishes met the criteria outlined above, though they were distributed disproportionately across the city. Within each of the Divisions a random sample of parishes was selected on the basis of the population meeting the criteria within the Division, required sample size and practical considerations. Within each Parish a sample of 45 householders were interviewed.

Systematic sampling of household

No existing frames of sampling for household within parishes existed. Therefore enumerators were instructed to walk through the parish and select every 5th house on the right. Respondents were women, men or children over the age of 14.

Sample size

The size of the sample as well as the design adopted are important in gaining reliable data which can be viewed as representative of the target population. Calculating the size of sample is based on a statistical theory that is beyond the scope of this manual to describe. However, merely increasing sample size will not necessarily increase reliability since other factors such probability and standard error also dictate sample sizes. Certain estimates may need to be made, such as the likely number of people engaging in a particular practice and the distribution of the practice within the type of population. Advice of calculating sample sizes can be found in any standard statistics reference book, alternatively advice should be sought from someone with statistical expertise.

However, statistical validity is not the only criteria that may influence sample size. Consideration of the available human and financial resources and the time that staff have to undertake a study should also be considered. A balance should always be maintained between the size of the sample surveyed and obtaining reliable data. In some cases, it may not be possible to complete the number of questionnaires required for a statistical design because there are limited funds or there are insufficient staff. In this case, a study may still be undertaken. Most social scientists stress that the reliability of data collected is as important as the sample size and also that studies that are not statistically based can still yield useful data

Enumerators and Training

Care should be taken when selecting the staff to undertake the study. They must be literate, as otherwise they will not be able to fill in a questionnaire. Consideration should be given whether to use field surveillance staff or independent enumerators. There are potential problems when using field surveillance staff to undertake water usage surveys. They may be known to the community for their role in health education and this may contribute to socially desirable responses being given, for example when questions are asked regarding treatment of water within the home. Similarly field surveillance staff may be tempted to use the opportunity to promote better practices, which is not appropriate when carrying out the study. These problems can be overcome though moving staff to areas where they are not operational and by proper training of enumerators to ensure they are aware of the potential bias they may introduce. If bias is expected to be a major problem, then independent enumerators should be used, for example other staff or students.

It is also particularly important that cultural taboos relating to the interaction of men and women are not contravened. It is likely that a significant proportion of principal respondents will be women as they commonly manage household water. Indeed, the study may deliberately target women. In this case, the cultural mores about interactions between men and women must be carefully considered and a decision made as to whether using male enumerators would be appropriate or whether only women should be allowed to interview women and only men interview men.

Training of enumerators in the use of questionnaires is critical in ensuring that the data collected is reliable. They must fully understand the purpose of the study and be competent in the administration of questionnaires. It is critical when using questionnaires that the enumerators do not influence the responses provided and that they ask questions directly from the questionnaire without providing explanations of the questions. Therefore it is essential that before each study is undertaken, training and pre-testing of the questionnaire by the enumerators is carried and any confusion or problems identified are resolved. In all studies of this nature, it is essential that enumerators obtain verbal or written consent from respondents and that confidentiality is guaranteed. Staff should understand that they cannot force participation in the study and should be polite and respectful to the respondent and not criticise or laugh at any responses inappropriately.

9.2.2 Participatory approaches

Participatory approaches involve more time and resources, but provide more detailed information on individual communities, thus they are of particular use when the findings of the study will be directly incorporated into implementation of activities in those communities. In these circumstances, the use of participatory techniques will often provide the basis for ongoing discussions with communities and in developing a joint planning approach. Participatory approaches such as focus group discussions can also be incorporated into triangulated studies with questionnaires and observations when little is known about water use patterns or likely problems in responses to questions.

There are many different participatory techniques that can be used to elicit information about water usage. These include the use of key informant interviews, focus group discussions (often covering several different groups within the community, e.g. youths, women), community mapping and transect walks to name only a few. However, as with broad-spectrum studies, it is essential to be clear about the objectives and the target population to be included in participatory studies from the outset. In literate populations, visual methods of information gathering may be less appropriate than discussion-based approaches where key conclusions and resolutions can be written down. Furthermore, in societies where the movement of women is restricted, transect walks may not be appropriate. Usually several participatory techniques would be used, with different techniques being used at different times and for different purposes. A full discussion of the merits of each technique is beyond the scope of this text and readers are referred to the suggested further reading in Annex 6. Two approaches, which may be particularly useful, when carrying out water usage studies, are focus group discussions and mapping exercises. In both these exercises, additional techniques can be incorporated, such as ranking of sources by use and seasonal calendars of seasonal use.

The people used to undertake participatory research must have had training in the use of such techniques and of working with communities. They should be sensitive to the cultural and social values of the community and be able to manage a group in a way that encourages participation from all the members, but remains focused on the issues under discussion. This approach is more skilful that a broad-based survey and hence training may need to be a longer exercise.

Focus Group Discussions

Focus group discussions are a means of exploring a small number of issues with groups of people. Often groups comprise of between 8-15 people chosen as representative of a target population. In many cases, a number of focus group discussions are carried out with different target groups or the same target group in different areas. A topic guide is usually drawn up by the researcher, which outlines areas or questions that are relevant to the objectives of the study. A topic guide is a general guide regarding the issues to be discussed and unlike a questionnaire it does not have to be rigidly followed. It is prepared to ensure that major issues are discussed and the exploration of related issues is encouraged.

It is useful to have two researchers involved in the focused group discussion. Each has a separate role - one as the facilitator, the other as secretary, taking notes. If resources are limited, a single researcher can use a tape recorder, but you must be certain that this will be acceptable to the target group.

Mapping Exercises

A mapping exercise is another useful method of collecting data for a water usage study. This is also a group exercise and as with the focus group discussion is carried out with small groups of people. The basic principles of a mapping exercise is to facilitate the group to construct a map of their locality indicating the key factors you are interested in. This is a useful way of collecting data about source availability, which sources are commonly used, activities that water is used for and reasons for choosing water sources in a particular geographical area. Group members are guided in the development of a map of their area. A topic guide of issues relevant to the study is used by the facilitator to lead discussion about the factors that the study is focused on. These factors are discussed and consensus opinions reached and are illustrated on the map.

Topic Guides

A topic guide has the same role in focus group discussion and mapping exercise as a questionnaire has in a broad based survey. It's purpose to elicit information relating to the objectives of your study. Hence it important that you carefully consider the items in your topic guide to ensure they allow for useful information. Given that participatory methods tend to be more time consuming, and that people in urban areas tend to have limited time, a maximum period of one and a half-hours should be given for the exercise. This will limit the number of issues you can cover and your topic guide should reflect this. An example of a topic guide is shown in Box 9.3 below.

Box 9.3: Topic Guide for focus group discussion

Aim: To determine which sources are being used for consumption

- What water sources exist in the locality

- Which water sources do people commonly use in the locality

- What are these sources used for

- What influences decisions to use the sources

Facilitators and Training

Where possible it is helpful to use facilitators who are known and trusted by the community. To some extent, the degree of willingness to openly discuss issues will depend on the level of trust and confidence participants have in the facilitators. A known and trusted facilitator is likely to develop good rapport more easily with the group and thus is likely to elicit more in-depth information. In addition, given that participatory techniques require greater skills, facilitators who have experience of participatory approaches are preferable and will reduce costs incurred through training. Facilitators should therefore have an understanding of the role of participatory methods of data collection within local development. They will also need the skills to utilise the specific techniques selected. A good understanding of the process of running a group exercise and managing difficulties will help ensure that the exercise is successfully carried out with co-operation of all group members.

However, where facilitators do not have previous experience, training is particularly important since the methods described are sometimes complex and involve the management of groups of people with different views and potentially raise expectations in a particular area as the community is being engaged in dialogue about the issue. Such training will take time and resources and incur additional costs to the study. The relative merits of costly training must be considered in the light of the benefits both to the study and the wider applicability of such techniques. Where there is no broader demand for such skills, this may not be a cost-effective approach.

9.3 Incorporating results into surveillance and intervention activities

The objectives of your study and the data collected will influence how you analyse the data and how it is used to inform surveillance and/or intervention. Following collection of the data, this should analysed in a way that enables clear information relating to the objectives to be determined. Initially this may be in terms of simple frequencies and tables providing a breakdown of water use patterns. This information can be provided to local administrations, health officials and other stakeholders (including communities) in the first instance in order to give a picture of water use patterns at the local level (e.g. Parish level) as discussed in Chapter 10.

There are many ways in which the data from a water usage study can be used to improve surveillance programmes and plan interventions to improve water supply. The exact use of the data will depend to a certain extent on the specific objectives of the study. Some broad guidance is provided below.

9.3.1 Informing surveillance programmes

The use of broad-based surveys is recommended for informing surveillance programmes and this section will focus mainly on analysing quantitative data. There are two major ways in which surveillance can change as a result of the water usage data: changes made to the zoning process, and refinements made to the monitoring programmes.

In order to make these refinements to the zoning process and monitoring programmes, similar information is necessary

- Primary source: Type & frequency

- Use of primary source   Consumption/non-consumption

- Multiple sources   Frequency

- Secondary source   Type & frequency

- Use of secondary source Consumption/non-consumption

- Vendors   Frequency

- Use of vendors   Consumption/non-consumption

9.3.2 Refining the zoning process

As zoning incorporates a water supply variable - the water economy - water usage studies can assist in the development of categories or zones that will be applied across the urban area.

Zoning is initially developed on the basis of availability and as this may dictate the number of samples to be taken, it is important to be clear how important different sources are and whether only certain sources are used for drinking.

If the water usage study indicates a significant part of the target population is using one source type for consumption, then it is important to make decisions about whether further sub-division of zone categories is required and whether certain categories should be no longer used. Once there is evidence that 80% or more of people use one particular source type for drinking, then it may more appropriate to use the characteristics of the predominant supply type as zone categories. For example, if over 80% of the population use a tap for water for drinking water, it may be more effective to use criteria such as service level or reliability.

Once over 95% of people use a single source type for consumption, then it is probably no longer worthwhile categorising Parishes as 'mixed water use' as this will not help target resources. In general once the level of use of a particular type of source drops below five percent there is little point in including this in a routine surveillance programme, although occasional visits may be made to the source.

The process of refining zones is shown in figure 9.1 below.

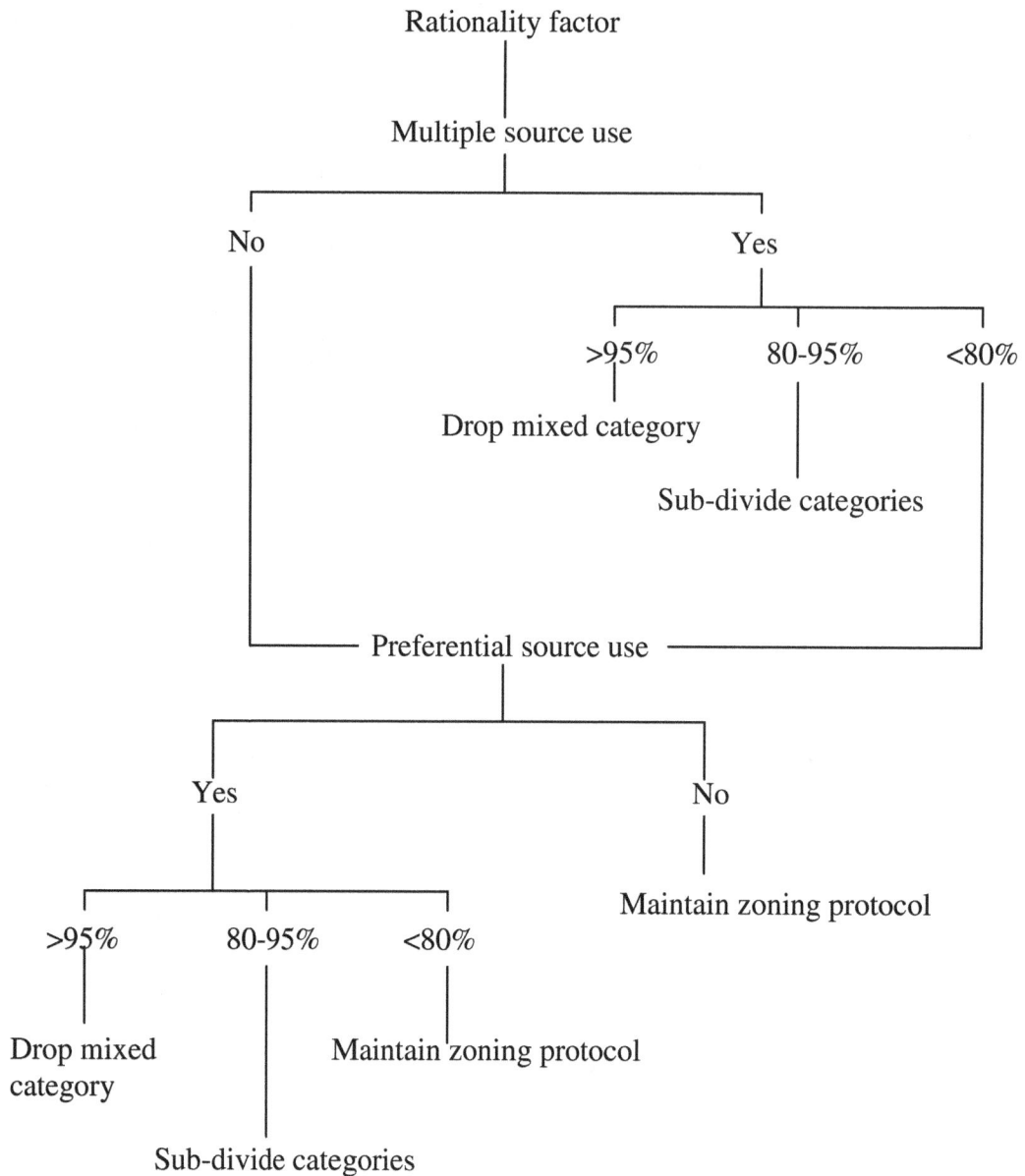

Figure 9.1: Refining the zoning process using water usage data

9.3.3 Refining sampling programmes

This process comes into operation once the zoning categories have been refined and can be implemented urban-wide or on a more local scale. As noted in the previous chapter, sample numbers are often based on population and it was stressed that such figures should be based on usage in preference to availability. In the initial zoning process sample numbers may be based simply on an estimation of the number of people with their own connection and an estimate of the number of people without a connection who use piped water. This would usually reflect the proportion of piped sources to non piped sources available as determined by the inventory. The water usage study will provide a more accurate estimation of the number of people using a piped water source and thus the sample can be adjust to reflect this. For point sources the level of use as opposed to availability may not have such a direct impact on the monitoring programme as in the case of piped water. However, some slight adjustments may be made in response to the data.

9.4 Key types of water usage data and their use

9.4.1 Rationality factor

(a) Are people using multiple sources?

If they are, then it is possible that there is a rationality factor in operation and particular sources are being used for consumption and non-consumption. If this is the case, it is important to focus the surveillance programme on those source types that are being used for consumption. If they are not, then there is no rationality factor and the population are not differentiating between sources which are for consumption and non-consumption. The monitoring programme may be adjusted to reflect the predominant source as discussed below.

If people are using multiple sources, is this based on the rationality factor?

If this is the case, then surveillance needs to focus on sources being used for consumption rather than those not used for consumption. If they are not, then the likelihood of a source being used for consumption is similar for all sources and surveillance cannot be based on differential use.

1. Predominant sources used

(a) Where there is no rationality factor, are particular source types being used as the primary source of water?

If one or more particular source types are being used by the target population as their primary water source (for example taps), then it is important that this source type is targeted in the surveillance programme, since no rationality factor is operating and this source type will be used for consumption. If there is no clear preference for source type, the likelihood of sources being used for drinking is similar across source types and the surveillance programme should reflect this on the basis of availability and likely variation in quality (see Chapter 8).

(b) Where there is no rationality factor and multiple source use, are particular sources (primary, secondary and other) being preferentially used overall?

In considering all the sources used by household, if one or more particular source types are being used by the target population overall in preference to others, then it is important that this source type is targeted in the surveillance programme. Since no rationality factor is being used it is likely that this source type is being used for consumption. If there is no clear preference for source type, the likelihood of sources being used for drinking is similar across source types and the surveillance programme should reflect this.

2. Vendor use

(a) Are vendors being used by frequently by the target population?

If they are then there is the potential for a rationality factor (as sometimes vendor water is seen as higher quality) and this needs to be explored. If not, then this is not an important factor to consider in the analysis of the data and subsequently in the monitoring programmes.

(b) Is vendor water being used for consumption?

If vendor water is being used for consumption, then it has to be targeted and the sources used by vendors targeted. If not, then this is not an important factor to consider in water quality monitoring programmes.

Using this information to inform surveillance in the areas where you have carried out the study is relatively straightforward. The urban wide survey is based on a sampling procedure deemed to be representative of the low income multiple source area and thus these results can be extrapolated to the non sampled areas, as it gives a crude indication of general pattern of where people get their water. Sample frequencies can be used to determine the relative importance of source types and monitoring programmes adjusted accordingly. For instance, if 70% of the sampled population uses piped water as their primary source sample numbers can reflect this by calculating the minimum number of samples required in each area based on 70% usage.

9.4.2 Characteristics influencing patterns of water use

Information gathered in the study represents a sample of the target population and a range of patterns may be identified using statistical analysis. This can be done at increasing levels of complexity and patterns can then extrapolated to the target population as a whole and used to refine the monitoring programme.

One approach that can be adopted is to look at other variables at a stratification level for example the divisional level that you think may influence water usage patterns. This would include available infrastructure (from the inventory), connection rates (from the piped water supplier), socio-economic level (from the socio-economic index) and population data (from the census). Analysis of association (correlation and chi-squared statistics) can then be used to establish whether there are relationships between these variables and water usage patterns.

For example an analysis of patterns of primary water sources in the sample may indicate that the lower the socio-economic level of the area, the less likely the community are to use taps and the more likely they are to use springs. In this case, the surveillance programme should focus on springs in the geographical areas that have the lowest socio-economic level.

9.5 Analysis and informing interventions

The water usage study can also be used to inform intervention programmes either a broad based survey or participatory approaches may have been used. The data collected may provide the following information:

- Reasons for using a particular source type

- Cost data

- Proximity data

- Collection data

- Storage data

- Treatment data

If this information has been collected using broad-spectrum survey techniques, quantitative data will be available for analysis using statistical methods. However if the data is collected using qualitative methods, the information will be richer, but less amenable to quantitative analysis and a situational analysis which describes the information would be used.

9.5.1 Analysis of quantitative data to inform interventions

Given the information gained from your study, key areas that could contribute to interventions may include the following:

What factors influence the source types people use to for water?

An analysis of reason given by household representatives by ranking frequency of reporting of reasons for using particular sources would highlight the predominant reasons. This information would help to prioritise actions. For example if the analysis suggests that distance is the primary reason for choice, then any intervention to provide public taps must take into account that if these are not substantially closer to the home, then alternatives will be used. If a household cost-distance assessment appears important, then attention must be paid to making water source both more accessible and cheaper to the user. If quality is a major reason, further promotion of safe sources may be all that is required.

Are household storing and treating water appropriately?

An analysis of storage and treatment data would give you an indication of efficacy of a health education message on treating water. However this information alone would not be sufficient to be ascertain whether people were storing or treating water appropriately. If this information is combined with household testing of water, a check on the evidence for good storage and handling practice is possible.

Is rainwater collected

In situation where no efforts have been made to promote rainwater harvesting on a large scale, an analysis of rainwater collection data which indicates that a significant proportion of the population are collecting rainwater may indicate that this is a potentially useful method to improve water supply. This is information that may form the basis of consideration of this method, taking into consideration of rainfall data and other environmental issues such as space and pollution. Where rainwater is not collected by any means, then promotion of rainwater collection may be less feasible and other approaches to improve water supply would be preferred.

Are point sources used by significant proportion of the population?

Where point sources are shown to be used by a significant proportion of the population, this may form the basis of a programme to improve or rehabilitate point sources. This may require changes in policy, technical improvement in rehabilitation or support to communities to improve operation and maintenance. These are discussed in more detail in chapters 12-14.

Are vendors being used?

Where significant use of vendors is indicated, interventions should be considered to improve vending practices. This may include ensuring adequate pressure and continuity at draw off points or working with vendors to ensure that water quality is improved that a code of practice is adopted and that costs remain affordable.

9.6 Issues to consider

As noted water usage studies should form an integral part of surveillance programmes. However, it is important to remember some key issues about water usage studies before planning to undertake them. There should always be a clear purpose for a water usage study, with clearly defined objectives, information needs and data collection methods. The collection of ill-focused data from the study may not provide useful information and whilst generating a lot of interesting data cannot be used to inform actions. Thus take time to decide what you wish to investigate, why it is important and the most effective way of collecting the data. Therefore, water usage studies are usually undertaken sometime after the initiation of surveillance once unresolved issues are identified and used to refine a surveillance programme.

Bear in mind that you are likely to share the information that is generated by a water use study with a variety of different professionals and communities. Therefore, it is essential that the information presented is simple to understand and does not require specialist knowledge to interpret. Simple surveys that collect a restricted range of data that can be quickly and easily understood are often more useful in decision-making than highly complex studies where interpretation is difficult and requires extensive explanation. Analysis of qualitative data requires a different approach to quantitative data and results in a less numerical output. This may be less influential in the decision making process made at policy levels. However, careful structuring of qualitative data can provide more accessible information for policy makers. Therefore bear this mind when planning social surveys and the approach you wish to adopt.

The data from collected either by means of a broad based survey or participatory approaches will produce data from which conclusions can be drawn with a varying degree of confidence based on results of varying degrees of power. Thus they provide data that is generally representative but not results that provide absolute certainties. Therefore, bear in mind that there may well be exceptions to general rules and that the results from any sample are an approximation of real life. Also bear in mind that conditions may change rapidly and that the results from individual studies may become less valid as socio-economic and water supply conditions change.

10.

Information management and analysis

It is critical that the data generated by surveillance monitoring programmes is stored and managed effectively and is analysed appropriately to ensure that it becomes useful information for decision-making. Data that cannot be retrieved and analysed easily and in a comprehensible form usually ends up by not being used and represents a waste of resources. As the principal benefit of surveillance is that it allows decisions to be based on a good understanding of the problems in water supply, a failure to ensure that data is transformed into information means that the surveillance function has failed.

As most monitoring and surveillance programmes will generate a significant amount of data, electronic data storage is generally preferred. Whilst paper archiving of data can be done, it requires manual analysis and the review of large volumes of data that may rapidly become unwieldy. In most countries the use of computers is widespread and therefore keeping data in electronic databases is the easiest method of data storage and retrieval for analysis. Furthermore, as some data will be linked (for instance water quality and sanitary inspection data) it is preferable to keep these in a way that ensures that simultaneous retrieval and analysis of both sets of data can be carried out.

One key thing to bear in mind with data management is that careful planning is essential. Careful consideration should be given as to how the data will be collected, how it is best stored and what type of analysis will be carried out. It is essential that duplicated entry of data is avoided. This is usually achieved through allocation of a unique identification code to each subject or water source. When this is done, all the data that relates to a particular subject can be stored and retrieved easily. Further information is available at the watermark web-site (www.lboro.ac.uk).

It is also essential to consider a number of data that may have links with each other – for instance they are all within the same town or area, or perhaps they are of the same source type. It is important that these primary data fields are borne in mind as this may represent a critical area of analysis – for instance to gain a breakdown of the frequency of different sources with a town or to compare costs between different source types. In many cases, a range of data may be collected on a single subject (for instance a particular water source or respondent in a survey).

Surveillance programmes collect a wide range of data and often there are multiple data sets for a single sources (or subject) that are related, for instance water quality and sanitary inspection data. When multiple sets of data are collected from a single source it is important to avoid creating data that is 'orphaned' – i.e. data that can be linked back to the subject or source from which it came. It is difficult to undertake analysis of orphaned data, as it is not clear to which subject or source to which the data relates.

10.1 Inventory, water use and other surveys

Where surveys are carried out to assess availability and use of water these are often based on questionnaires. Such data can be stored in a variety of database packages that allow fields to be defined that include part or all of the questions asked. This is often important as the question structure may need to be revised and with time the original questionnaires may become lost.

When questionnaires are used, a relatively large amount of data may be collected on each questionnaire. For instance, the inventory will collecting data on aspects such as construction date, operation and maintenance responsibility and frequency, rehabilitation works, costs of water and reliability of the supply. The water usage questionnaire also includes a wide range of data on the source used, the reasons for source use and costs as well as socio-demographic data. In both these examples, it there is an important need to ensure that all the data relevant to each subject (i.e. each questionnaire) is stored together as otherwise once the survey has been completed it may become difficult to relate different factors within each subject.

Setting up an effective database takes time and experience and it is beyond the scope of this manual to describe the ways in which each database functions. In general, it is best to select those databases with which staff are most familiar and which allow easy data entry and at least basic analysis. In the case of Uganda, the data from the inventories and water usage studies was stored on Epi-Info, an epidemiological, statistical and world processing programme developed by the Centre for Disease Control in the USA in conjunction with WHO. This package was selected for several reasons:

1. The format allowed the data to be stored exactly as it appeared on the questionnaire, which made data entry easy for users.

2. The package allows simple analysis and can export data to other packages such as SPSS for more sophisticated analysis.

3. Once one copy of the software is purchased, multiple copies can be made under the purchase agreement. This also ensured that public health departments had access to this software for other data storage such as epidemiological studies.

4. The memory requirements are not high and so can be loaded even where computing facilities are limited.

These properties are not unique to EpiInfo and similar databases could have been set up using other packages. For detailed information regarding setting up EpiInfo databases for inventories and water usage studies, please consult the watermark web-site mentioned above.

All data from social surveys, including inventories and water usage studies should be entered into the database as soon as possible after the data has been collected in order that the data can be analysed and reports provided to key stakeholders.

Data on connections will also typically be stored in either a simple database package or spreadsheet. In some cases, specific databases may be used such as Foxpro or Xbase if there is a need to link the database to a GIS system or to where reports must be generated to a specified format using report writing software such as R&R Report Writer.

10.1.1 Data analysis

Different types of data require different types of analysis from simple frequencies and descriptive statistics to those that require complex analysis requiring multiple steps of data manipulation. Planning data analysis is therefore important and it is essential to carefully consider what type of information is required from the data collected, the target audience for the information and their level of understanding of statistical concepts.

Inventories and connection reviews

The analysis of data from inventories and connection reviews is simple as the main output from such data are simple descriptive statistics such as frequencies, averages and measures of association and independence. Usually the inventory data will provide simple summaries of frequency of source availability (both in terms of number and type) for the whole urban area and smaller units.

The data collected on cost would usually be presented in terms of the frequency of payment for water by source type and the average and range (by quartile) of costs charged per unit volume. Comparisons between the costs of different sources where charges are commonly levied would be carried out and in particular between public taps and water purchased from individuals with a private connection. It may be interesting to compare the different charges levied by different types of piped water source within different parts of the urban area and between different urban areas to see if any associations or major differences become apparent. For instance, in towns with greater numbers of public taps, the average costs of piped water may be substantially lower than in areas where purchase from neighbours predominates. Comparisons may also be made between different types of water supply utility (parastatal, municipal or private) as these may illustrate association or difference worth more detailed investigation

In addition to details on availability and cost, simple frequencies may also be provided for the number of community-managed supplies, the age of supplies, frequency of operation and maintenance activities and whether sources dry up or their use is restricted. The type of analysis for inventories is shown in Table 10.1 below.

Analysis of connection data would in general also be limited to frequencies of connection (possibly by category) within different parts of the urban area and as a total for the town. The connection analysis within the town is primarily used for the zoning process but also may be used later in analysis of water usage data. The breakdown of connection by community or area within the town or city also allows a picture to be built up about the equity of access to piped water at higher service levels. This can be correlated with other data such as socio-economic level, availability of point sources and costs of water purchased from communal piped sources. Comparisons may also be made between different towns to assess differentials in access and between different types of water supply utility (parastatal, municipal or private) as again this may illustrate association or difference worth more detailed investigation.

Type of data	Type of analysis	Degree of detail
Source types available	Total number of publicly available sources Frequencies of all categories available (including different types of piped water and point sources) Summary frequency of piped, point and unprotected sources	Overall urban area By administrative sub-unit
Cost of water	Frequency of payment being required Averages and percentiles of cost	Overall urban area By administrative sub-unit By source type
Ownership of sources	Frequency of different forms of ownership	Overall urban area By administrative sub-unit By source type
Responsibility for operation and maintenance	Frequency of identified persons or agencies	By source type
Rehabilitation or repair	Frequency of occurrence Types of repair Who funded work Who carried out work	By source type By agency
O&M, cleaning activities	Frequency	By source type
Restriction on volume	Frequency of occurrence Frequency of reasons	By source type By administrative sub-unit
Whether source dries up	Frequency of occurrence Average of down-time	By source type By administrative sub-unit

Table 10.1: Inventory data analysis

10.1.2 Water usage studies

Water usage studies will typically yield a wide range of data and therefore the analysis of data may be more complex. The data may also come in several forms if a triangulated study is used and therefore data storage must be carefully considered. The rest of the section discusses the types on information and analysis that can be carried out and how to relate different types of data to each other. A simple broad-spectrum survey using a questionnaire approach is discussed first and followed by some discussion of triangulated approaches.

Broad spectrum surveys

When a study is carried out over a number of communities to look at what sources are being us used and why, there is a simple set of descriptive statistical analyses to be initially carried out. These would typically be simple frequencies and averages for the whole urban area and then by sub-units as shown in Table 10.2 below.

Type of data	Type of analysis	Degree of detail
Choice of principal source	Frequency of source types	Overall urban area By administrative sub-units
Numbers of people using multiple sources	Frequency	Overall urban area By administrative sub-unit By source type
Choice of subsidiary sources	Frequency of source types	Overall urban area By administrative sub-unit By source type
Reasons for source 1 selection	Frequency of reporting	Overall urban area By administrative sub-unit By source type
Reasons for source 2 selection	Frequency of reporting	Overall urban area By administrative sub-unit By source type
Use of water of source 1	Frequency of nature of use	Overall urban area By administrative sub-unit By source type
Use of water of source 2	Frequency of nature of use	Overall urban area By administrative sub-unit By source type
Use of supplementary household sources (vendors, rainwater)	Frequency of use	Overall urban area By administrative sub-unit By source type
Number of households paying for water	Frequency of payment	Overall urban area By administrative sub-unit By source type
Costs of water	Average costs, range of costs, percentiles, distribution	Overall urban area By administrative sub-unit By source type
Number of people treating water in the home	Frequency of reported treatment, frequency of reported boiling	Overall urban area By administrative sub-unit By source type
Quantities of water used	Averages, range and percentiles	Overall urban area By administrative sub-unit By source type

Table 10.2: Water usage data analysis

This simple initial analysis will then allow further statistical analysis to be carried out. This would include measuring whether significant differences are found between aspects such as reasons and use of different water sources. Such analysis would typically involve tests such as chi-squared or s or more detailed analysis, logistic regression. Once a set of associations or differences have been identified, a more detailed analysis can be carried including analysis of other data thought to be significant in determining the observed outcomes. This will be likely to include source availability and socio-economic data as well as coverage rates.

The first step should be to assess the data obtained through the survey itself, for instance comparing the numbers of people using different sources as their principal source and the use of multiple sources. Analysis of reasons should also focus on the differences between different sources. Of particular importance will be to evaluate whether different uses are associated with different source types as both principal and subsidiary source. Other analysis may include comparing use of multiple sources and the type of source used for both first and second choice sources, and whether water from different source types is used for different purposes and whether different reasons are associated with the use of different source types.

Once the simple analysis has been done, then other data may incorporated into the analysis such as overall socio-economic status of the area, the availability and density of different sources and the percent of households in the areas with a direct connection. This may well require use of more sophisticated statistical programmes and such analysis should only be undertaken if there is a value in determining more exactly the nature of causes of source selection and use.

For instance, in Kampala, analysis included initial correlation between source use and a range of factors including socio-economic status, source density, numbers of sources and connection rates. This was evaluated to review the strongest associations in terms of odds ratios and from this, it became clear that the major causative factor for multiple source use was socio-economic status and that the use of protected springs was correlated with availability of springs within the Parish.

Other analysis will include assessing the costs of water and quantities of water used. When assessing costs, two principal areas of interest may be investigated: how many families are collecting water that must be purchased and the differences seen by type of sources; and the average and range of cost of water. When looking at the average and range of costs, it may be worth analysing the data in relation to data obtained in the inventory to assess whether there is change in price over time. For instance in Kampala, no change in price was seen between the inventory and water usage study, despite a two-year gap between them. Quantities of water may be estimated by calculating the amount of water used each day - usually based on responses to the number of containers of water collected with a calculation of daily per capita consumption based on the size of the household. For instance in Kampala, the study showed an average daily consumption of 18.5 litres per capita, with very little difference between different source types.

The degree of detailed analysis depends partly on what the simple analysis of raw data indicates. For instance, it may be that a very clear association can be made between the sources selected and key variables within the study data. If, for instance, all the sub-units of interest are included within the study, then it may not be necessary to undertake detailed analysis. This may often be the case in smaller urban areas where the number of different sub-units is small and there are already marked differences between socio-economic status or access to water supplies at higher service levels. Thus detailed analysis is only likely to be necessary in large urban agglomerations.

Triangulated studies and data from other survey techniques

Social surveys sometimes collect similar data through several different means including questionnaires, focus-group discussion and observations. Such approaches may be used for a number of reasons, but within the context of a water usage study as part of a surveillance programmes, the principal purpose will be to utilise a triangulated approach of validating information given by collecting this in several different ways.

Data collected from observation of the number of people using a particular source is very simple to analyse and it will usually be a count of the numbers of people using the source and a percentage use of each source will be derived. This obviously allows a check on responses regarding source type use collected in a questionnaire.

The data from focus group discussions is more difficult to analyse as it is not quantitative data but qualitative. The analysis of qualitative data requires a different approach to analysis that is not based on observable frequencies, but rather the identification of common themes that can be analysed. It is beyond the scope of this manual to discuss qualitative analysis in detail and in the majority of cases, such detailed analysis would not be required for surveillance programme but would be restricted to specific social research or interventions planned in specific communities.

When using participatory methods, the data collected of importance for the surveillance and improvement strategy will be aspects such as importance of different sources and source types and their proximity to major centres of settlement within the area. This is best illustrated on a map. The other major areas for analysis may be what volume of water is collected each day – in Kampala this was 5-7 Jerrycans a figure that validated the questionnaire data - and reasons for source selection. The data can be used to prepare a situational analysis, which is often best undertaken if the purpose of the study is to provide baseline information prior to an intervention.

10.2 Water quality and sanitary inspection data

Sanitary inspection and water quality data should be stored in a database that ensures each data can be retrieved simultaneously for analysis of causes of failures. As the database grows, it will also be important to ensure that the data can be linked to the geographical area, town, populations served and type of supply. This is particularly important for national databases where data from a number of towns and for a wide range of source types will be stored and analysed. Usually diverse information will be stored in separate data tables and these will have to be interfaced in order to store and analyse data effectively without requiring extensive and frequent data manipulation. Thus a relational database is generally required as this will provide the links between different data tables automatically and provided data is inputted correctly, analysis will be reliable.

When establishing a database, there are a number of things that should be borne in mind. Firstly, the same water source is likely to receive multiple visits over time (particularly piped water sources) and therefore it will be important to be able to easily retrieve, view and analyse time series data for the same source. There will be sources of a similar nature and the database should therefore make it easy to review and analyse data from similar sources in different areas. Within each urban area or sub-unit of the urban area there will be a variety of sources and households that data is collected for and the database should make it easy to review and analyse data for a specified area. Finally, if the area or system is zoned, then the database should enable the data for individual zones to be reviewed and analysed.

Developing relational databases require programming skills and unless these are available then this may limit the possibility of storing this data in an electronic format. However, dedicated software is available and a good example of this is the 'Sanman' database that was specifically developed for low-cost surveillance programmes.

This software is a relational database written in X-base with a number of inter-linked tables. The database ensures that important data cannot be orphaned – for instance it is not possible for a sanitary inspection form to be selected without defining a category beforehand. Equally, it is not possible to enter water quality data without first establishing a new sanitary inspection. The sanitary inspections in the programme are defined by the user which allows flexibility in allocating risk scores and in refining sanitary inspection approaches. If an alternative database is used, then this flexibility should be maintained. Other data tables such as towns, area, zone and population served allows more focused analysis on areas of key importance.

This manual will not review in detail the use of the 'Sanman' programme as it includes a reference manual, but a brief description is included here as the key points would common to all relational databases. The crucial first step is to define categories of water supply with associated sanitary inspection forms and risk score. The categories are the description of the source – protected spring, borehole with handpump, dug well, piped water etc. The sanitary inspection questions on the database must the same as those used during field collection. These can be periodically updated as revisions to the inspection forms are made. The different types of water supply (community owned, privately owned, utility supply, Municipal supply etc) are included in data tables that reflect the type of management of water sources. Once this is done, the next set of pre-defined variables - town, area, zone and population bands - which are used to define groups of sources are set up. The final stage is to define any user water quality parameters not already in the database.

Once this is established a unique record for each source can be assigned, that is controlled by the water source number. This approach means that all the data for a particular source can be stored together allowing easy viewing and analysis of time series for each source. Each source should be given a unique record number and in the 'Sanman' database, duplicate records are prevented by a screening process that allows the water source number to exist only once.

The data can then be put into the database as it is generated. It is preferable that the data is put in chronological order for viewing, but not essential for the analysis as this allows the records to be analysed by the date on which data were collected. Water quality surveillance databases often grow rapidly and it should be borne in mind that data will require regular back up and it may be necessary to discard historical data once it reaches a certain age. The 'Sanman' database can store up to 999,999 sanitary inspection records and the same number of water quality records. However, it may be questionable whether all these records need to active and it is often more effective to create electronic archives of historical data and only to keep the more recent data in the active database. This will simplify analysis and prevents the database becoming slow, as too much data must be reviewed.

10.2.1 Analysing data

The analysis of data is the principal mechanism by which raw data can be transferred into usable information for managers, communities and other decision-makers. Raw data is of relatively little use – most people will not understand what it means unless that have been directly involved in its collection and few will have sufficient time or interest to analyse raw data. What is required is simple, direct and comprehensible information that can be used without further manipulation and is meaningful to the target audience. The latter is extremely important, as the type of information that is of most use to communities is unlikely to be the same as that required by policy-makers.

The need for regular simple reports to users of the data has already been discussed. Most routine reports should present data in a simple format and include aspects such as the number of samples taken, minimum and maximum contamination found as well as other water quality parameters and the overall risk score. This can then be used to make recommendations for action on an ongoing basis. Such summaries may be given by date, zone, source category, town or area and complex stratification can be developed. Such summary reports would usually be given on a monthly basis, but could also provide annual reports.

The routine collection of water quality data will allow seasonal influences on water quality to be evaluated. This may used to define times and areas of particular risk of drinking contaminated water and the increased risk to health. By combining water quality data with other data used in the zoning process, a vulnerability map can be prepared that will help in ensuring health and other bodies are better prepared for potential epidemics.

When analysing water quality data, in most cases simple descriptive statistics such as averages, range and percentiles suffice. One crucial point to remember, however, is the selection of the average used may influence the results significantly, particularly where results are obtained that are too numerous to count (TNC/TNTC). In numerical databases, a default value must be assigned for such results. This is not a 'real' number – it is made up and may be twice the maximum recorded result or be based on previous analysis of diluted samples. Where analysis includes default values, a median rather than a mean should be used in analysis as a single high value assigned for a TNC result will result in a mean that does provide a reliable representation of the true state of water quality. Where TNC results are not found, then means are a more powerful average to use. More complex analysis may be done in relation to sanitary inspection such as regression to identify what were the major causes of failure observed as discussed in the following sections.

A final method of analysing data is to record the results obtained that show exceedence of national standards or WHO Guidelines Values. The proportion of samples that failed to meet national standards can be used to determine the degree of compliance of different water supplies. This data becomes useful in identifying problem areas within particular supplies and in comparing different water supplies. Both types of analysis helps planners and managers decide where to direct resources and attention in improving water supplies. However, when undertaking such comparisons, make sure that proper account is taken of the differences in sample numbers between different areas within a supply or from two or more water supplies. Where small numbers of samples are taken, low numbers of failure may lead to significant reductions in compliance.

10.2.2 Analysing operation and maintenance

The monitoring of operation and maintenance is an important element in surveillance as many water supply problems relate more to weaknesses in the operation and maintenance of the water supply rather than design, construction or siting problems. This requires an approach that looks at both water quality and sanitary inspection data. As sanitary inspections provide an integrated assessment of the status of a water supply from a water quality risk perspective, they can be valuable tools in monitoring operation and maintenance performance.

Most of the risks commonly covered in a sanitary inspection relate to physical measures put in place to prevent contamination (e.g. headworks or protection works) or to limit deterioration of infrastructure (e.g. fences and diversion ditches). They tend to be measures that water managers would be able to control through operation and maintenance. The presence of these risks therefore indicate a failure in the operation and management of the supply. Supplies with a high risk score can therefore be seen as those with weak operation and maintenance. Once an overall risk score exceeds 60%, the supply can be categorised as poorly managed and likely to be contaminated. Measurement of operation and maintenance can also focused on certain critical factors whose presence as risks indicate fundamental weaknesses in O&M performance.

Piped water

Water quality results may also indicate failures in operation and maintenance of the supply even where sanitary risk data is limited. For instance, in piped water supplies, sanitary inspection must take into account that microbiological may result from either failure in supply or because local sources of faecal matter gained entry into the pipe system, often very close to the sampling point.

Where water suppliers carry out routine (preferably daily) testing of final waters, regular review of final water may be adequate in assessing whether microbiological failure is likely to have resulted from poor treatment or subsequent contamination during distribution. Clearly where final waters show contamination then a treatment failure has occurred and operation and maintenance has been poor. Using sanitary inspection forms for treatment works provides an effective way of assessing operation and maintenance performance during the water production phase and should be routinely undertaken by suppliers of water. By undertaking regular routine inspection of treatment plants, the operation and maintenance of treatment can be easily assessed and recommendations made for action as discussed in Chapter 13.

The supply risks incorporated within a sanitary inspection cover the basic aspects of good sanitary risk management that it would be expected that a water supplier would control. These include aspects such as signs of leakage or reported pipe bursts and discontinuity within supply. These factors may not only influence water quality, but also reflect a broader supply inadequacy that may force the use of alternative water sources or reduced quantities of water used due to limitations in supply. Whilst water quality failure may result from either supply or local faults, supply risks are of particular importance as they affect a larger number of people.

The frequency of reporting of supply risks over time provides a good indication both of long-term performance and the impact of short-term deviations from good practice on water quality. Clearly, the presence of supply risks indicates that operation and maintenance has been compromised and provides a sound basis for recommendations and action to be taken by the water supplier.

A further means of assessing operation and maintenance and in particular adherence to cleaning and flushing schedules, is to plot chlorine residual levels within the system and in particular to relate these to zones based on service reservoir. The loss of free chlorine residuals during bulk distribution storage is a global problem. In temperate climates this often relates to storage of water for fire fighting. In tropical climates, both free and total chlorine residual losses are common as high ambient temperatures promote accelerated loss of a volatile substance. In both cases, however, the loss of free chlorine is also related to poorly maintained and cleaned distribution networks, including service reservoirs. The state of the interior of service reservoirs should be checked regularly, but this may be difficult sometimes as access is often problematic and the levels of water in reservoirs vary with demand. Thus at the time of a visit, the dirty areas may be below the water level, making inspection difficult.

Mapping of chlorine residual loss provides information regarding whether the loss is due to volatilisation or due to chlorine consumption. Free chlorine loss during distribution that is not associated with total chlorine loss would be associated with chlorine consumption and would indicate that operation and maintenance has been poor and that cleaning and flushing are required. Free and total chlorine loss indicates that loss through volatilisation is part of the cause and whilst cleaning of reservoirs and flushing of lines may provide some temporary improvement, it may not deal with the fundamental problem of chlorine loss. In the latter case, it would be more realistic to recommend that booster chlorination be practised.

The sanitary inspection forms for piped water supply will also typically include local risks that are within the remit of the household or community to control. This covers aspects such as exposure of the household main, water collecting around the base of taps and leaks within the household main. The presence of these risks will indicate whether local operation and maintenance around the facility has been compromised and therefore remedial action and strengthening of local maintenance is required, as discussed in Chapter 13.

Point sources
The operation and maintenance of point sources, which are typically managed by communities or user groups, is also easily monitored using sanitary inspection and water quality data. There are a number of key measures of the operation and maintenance of point supplies. As point sources are community-managed, there are not the same differential responsibility issues as there are for piped water supplies and it could, for instance, be expected that control of land-use around point sources would fall under the remit of the water source managers to control. Thus all the risks included in the sanitary inspection reflect on the operation and maintenance of the water supply.

Sanitary inspection can be used as an early warning indicator of potential future problems as risks such as the absence of fences and poorly maintained diversion ditches will provide early indications that there is poor operation and maintenance and that direct pathways for contaminants are likely to develop. This can be evaluated by analysing how often pathway factors occur when the contributing factor is present and how often when there are absent. This could be done through analysing odds ratios or chi-squared statistic. This may be useful to do as very often the indirect factors do not show direct associations with contamination, which would be expected by their nature. Thus, for instance, in protected springs in Uganda, strong associations were noted between the lack of a fence and lack of diversion ditches and the erosion of the backfill area.

Water quality data should also be analysed in relation to season and rainfall to allow an evaluation of seasonal peaks in contamination. This is important both for health education as the times when activities need to be targeted can be established and for improvement strategies once this data is linked to sanitary inspection data as discussed below.

10.2.3 Identifying causes of contamination

The above sections described analysing data to determine whether operation and maintenance is adequate. However, a second major use of the water quality data is to analyse what are likely to be the main controlling factors on microbiological contamination, as this provides the rational basis of an intervention strategy. In order that the most important sanitary risks are addressed and interventions are planned in a cost-effective manner, there is a need for a thorough understanding of the ways in which sources of contamination and the pathways for the contaminants to enter the source interact. In particular, the degree to which source or pathway predominates as controlling factors is important to determine as in the former case there may be little justification for action, whereas in the latter improvement of the sources is possible. Such analysis of data is most effectively done when water quality and sanitary inspection data are evaluated for a number of sources over a period of time.

Point sources

When evaluating the impact of risk factors on water quality, analysis can be relatively simple or highly complex. However, it should be emphasised that the complexity of analysis will not necessarily mean that the power of the conclusions are any stronger. In some cases simple analysis will provide results in which a high degree of confidence can be placed. In other cases, more complex analysis may be required in order to provide a more accurate reflection of the factors in water quality deterioration. In some cases, only simple analysis is required as there is little variation in water quality – i.e. the same source either remains significantly contaminated or free of contamination. This may be the case where hazards are the primary cause of failure and when deeper point sources are used. In very shallow groundwater, such as gravity springs, individual sites may show very significant variation in quality over time and it may be less easy to determine which factors are causing the failure. This then requires more complex analysis of data and development of models.

The purpose of such analyses should be, in part, to see where interventions are required and also to identify whether rehabilitation could be effective. For instance, if contamination of a protected spring is primarily caused by hazards such as on-site sanitation, rehabilitation is unlikely to be successful without treatment of water as little can be done to provide an engineering solution. In this case, a more appropriate response would be to install a public tap. However, if the cause of contamination is found to primarily relate to poor sanitary completion, rehabilitation (usually involving an improved design) may well be effective. For instance, in Uganda, analysis of sanitary inspection data indicated that failures sanitary protection was the critical cause of failure. A pilot project to re-protect springs was carried out using a more effective design and improving sanitary protection. Despite the presence of latrines uphill, this yielded a two-log reduction in faecal coliform presence in the wet season from over 200/100ml to a maximum of 13/100ml. In addition to comparing the risk factors and contamination, it is also important to analyse data in relation to rainfall as this may exert a significant influence on water quality. By assessing the importance of different risk factors and rainfall, the most important routes of contamination may be identified.

The process of risk factor evaluation can follow a simple procedure. Critical to this is to decide what exactly is being assessed and in particular an evaluation is being made regarding the incidence of contamination above a specified level or severity of contamination found in an open-ended format. These are fundamental different measures and different risk factors may be important in different aspects of contamination.

118

It is important to assess whether evaluations are based on a small number of sources that have received repeated inspections and sampling or whether a larger number of sources with single or infrequent inspections and sampling. In the first case, a much more detailed analysis can be made of causes of failure and is in many cases preferable as some risk factors may be as strongly influenced by season as water quality, a good example being the presence of surface water uphill of a source. This allows the use of more complex statistical analysis such as multiple logistic regression or factor analysis when other parameters such rainfall can be incorporated into the analysis. Single sampling rounds may be useful in developing a good initial evaluation of the importance of different risks in controlling contamination, but with the obvious limitation that data on seasonal-dependent risks may be biased.

The simplest way to evaluate controlling factors on contamination is to define categories of water quality (e.g. <10cfu/100ml and >10cfu/100ml etc). By comparing frequency of risk factor reporting under the different conditions of contamination, the relative importance of different factors in controlling contamination can be evaluated. If there is a positive change in frequency of reporting in a factor between the lower and higher condition of contamination, it is likely that there is an association between the presence of the risk factor and increasing contamination. If a negative change is noted, then it is unlikely that an association exists. The relative size of the difference can indicate the relative strength of the associations between risk factors and contamination above a specified level.

Examples are shown in Tables 10.4 and 10.5 below

Risk factor	Frequency ≤10 FC/100ml	Frequency >10FC/100	Difference
Surface water uphill of spring	45	95	+50
Other pollution uphill	43	84	+41
Eroded backfill	35	58	+23
Diversion ditch absent or faulty	76	95	+19
Masonry faulty	12	26	+14
Flooding of collection area	76	89	+13
Fence absent or faulty	82	95	+13
Animal access within 10m	76	84	+8
Latrine uphill within 30m	4	0	-4

Table 10.4: Combined sanitary inspection and water quality data analysis for protected springs, Kabale, Uganda

More sophisticated analysis of this data includes the development of logistic regression models. These often provide a way of identifying the factors of greatest importance in causing contamination and often reduces the number of critical factors. However, although useful, such analysis does not necessarily mean that any stronger conclusions can be drawn and tend to require much greater explanation to non-specialists.

Risk factor	Frequency <1FC/100ml	Frequency >1 FC/100ml	Difference
Latrine <10m	12	41	+29
Latrine uphill	18	45	+27
Other pollution <10m	13	41	+28
Ponding <2m	19	23	+4
Water collects on apron	14	18	+4
Handpump loose at attachment	1	0	-1
Apron <1m	2	0	-2
Fence missing/faulty	93	86	-4
Apron cracked/damaged	19	9	-10
Drainage cracked, blocked, dirty	68	0	-68

Table 10.5: Combined sanitary inspection and water quality data analysis for boreholes, Soroti, Uganda

A second area of analysis of data is related to the severity of pollution. This is often useful as the simple incidence of contamination may not provide clear-cut answers in all cases and may leave critical questions unanswered such as which factors are most responsible for gross contamination and if a hazard is shown to contaminate a water source, what degree of contamination may result. This is important as particular risk factors may be of limited significance in causing a contamination event, but when in those cases when they do contribute to contamination, this is very high. This can be done by comparing the average contamination of when a factor is present and when it is absent and test the significance of any variation.

Piped water
When using the sanitary inspection data to determine whether water quality failure relates to either local or supply risks, it is important not simply to look at microbiological data but also chlorine residual levels. The effective of chlorine and other disinfectants on micro-organisms in water is a function not only of the concentration of the free chlorine that causes inactivation but also of the time for which a micro-organism is exposed to the chlorine – the Ct value. When water undergoes terminal disinfection, dosing is usually based on the chlorine demand - i.e. how much chlorine is required to achieve full disinfection. It is usual for a chlorine residual to be maintained during distribution to ensure that protection is provided against subsequent ingress of contaminated surface or groundwaters. For chlorine this is usually a minimum of 0.2mg/l, although in some countries lower levels (such 0.1mg/l) are accepted. Given that disinfectants rely on both concentration and time, microbiological failures may occur if the source of pollution is close to the sampling point and there is a direct entry for the pollutant into the pipe. This typically relates to stagnant water around the riser pipes or the presence of wastes either directly in contact with or very close to pipes. The free disinfectant residual in such cases is unlikely to be able to inactivate all bacteria and other microbes unless it is at a very high level (e.g. exceeding 1mg/l for chlorine).

An example of how data can be analysed or tabulated for piped water is shown in table 10.6 below.

Division	Parish	Quarter	Local risk	Supply risk	Chlorine adequate
Central	Kagugube	Jan-Mar 98	Yes	Yes (10)	No
	Kisenyi II	Jan-Mar 98	Yes	No	No
Kawempe	Bwaise III	Jan-Mar 98	Yes	No	No
	Kawempe II	Jan-Mar 99	Yes	No	Yes
	Kyebando	Jan-Mar 99	Yes	No	No
	Kawempe I	Jan-Mar 99	Yes	No	Yes
Makindye	Makindye II	Jan-Mar 98	Yes	Yes (7)	No
	Kabalagala	Apr-Jun 98	Yes	No	No
	Kibuye I	Apr-Jun 98	Yes	No	No
	Kisugu	Apr-Jun 98	Yes	No	No
	Makindye II	Jul-Sep 98	Yes	Yes (7,8,10)	No
	Katwe II	Oct-Dec 98	Yes	No	No
	Kibuye I	Oct-Dec 98	Yes	Yes (10)	Yes
	Kibuye I	Jan-Mar 99	Yes	No	No
	Katwe I	Jul-Sep 99	Yes	Yes (9)	No
	Kibuye I	Jul-Sep 99	Yes	Yes (10)	No
	Kisugu	Jul-Sep 99	Yes	No	No
Nakawa	Banda	Apr-Jun 98	Yes	No	No
	Bukoto I	Apr-Jun 98	Yes	No	No
	Bugolobi	Apr-Jun 98	Yes	No	No
	Luzira	Jan-Mar 99	Yes	Yes (7,8)	No
	Nakawa	Jul-Sep 98	Yes	Yes (8)	No
	Naguru II	Jan-Mar 99	Yes	Yes (7,8)	No
	Naguru II	Apr-Jun 99	Yes	Yes (8,9)	No
	Luzira	Jul-Sep 99	Yes	Yes (7,8)	Yes
Rubaga	Ndeeba	Apr-Jun 98	Yes	No	No
	Lungujja	Apr-Jun 98	Yes	No	No
	Nateete	Apr-Jun 98	Yes	No	No

Table 10.6: Microbiological failures related to sanitary risks
Notes: 7 = discontinuity within 10 days previous to sampling; 8 = sign of leakage; 9 = reported pipe breaks within week previous to sampling; 10 = main pipe exposed

Where local risks are present, but no supply risks are noted, contamination is likely to have derived from the immediate areas surrounding the sampling point. If supply risks are noted then there is an indication of fault by the supplier even if local risk may have also contributed significantly to the contamination event.

If a microbiological water quality failure has been noted and the free chlorine residual is below 0.2mg/l, it is important to decide whether the loss of free chlorine related to inadequate dosing in supply (a supplier fault) or due to consumption by local contamination (non-supply fault). It is important therefore to also analyse the total chlorine data.

If the dosing rate at the works is known or a figure for free chlorine is obtained from either the outlet of the clearwell or nearest tap, the cause of loss of free chlorine can be determined. Where total and free chlorine levels leaving the plant are adequate, attention should be paid to potential chlorine loss in bulk system storage by looking at the total and free chlorine values at the inlets and outlets of service reservoirs. Where both are adequate, it is unlikely that storage has caused free chlorine loss and the problem would therefore be linked to piped distribution in the area of the sampling point. If no supply faults are noted and other samples from the area indicate an adequate free residual, the likelihood is that free chlorine consumption occurred close to the sampling point. Where free chlorine shows a reduction after storage then clearly, a supply fault can be identified. Furthermore, if samples in the same zone show similar losses in free chlorine, then blame can be apportioned at least in part to a supply failure.

Using data to categorise systems

By using the water quality analysis and sanitary inspection data, the systems covered by surveillance can be categorised on the basis of contamination found and most likely cause. This not only allows a focus of attention to the areas of greatest importance in individual supplies or supplies within an urban area but also allows evaluation of the national situation regarding whether problems exist in design, construction or operation and maintenance. This then allows the development of a regional and/or national improvement strategy. A further use of such categorisation is that when new or modified standards are proposed, it will allow the water sector to evaluate whether supplies can meet the current draft standards without extensive upgrading and also be to identify major remedial work that may be required. An example from an assessment Ghana is summarised in table 10.7.

Category	Description	Assessed systems
Category 1	No contamination	Barakese direct; Owabi direct; Berekum; Kpandu
Category 2	Contamination derived from local problems	Accra MPZ/HPZ; Bolgatanga; Cape Coast; Ho; Takoradi; Tamale; Tema
Category 3	Contamination from both supply failure & local problems	Accra LPZ; Kpong direct; Keta; Kumasi High level; Obuasi; Sekondi; Sunyani; Weijja direct
Category 4	Contamination derived from major supply failure	Kibi; Koforidua; Navrongo; Nkawkaw; Shama/Elmina

Table 10.7: Categorisation of systems from an assessment in Ghana, 1999

From this table, it is possible to see that from the evidence of microbiological contamination, improvements in supply performance were required in supply problems are noted 13 of 23 systems covered. This indicates that in this case substantial improvements in operation and maintenance were required within these supplies in order to deliver safer water supplies.

Household water

When analysing household water quality a number of simple analyses may be performed and care should be taken to decide what the analysis is designed to show and what is being evaluated. The most obvious analysis is to assess whether the water being consumed shows evidence of being contaminated. Causes of failure can be analysed by the same approaches as for point sources. A simple household water storage inspection form is show in Annex 3 and this can be used to evaluate what the most important controlling factors in contamination of household water quality using similar techniques as discussed for point sources.

By assessing the quality of water stored and used in the home compared to those of the source where the water was obtained, the importance of re-contamination can be evaluated. This can be evaluated further by analysing samples taken from a source, collection vessel and household water storage, which may identify where contamination occurs during the water chain and whether household treatment limits contamination at the point of consumption. The analysis of household water quality will also indicate where the major focus of an intervention strategy is required. For instance, where point sources are of good quality, but household quality is poor, the most appropriate response is clearly aimed at the household level rather than source improvement.

The basic analyses to carry out are simple descriptive statistics such as the average (mean and median), range and percentiles, as shown below in Table 10.8. This can be used to evaluate the effectiveness of health education linked to water quality surveillance. For instance, the data shown in the table 10.8 for Kampala showed that household water contamination decreased significantly in most areas during a 12 month period of household testing and routine community feed-back and health education.

Division	Oct-Dec 1998		Jan-Mar 99		Apr-Jun 99		Jul-Sep 99	
	Median	% 0	Median	% 0	Median	% 0	Median	% 0
Central	0	86.67	0	94.29	0	93.33	0	100
Kawempe	9	38.89	28	22.22	3	20.69	1	45
Makindye	24	35	3	22.73	1	44.44	3	43.75
Nakawa	0	56.25	29	4.76	42	6.06	11	16
Rubaga	50	35	0	72.73	0	93.1	0	84.78
Total	1	48.31	1	45.69	0	51.54	2	54.12

Table 10.7: Household water quality results for Kampala

11.

Regulation

The regulation of the water sector is one mechanism by which improvement and maintenance of high quality water supplies that represent a limited risk to public health can be achieved. Regulation of the water sector commonly encompasses issues such as cost to the consumer, cost-recovery and sustainable financial performance, water quality and continuity of supply as well as social provision and increasing access. It would also typically cover sanitary codes to be followed for protection measures around sources, minimum treatment requirements and best practice codes for pipe-fitting.

Although regulation may provide a very effective method of water sector improvements, it is not a panacea for all problems. Furthermore, it is essential that regulatory activities in different areas are complementary, do not conflict and are perceived as constructive rather than unduly proscriptive. When regulation is effectively implemented it provides functions that are supportive of improvement in the sector and is sensitive the priorities, needs and demands of the population it is designed to serve.

It is important that priorities are balanced. For instance, improvements in water quality achieved through enhanced treatment will have an impact on the cost of producing drinking water. Increased costs, in most cases, will be passed onto the consumer. It is essential, therefore, that regulators keep in the mind the broader implications of any intervention they suggest to prevent the resolution of one problem becoming the cause of a more serious health problem. It should also be noted that many of the criticisms levelled at water quality improvements in drinking water supply is precisely because such interventions very often only provide benefits to the wealthy and may often entail significant disadvantage to the poor. A good example is the concern over disinfectant by-products, whose impact on health will be felt more by the rich (given longer life expectancy and more limited exposure to pathogens) than the urban poor who use multiple sources and suffer the greatest burden of infectious disease. Control of by-products may exacerbate the health problems of the poor by reducing the level of protection provided by residual chlorine in distribution and by increasing costs of supply that make access to water supply at higher service levels difficult.

Where private sector involvement is encouraged in the provision of water services, the independent verification of water quality and enforcement of compliance with standards is an important function of Government. Essentially, regulation is designed to protect the interests of the general public and to ensure water is not provided that is a risk to health. Compliance orientated monitoring, therefore, is driven by a legal process where failure to meet required standards leads to some form of enforcement or punitive action to comply with standards. Implicit in this process is that the legal responsibility of the supplier is clearly defined, both in terms of standards to be met and the limit of responsibility.

Responsibility for good management of delivery of the water supply – 'the duty of care' – lies ultimately with the water supplier. Thus the supplier is responsible for ensuring that they fulfil all performance criteria that may be regulated (water quality, continuity, leakage etc) and the burden of proof of meeting these criteria lies with the supplier, although the criteria themselves are set by an external regulatory body. However, such duty of care only applies up to the limit of the responsibility of the supplier. Once the water enters the pipe system of a house, responsibility for maintenance lies with the occupant or owner, although sanitary codes governing plumbing quality may also be applied.

When considering the most appropriate form of regulation and defining how regulatory bodies will function, it is important to review key concepts in regulation and which water supplies can be realistically regulated, where regulation should be targeted and liability in circumstances of failure.

11.1 Ownership, responsibility and liability

It is important to be clear about the implications of ownership, responsibility and liability with respect to the objective of regulation. The objective of regulation is to ensure that the water suppliers distribute a product that meets certain standards and norms set out in the legislative code, usually defined on the basis of risk to public health.

Ownership of the means of supply of a product (in this case water) implies a certain degree of responsibility (and hence liability) as it is expected that the owner of the supply retains some control over actual distribution. Whilst some of this responsibility may be deferred to second or even third parties (for instance in the case of contract management or operation and maintenance), some degree of liability will reside with the owner of the supply. Also fundamental to this concept of liability is that there is a separation between the supplier of the product and the consumer. This implies that consumers of the product are not directly involved in its production and distribution. This has important implications for which supplies can be regulated and the process of regulation to achieve national standards and norms. The rest of this sub-section is divided into four parts dealing with key areas that should be considered: private sector operation; government and parastatal supplies; community-based water supply (including water user associations and groups); and, informal water sale.

11.1.1 Private sector operation

In the case of private sector involvement in provision of water supplies, regulation can be implemented successfully as the body responsible for the production and distribution of the product is separated from the end-users of the product and furthermore operate on a profit basis. Whilst it may seem that the allocation of liability in these circumstances is simple, this is not always the case and liability will largely be determined by the nature of the private sector operation and where ownership of infrastructure resides.

In very few countries has full ownership of the water supply infrastructure been transferred to the private sector. In this situation, liability can be readily allocated to the organisation that produces of water. However, in most countries, private sector operation has taken the form of leasing or granting of concessions in the use of the infrastructure with ownership remaining with a local or national government body.

In private sector arrangements, it is essential to define exactly what responsibilities lie with the operator and what is retained by Government. These should be clear and included within any contract entered into. In particular, it is essential to know where responsibility lies for infrastructure improvement. The private operator under most circumstances will be responsible for the correct operation of treatment works and basic maintenance of distribution

126

systems and are liable for failures of defined operational procedures and may be responsible for small-scale investment in supply improvements. However, unless the private sector operation agreement takes the form of an enhanced lease or concession, it is unlikely that the operator will be responsible for large-scale rehabilitation, extension or replacement work, a function that may be retained by the owner of the infrastructure (i.e. government). In such a situation, therefore, it is critical that the regulator clearly understands where liability lies with regard to different parts of the water production and distribution organisation.

For instance, it is well known that the age of pipes and the pipe material may exert a very significant influence on water quality as older pipes are more likely to break, increasing leakage and the potential for discontinuity and back-siphonage, and that galvanised iron pipes more readily support biofilm development and cause chlorine decay. All these factors may lead to a failure in water service quality. The issue of liability then revolves around who was responsible for the distribution failure. Unless the agreement with the private operator explicitly states that they are responsible for mains replacement and rehabilitation (unlikely outside of a long-term enhanced lease or concession), in most cases failure to meet standards or norms is the liability of the owner of the infrastructure (i.e. the Government). However, in some cases, it may be proven that the operator was negligent in notifying the owner of required investment can be shown or the operation of the supply has led to a reduction in working life-span of the infrastructure, in which case the operator would be liable.

In cases of routine operation failure, for instance water quality deterioration as a result of poor treatment or basic maintenance practices such as repairing leaks, flushing and cleaning of service reservoirs and distribution mains, liability clearly lies with the private sector operator. A further case of liability is where the operator has failed to ensure that adequate continuity can be maintained failing to ensure back-up power supplies are available.

In the case of other aspects that may be regulated, such as tariffs, the regulator will define acceptable tariffs to be applied to different types of water service (this may often include a band rather than specify exact figures). The supplier will be expected to apply these tariffs and deviations can be expected to lead to action. The need for cost-recovery may also be regulated in this way, with targets for cost-recovery set. In the case of social provision, targets may be set for private operators for increasing connections within existing infrastructure, with government (as the owner) responsible for provision of the infrastructure to new areas, which may again be subject to targets by the regulator. Where a concession or enhanced lease is in existence that requires the private operator to invest in infrastructure, targets for increasing connections in existing infrastructure and for expanding distribution may be set for the operator and regulated.

11.1.2 Local government and parastatal operated supply

Much of the urban water supply in developing countries remains under the control of either local governments or national parastatal organisation operating with a certain degree of autonomy but still falling under line Ministries in national governments. The role of local government as an effective water supply provider is gaining more acceptance, whilst parastatals often provide efficient and effective services. Local government run water supplies can be covered by regulatory models, with a national regulator typically residing within a Government Department or independent commission. Clearly, the national regulator should not be directly or indirectly involved in the provision of water supply services as a facilitator. Thus in some countries, where a national Department makes grants available to local authorities to supply water, the regulator should be within a separate Government department or commission, because of conflicts of interest in facilitation and regulatory roles. However, it should be noted that surveillance of water supply at local levels can still be operated where the local authority also undertakes water supply provision, provided this is carried out by a separate department and where the purpose of surveillance is not directly related to the enforcement of compliance.

Parastatal organisations can also be regulated provided that the regulator is situated outside the Government Department or line Ministry that houses the parastatal. This does raise some complicated issues that should be resolved. As parastatals are essentially part of government, an immediate issue arises as to whether any regulation is truly independent. This problem may be overcome either by locating the regulator in another Ministry, such as Health or in the establishment of an independent Public Utilities Regulatory Commission (an approach gaining interest in Africa). An alternative approach is for local authorities to undertake the regulation of water supplies provided within their areas by the parastatal organisation.

11.1.3 Community-based supplies

An increasing emphasis has been placed in lower-income countries on the transfer of ownership of water supplies to communities. This is driven largely by a belief that such approaches are more sustainable and follow a principle of devolving responsibility to the lowest feasible level. Under such arrangements, an external agency (whether private contractor, NGO or government) carries out the construction of a water supply in collaboration with a community. Once the supply is completed, responsibility for the management, operation and maintenance of the water supply is assumed by the users. Whilst this is usually seen as being primarily a rural approach to water supply, such water supplies may constitute a significant proportion of the water supply in urban and peri-urban areas, particularly in low-income communities.

Where ownership and responsibility of the means of supply is transferred to the users, regulation becomes much more difficult unless there are circumstances that identify an external body as being responsible for water supply failure that was beyond the capacity of the supply managers (the community) to control. In this situation, it can been seen that there is no organisational separation between supply and use and therefore it becomes a user choice whether to improve the water supply. In such circumstances surveillance should be carried out to provide support to communities to improve their supply rather than force them to do so. Where communities have established a water committee, it could be argued that they could be held liable for water quality failure, although it is debatable whether this would be constructive or simply make few people willing to serve on such committees. What is clear from the high rates of non-compliance in many small water supplies in Europe and North America (typically 40-80% against national and regional standards) is that regulation of this sector is unlikely to be achievable.

There are three circumstances where it can be suggested that regulation of community supplies can be effective: during construction; government support requirements; problems caused by factors beyond the reasonable limit of community control.

Regulation of the construction of community supplies is clearly feasible and desirable. During construction, responsibility for the provision of the good is outside the end-user responsibility and the liability of the constructor in providing a safe water supply can been seen. There is great potential for regulating construction practice through the establishment of norms and best practice in relation to concrete works, pipework and establishing a sanitary code. A sanitary code for point sources, should specify the minimum sanitary protection requirements, for instance fences, diversion ditches, wastewater drains and the distance from the sources that these should be built. Sanitary codes for plumbing should cover aspects such as the materials and methods to be used in pipe joining as well as basic hygiene for plumbers.

The second issue of government responsibility for support is more debatable. Some workers have suggested that surveillance should only be carried out when there is a legal requirement for action by Government. Not only does this greatly restrict the role of surveillance in promoting water supply improvement, it may have a dubious legal basis. In order for government support programmes to be held liable, it implies that such programmes retain an ownership or fundamental responsibility over the supply of water that is at odds with the ethos of community management and potentially national laws regarding water supply management. It is far better for government support programmes to be viewed as a constructive process to help communities improve their water supply rather than make them liable for action.

The third issue is an area where regulation appears possible. For instance, if water quality deteriorates because of the establishment of new industries or activities in the vicinity of the area, a liability of the owners of the polluting industry and planners who approved its location may be possible to demonstrate. In other circumstances, a case for liability may be made in situations where water quality deterioration has resulted from improper water supply development and water resource management. The improper management of water resources (whose ownership typically resides with national government) that leads to water supply quality deterioration does offer an avenue for regulating community-owned water supplies.

11.1.4 Small-scale and informal water sale

In many towns, water may be supplied through vendors. These may either be licensed and sell large volumes of water or individual vendors who sell small quantities of water to neighbours or specific communities. In the first case, regulation is simple through establishing enforceable best practice norms and standards relating to where water can be collected, any additional treatment requirements and the allowable tariff. Where vendors are small-scale and typically collect a few containers of water, which are then sold to individual households, regulation may be difficult and expensive. In these cases, it is preferable to work with vendors to establish good working practices. Banning of such vendors, whilst possibly attractive to the national water sector management, is unlikely to be successful and may not enjoy support from the populations that utilise such vendors. It should also be stressed that households only use vendors because either they lack a water supply close to their home or because the piped water supply is unreliable. Therefore, increasing access to higher levels of water service will be more effective in reducing the use of vendors than trying to control the practice.

Informal water supply is a common feature in many urban areas and typically involves the sale of water by households with their own direct connection to the piped water supply to unserved households within their community. Whilst the informal sale of water often results in much higher costs being paid by the poor for water and may be perceived by the supplier as being undesirable as their revenue may be less than if a commercial rate was applied, it does provide a useful service. The control of such supplies would be largely impossible due to the enormous expense involved in trying to prevent sales. This would in any case be likely to fail as the households purchasing water from their neighbours will appreciate a service that is close and where occasional credit may possibly be obtained. Furthermore, despite a perceived loss to the water supplier as revenue is collected on a domestic rather than commercial rate, in real terms the revenue collection is often higher than the rates that would be typically charged for the principal alternative mode of supply through public taps. Again, it should emphasised that people buy water from their neighbours because they lack access to their own connection or public taps within a short distance of the home. Attention should be paid to increasing the numbers of connections and provision of public taps rather than controlling informal sale. However, support can be given to communities to help reduce the price of informal sales by passing local bylaws.

11.2 Models of regulation

The nature and form of regulation may vary between countries and regions. There is no 'blueprint' for regulatory framework development and no one approach that is universally applicable. It is essential in the development and implementation of regulation that the current and planned legislation relating to the water, health and local government sectors is taken into account and that the capacity of potential regulators in the country is assessed. Approaches that may have worked in one country or region do not necessarily transfer to other countries. It is essential that each country reviews its needs and capacity for regulation before embarking on the development of a regulatory framework.

As discussed in Chapter 3, there are a number of key stakeholders in the water sector and their needs and priorities must be considered when developing the regulatory framework. In addition to national institutions, the external donor community also has a stake in ensuring that the investments they make yield the greatest benefit, whether expressed in terms of improvement in social conditions or re-payment of debt. All these interests have to be take into account and it is not uncommon to find more than one regulatory body existing addressing different issues. Whilst this does not inherently represent a problem, it should be noted that co-ordination amongst regulators is vital and usually most effectively achieved when they fall under the same umbrella organisation.

In the case of regulation of costs and social provision, regulation would normally be achieved through an independent commission that regulates the performance of water utilities. Regulation and enforcement is then carried out on the basis of tariffs listed and charged and the degree to which targets on new connections are met. A similar approach can be used to establish rates of leakage, although this typically may also include consultations with the water resource management body in order to reduce over-abstraction of water. Targets would be set for leakage rates and suppliers required to provide evidence from leakage detection programmes and unaccounted-for-water.

In the context of water quality regulation, there are two key models are available that have evidence of providing effective regulation of the water sector. These are discussed below.

11.2.1 Independent analysis approach

The model adopted in some countries is for the water quality regulatory body to carry out completely independent testing of water supplies. Such an approach implies that the regulatory body has access to analytical facilities of its own, with staff trained to carry out sampling, analysis and sanitary inspection.

Such approaches have a number of advantages. It tends to be higher profile amongst the general public who see people from an independent surveillance body as proof of public health concern and protection. Clearly, the results generated from independent testing are often treated with more respect by the public than those generated by water suppliers where suspicion may remain (usually unjustified) about the reliability of such results. Also, independent testing provides a reliable way of detecting problems, particularly where samples are taken based on stratified random sampling.

Whilst this approach has many advantages, it is expensive and shifts the burden of proof onto the surveillance agency rather than the water supplier. In practice such approaches may be difficult to sustain in lower-income countries. Funding difficulties often mean that laboratories are built but not efficiently used and insufficient numbers of samples are taken because of transport difficulties and the time spent in travelling to and from sites. Such approaches will also entail significant transport of samples therefore requiring sample preservation and cold boxes.

The use of on-site equipment is widely used for independent surveillance. Such equipment is highly appropriate where compliance-based monitoring does not drive surveillance. However, in the context of enforcing compliance with standards, the use of on-site equipment has major drawbacks. Although the reliability of results from field equipment is often comparable to laboratory-based testing (and in some cases more accurate), from a legal viewpoint guaranteeing quality control and assurance remains problematic. Analytical quality control can be exercised in the field, and is done in Uganda, however, the lack of control over the analytical environment is inevitably restricted and guaranteeing aseptic techniques may be difficult to prove.

11.2.2 Audit approach

The alternative approach to regulation of compliance is to use the audit approach. In this approach, the burden of proof of compliance is shifted onto the water supplier who have a legal responsibility to carry out sampling and analysis of water quality, supported by sanitary inspection, with sample numbers and strategies defined under national and regional water laws.

Under an audit approach, results of analysis undertaken by suppliers are sent on at least a weekly basis to an Inspectorate. A system of notification is established to provide immediate warning of failure on key parameters, which triggers an immediate inspection of the works. In addition to results from water quality analyses, results from quality control exercise and proof of good laboratory management (for instance ISO accreditation) are provided. Additional verification is carried out by inspectors who make both announced and unannounced visits to supplies and laboratories and carry out comprehensive reviews of analytical data, sampling strategies, quality control procedures and laboratory management. In addition, assessments may also be made of treatment works and distribution operation records.

As the burden of proof is transferred to the supplier, enforcement action can be based solely on the results generated by the water supplier. In cases where the Inspectorate feels that the results obtained are unreliable, samples can be taken to an independent laboratory for verification. This requires that the Inspectorate either has access to its own laboratory or enters into contract agreements with laboratories to undertake such work.

The advantages of the audit approach are that it has a lower-cost to the Government as a regulator whilst providing a means of enforcing compliance. The number of inspectors required is relatively small and there is no requirement for construction and maintenance of expensive laboratories. However, there are disadvantages of this approach. It is far less visible than an approach based on independent analysis. It relies on good communications in order for suppliers to send results to the Inspectorate and it limits the ability to carry out testing on a local scale. However, these issues can be easily overcome by adopting the following strategies:

1. Decentralisation of the Inspectorate so most inspectors are based in the areas where the water supplies are rather than being based centrally

2. Linking to a decentralised system of local water quality surveillance carried out by non-Inspectorate staff to provide independent results

3. Making timely communication of results a legal requirement for water supply operators.

A suggested organogram for an audit based regulatory body is shown overleaf in Figure 11.1. The Chief Drinking Water Inspector is supported by two Assistant Chief Inspectors, each taking responsibility for an administrative area in which they are based. These persons would take responsibility for management of the Inspectorate activities in their areas, for liaison with the suppliers in the area and support to local authorities in surveillance activities. They prepare drinking water quality reports for the area on a monthly and annual basis and assist the Chief Inspector in preparation of the national annual report. They identify independent laboratories and undertake inspections of supplies in support of Regional/Zonal Inspectors. They will be responsible for the preparation of proposed exemptions and relaxation's applying to supplies within their area and for issuing of contracts to independent laboratories. They would be expected to assist the Chief Inspector in preparation of enforcement cases.

Within each area a number of Regional or Zonal Inspectors based within a smaller area of responsibility, but more typically would take responsibilities for a group of supplies defined under an Inspectorate zone. These Inspectors are expected to receive and review all water data from water suppliers and results from piped water testing by local authorities and maintain a Regional/Zonal water quality database. They will be responsible for carrying out audits of supplies and laboratories and for direct liaison with system operators on failures and the need for exemptions. They will also provide support to local authorities and carry out training in sampling and analysis as appropriate. They will be responsible for notification of Assistant Chief Inspector of failures and preparation of enforcement cases.

Local authorities would need to appoint a liaison officer on water surveillance to deal directly with the Inspectorate and water suppliers and to ensure that water quality data is sent on at least a monthly, preferably weekly, basis. They will also establish a notification procedure in case of failure on critical parameters and liase with the Inspectorate in legal cases.

Organogram for an audit-based regulatory body

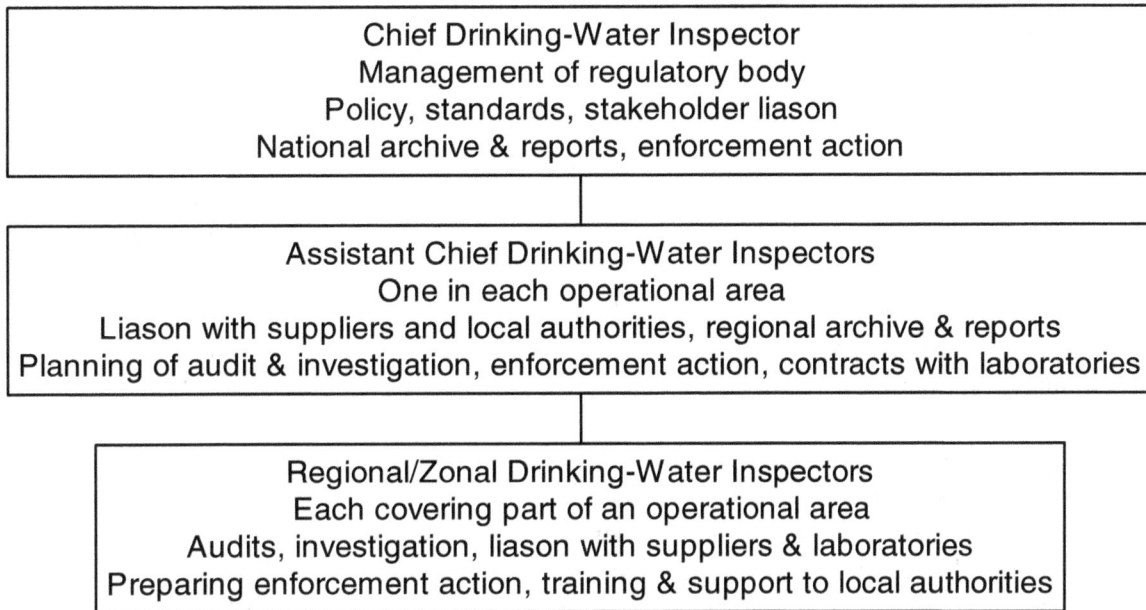

Chief Drinking-Water Inspector
Management of regulatory body
Policy, standards, stakeholder liason
National archive & reports, enforcement action

Assistant Chief Drinking-Water Inspectors
One in each operational area
Liason with suppliers and local authorities, regional archive & reports
Planning of audit & investigation, enforcement action, contracts with laboratories

Regional/Zonal Drinking-Water Inspectors
Each covering part of an operational area
Audits, investigation, liason with suppliers & laboratories
Preparing enforcement action, training & support to local authorities

Figure 11.1: Organogram for an audit-based water quality regulatory body

11.3 Standards

A key component of regulation is the establishment of standards within a statutory instrument linked to the basic water law. It should be emphasised that standards (whether relating to cost, quality or access) should not be included within an actual water law as this approach makes changes cumbersome and time-consuming. For instance, evidence for health impacts from different parameters of water quality changes very rapidly as it is area of extensive research. Standards set in a law will not be amenable to rapid change to take into account new information.

Standards are designed to set norms and define the practices to be followed by water suppliers in order that water supply is maintained at an acceptable level. Standards are also used to measure compliance and therefore what constitutes a breach of acceptable practice leading to punitive or enforcement action. When establishing standards, it must be clear what standards are designed to achieve and how they relate to other instruments available in regulation. Furthermore, as in other aspects of regulation, the appropriateness of standards for each type of water supply should be carefully considered. For instance applying strict water quality standards on small community-managed supplies is rarely feasible and given that compliance is difficult to enforce it is preferable that small or community-managed water supplies are covered by water quality targets or guidelines rather than standards.

Standards for aspects such as leakage rates and tariffs will usually be set by a regulatory body in consultation with stakeholders, including the supplier. Typically, economic levels of leakage will be set taking into account source sustainability and the impact of leakage in failing to meet demand for water. Tariffs would usually be set in consultation with users, suppliers and set against the needs for cost-recovery and social provision. Water quality standards will also entail consultation with suppliers regarding achievability and additional production costs and in consultation with user groups.

The following sections review the purpose of water quality standards, highlights alternative methods to establish water quality objectives and reviews the regulatory instruments available in applying water quality standards.

11.3.1 Water quality standards

Water quality standards are legally enforceable measures of performance designed to limit public health risks and thus they must be of importance to health or acceptability; they must be a known problem; they must be measurable in the country; and, there must be a means of either preventing their presence in water through source protection or removal through treatment. It should also be recognised that unless compliance is enforced, the establishment of standards is not appropriate and either targets or Guidelines established until such time as enforcement is possible.

Prioritisation of parameters to be included in standards is essential. The priority should be given to microbiological quality and those parameters that affect acceptability of the water to the consumer. However, where particular chemical substances given rise to significant health concerns, these should also be included in the standards from the outset. Substances of lower health concern should be accorded a lower priority and this should be reflected in sampling rates and possibly by not defining standards, but issuing guidelines or targets.

In some cases, it may be necessary to demand improved treatment of water supply to remove contaminants given the current quality status of source waters. Where treatment could be used to remove contaminants from domestic water, careful consideration has to be given to the impact that this may have on production costs (and hence costs to the consumer). More significant problems may result from price increases which exceed the willingness or ability to pay of low-income communities leading to forced use of more contaminated sources and increased health burdens. Where the use of sophisticated treatment processes would lead to significant increases in tariff, it may be more effective to use other measures to promote water quality improvement.

The process of establishing standards that are appropriate takes time and resources. However, it should be emphasised that this is far preferable to the practice in some countries of adopting WHO Guideline Values without consideration of local climatic, social and economic factors or of the capacity to remove and monitor substances. The WHO Guidelines provide the basis from which standards should be set, but do not provide a 'blueprint' for standards to be adopted wholesale.

In order to set appropriate standards, it is preferable that this should be based on a lengthy and reliable analytical record, up to date information regarding the infrastructure (including the condition of headworks, treatment plant and distribution systems) and a sound knowledge of the environmental and health problems in the country. Therefore, periodic systematic evaluation of water, environmental and health problems is most appropriate as a form of establishing standards.

11.3.2 Water quality targets

Water quality targets (or objectives) may be legally binding, although are not as powerful in this sense as standards. Essentially, targets are used in situations where compliance with a standard is unlikely to possible in the short-term without significant investment in infrastructure. When targets are set for suppliers, they should be time-limited and linked to a process of improvement in the water supply to allow eventual establishment of the standard.

11.3.3 Water quality guidelines

Water quality Guidelines are not usually legally binding, but provide the supplier with an outline of the water quality desired by the population and regulatory body. Guidelines are usually set based on risk to health (e.g. the WHO Guidelines for Drinking-water quality). Guidelines are generally set because:

- the nature of water supply makes standards inappropriate (e.g. community-managed or small systems);

- the parameter involved is of no importance to health or acceptability (e.g. operational parameters such as corrosivity or hardness whose impact is felt primarily by the supplier in terms of reduced efficiency);

- achievement of a standard for the parameter may cause costs to rise unacceptably (e.g. organics removal);

- the parameter cannot be analysed for in the country and the extent of the problem is unknown (e.g. pesticides);

- the principal cause of failure is beyond the control of the supplier and requires action by other bodies (local Government, Environment Protection Agency etc) in order to improve water quality.

Guidelines may be subsequently upgraded to targets or standards as the sector develops and regulatory bodies, the public and suppliers recognise achievement of a certain level of water quality is achievable, affordable and desirable.

11.4 Regulatory instruments

In some circumstances, the application of a standard may be warranted for the whole country, but there may be mitigating factors in some supplies that make achievement problematic. In other circumstances, whilst a high standard is desired, it may be difficult to achieve and a progressive approach is required for improvement of water quality. In such circumstances, it is important that regulation is flexible and has instruments that can be used to modify standards and enforcement. There are two key instruments that may be used when regulating water quality supplied by utilities. These are:

- Relaxations

- Exemptions

11.4.1 Relaxations

A relaxation is generally used in a universal fashion – i.e. it applies to all systems. Effectively a relaxation is usually an allowed percentage of samples allowed to deviate from a standard and may also include an upper level of the degree of deviation allowed. However, it is important to note that the actual standard for the parameter is not changed. Additional caveats may be put in the relaxation such as contamination not allowed in consecutive samples taken from any individual sampling point and an upper limit set of the level of deviation from the standard that will be accepted. Relaxations may be time constrained or left open, depending on the nature of the parameter and its importance to health. Where achievement of the standard will not be realised in the majority of supplies or most of the time, it is better is establish a water quality target or guideline rather than use a relaxation.

11.4.2 Exemptions

An exemption is usually parameter and locality specific, is usually time constrained and linked to a programme of action to improve water quality. As exemptions are specific to particular supplies they are different from relaxations. In an exemption, the standard for the parameter is set, but for a particular supply, deviation is allowed. The degree of deviation may also be set within the terms of the exemption. Exemptions are often put in place where a particular supply has a specific water quality problem whose resolution will be likely to take some time (i.e. construction of new infrastructure) or will raise costs unacceptably. For example, where nitrate is raised at a few supplies, an exemption may be granted to allow the supplier more time to implement improvements progressively or await action of other bodies in reducing nitrate loads in source waters.

11.4.3 Establishing instruments

The powers of regulation are usually vested within a Government Department and relate to primary laws governing water and health. In most cases, these laws should be used to set the legal principle for regulation of the sector and the definition of institutional responsibility would be typically included within an Act of Government.

However, the actual tools of regulation – standards, norms, codes of practice, exemptions and relaxations should not be included within the primary law. The actual performance criteria and targets will be expected to change, sometimes rapidly. For instance, the influence of water on quality on health remains an area of substantial research, changes can be expected in information available. This may include evidence of health impacts of relatively recent synthetic chemicals, or in improvement in the understanding of the health impacts of chemicals that have been of concern for many years. Equally, there is increasing evidence of 'new' or 'emerging' pathogens for which data on health impact and required remedial action is being steadily accumulated. Also, as socio-economic conditions change, tariff levels will be expected to change.

A suite of statutory instruments should be defined that are linked to the primary law. In this case, the primary law will define the areas that will be covered by statutory instruments in relatively broad terms with a provision for statutory instruments to be updated by the relevant Minister on expert advice. The advantage of this approach is that it allows standards, norms and other regulatory practice to updated simply without the need for debate within the political framework of the country. Clearly, however, safeguards must be put in place to ensure that updating of statutory instruments is only carried out when there is strong evidence of a need based on robust data.

In some cases, existing legislation may be outdated and undergoing review. In these cases, it may be possible to develop statutory instruments prior to the passing of new legislation, providing the current legal code makes provision for the establishment of statutory instruments. This is may be important as the revision of the basic or primary water law is often time-consuming. However, it is important that such instruments do not become 'orphaned' – i.e. that once the basic law is revised, the statutory instruments can pass directly to the new law from the old law.

Another key aspect is to ensure that either the basic law or statutory instruments outline what the basis of standards will be (e.g. evidence from the WHO Guidelines for Drinking-water Quality). In addition, it should be stated which institutions must be consulted during the revision process, the frequency of revisions allowed (e.g. review once per year) and the process of revision (number of expert meetings, consultation etc). Such information is often critical to ensure that the statutory instruments are seen as transparent and accountable.

Relaxations and interim standards should be set by the regulatory body in consultation with other stakeholders including suppliers. Exemptions are essentially contracts drawn up between the regulatory body representing the public interest and the operator to allow deviation on specific parameters. The process of setting the exemption should be primarily driven by the operator rather the regulator and based on a case being made by the operator as to why an exemption is required. If the operator feels that meeting a certain standard is not possible at an individual supply they should apply for an exemption to the regulatory body outlining why achievement of the standard is not currently possible and what additional investment is required to meet the standard. Through a process of consultation between regulator and operator, an exemption can be granted, specifying the time limit allowed under the exemption and the improvement work to be carried out and by whom in order to achieve the standard.

11.5 Other standards

Other aspects also require standards to govern water supply provision. Typically this will cover aspects such as:

- Tariff charged for water supply services

- Allowed levels of leakage from piped water supply and reliability of supply

- Access to water supply, including social provision.

The regulation of tariffs and leakage would typically be included in statutory instruments that will set allowable limits. However, these require careful consideration of the full range of requirements applied to the water supply sector. For instance, if a water supplier is expected to be fully cost-recovering (including capital investment costs) the tariff that can be set must take this into account. Tariffs should be set that provide incentives for households and communities to access piped water supply and that differentiate between domestic and other uses including commercial or industrial uses. The latter uses would typically be expected to pay more per unit volume than domestic users. It is also likely that a sliding scale of tariff would be set that make lower service levels less expensive than higher service levels.

Tariffs should address not only ongoing consumption but also the cost of connection as this is sometimes used by suppliers to subsidise poor operational performance or to make cost-recovery performance appear better than in reality. In some situations, utilities may have limits set on the level of surplus that can be accrued within a one year period in order to ensure that re-investment in the supply is maintained at a realistic level and that tariffs are not set at levels that are too high. This may apply equally to public utilities or private sector operators (where shareholder dividends may be restricted).

Leakage control should set standards that are as low as possible taking into account source sustainability, cost of reducing leakage and expected benefits to the consumer. Clearly, lower leakage rates make water supplies more efficient and therefore cost-recovery should be enhanced as production will more accurately reflect demand. However, complete elimination of leakage is unrealistic and a balance should be struck between the cost of controlling leakage that will be passed on to the consumer and the reduction in costs derived from more efficient performance.

The regulation of access to water supplies at different service levels would typically be carried out through a policy document and in setting targets that must be met by water suppliers. This clearly links to the Government social policy and may be subject to standards but to targets.

12.

Policy and planning of interventions

The purpose of surveillance programmes should be to generate information that can lead to improvements in water supply. However, a certain degree of realism should be exercised in expectations of surveillance leading to changes and improvements. The purpose of surveillance is to generate information that leads to *informed* decision-making that addresses health and equity. In order for informed decision-making to result, there is often a need to develop convincing arguments based on sound data that are reliable and accurate and that reflect real-life situations that may vary with time and space. Therefore it is often necessary to collect substantial amounts of data before decisions are made in order to ensure that these are well founded. Evidence-based approaches are increasingly demanded in all sectors of socio-economic development and evidence for problems and solutions takes scientific rigour in collection and analysis of results.

The success of technical, social or regulatory interventions to improve water supply are often dependent on the policy environment within which they operate. Without policies that support the development of improved water supply and which place an emphasis on providing improved services for the poor, advances in other areas may produce little benefit. Policy interventions are particularly required to focus resources on those at greatest risk from poor water supply and in particular to address the causes of restricted access by the urban poor to higher levels of water supply service. This will usually require a commitment to address tariff and charging policies.

A key role for the use of surveillance data is to identify the short, medium and long-term needs in improving water supplies based on assessments of coverage, water quality and sanitary risk, cost and water usage patterns. Short and medium-term solutions will address immediate needs for improved water quality supplied to the population and typically will focus more on communal sources and in-house water treatment and health education. The long-term objective should be to increase access at higher service levels that promote improved health.

There is likely to be some degree of conflict between the needs and most appropriate responses to poor water supply over short periods of time and those demanded to achieve long-term improvements in health. What is most important is that the differing needs are well balanced and although care should be taken not to jeopardise long-term solutions through short-term action, it is equally important that improvements possible to reduce health risks in the short term are not ignored because of plans for future improvement. This is particularly the case where such plans remain on paper or in policy documents and not in concrete action on the ground.

The outputs of surveillance data should be used to influence policy making with regard to water supply improvement and in linking to other surveillance programmes, such as disease surveillance. These are discussed further below. Technical and health education interventions are discussed further in the next two chapters.

12.1 Policy level

At the policy level, surveillance data can be used to influence both national and local decision-makers in a number of ways. One of the key outputs from the broad range of data collected from surveillance programmes should be identification of appropriate solutions for improved water supply in low-income areas. This should take into account water use patterns, cost issues, current water quality and the socio-economic and demographic circumstances of each community.

One of the principal issues to assess is the level of current access to higher service levels of water supply and to examine where the bottlenecks in increasing access may lie. In many urban areas, relatively few households have at least one tap at their house and as a result use less water, use sources more likely to be contaminated and, where sources are of high quality, consume water that is subject to re-contamination during transport and storage.

Surveillance of cost and access can help to define the critical barriers to access to higher service levels and advise policy-makers on the ways to overcome these barriers. Such barriers may typically be related to:

1. Inadequate distribution infrastructure that limits the numbers of people that can be served

2. Poor water supply management with high unaccounted-for-water that limits the number of people that can be served by the supply

3. High cost of connection and high recurrent costs

4. Poor perception of piped water supplies due to unreliability or suspected poor quality

In the case of the first problem, surveillance should be able to influence policy regarding the need to develop water supply infrastructure that can provide water to the whole urban population. Inequities in current access and the poor quality of the alternative sources currently used by the population can direct further investment in infrastructure to ensure access can be improved.

In the case of the second problem, routine surveillance can indicate the current level of water losses and this can be integrated within a regulatory framework to improve water supply management and operation and maintenance. Again, the knowledge of water use patterns and the risk to the health of users from alternative supplies can be used in identifying investment needs and management performance improvement.

In the last two factors, surveillance can identify critical bottlenecks and identify the appropriate solutions to these problems. In particular, surveillance can identify those elements of the payment system that act as disincentives to connect and those that provide incentives.

12.1.1 Communal services to the poor

In many urban areas, point sources are available and commonly used. These may include supplies that have been provided at some point by local administrations or NGOs or may represent community initiatives. Whilst some point sources are well maintained and provide water of good quality, other have been allowed to deteriorate and as a result no longer produce water of adequate quality to be consumed without additional treatment. There is often an urgent need to improve these supplies to reduce the public health risk.

However, in many urban areas when plans are drawn up to improve water supply in low-income areas, this is often limited to the provision of public taps. This is despite evidence that existing facilities may be substantially under-utilised, may not meet the demands of the population, are unsustainable and in many cases do not provide significantly greater comparative advantage over alternative supplies.

The assumption that public taps represent the best available solution is in many cases debatable. The principal benefit from a tap is that it can be located closer to the home than most point sources and is often of lower capital cost than alternative supplies. However, the recurrent prices of water at public taps are often high and usually bear little relation to the utility charge. Disconnection is a common problem, with disconnection often occurring within a short period of time from commissioning.

The identification of appropriate solutions require an understanding of the current water use patterns in different communities, their perceptions of what interventions will best meet their current and future needs, their socio-economic and demographic status, the reliability of supplies and the degree of contamination and causes of water quality failures. Critical to this is to ensure that interventions are deemed appropriate and acceptable to the users and to ensure that the needs of all the potential target users are met and that no group will be particularly disadvantaged or marginalised because of the intervention selected. The latter is particularly important when taking considerations of equity into account.

For instance, water from a public tap may be affordable for 80% of a target community but may leave the remaining 20% with little choice but to use alternative sources of poor quality. The remaining community may struggle to support the lowest 20% by providing water either free or at a lower cost. Equally, whilst the price of water may be affordable, the reliability of the supply may be poor resulting in use of alternative supplies or the supply may be prone to frequent failures in quality that expose the population to risk of infectious disease. These factors may reduce willingness to pay for supplies that are unreliable or perceived as poor quality.

Therefore, in some cases, alternative approaches may be required to improve water quality either through the improvement of point water supplies or by initiating household treatment of water within the home. Where piped water supplies are not believed to meet the full needs of the low-income population, then surveillance data can be used to influence the decision-making process to allow for alternative approaches to be used.

For instance in Uganda, the surveillance data was used to influence policy makers in considering a broader range of water supply improvements, rather than only focusing on the construction of public taps. The re-protection and improvement of protected springs in low-income areas of towns was one such intervention. This was supported by the data showing the level of use of springs, the close association of the use of springs and cholera cases and limited increases in household access to piped water supply. It should be noted that this was only one option that was considered for each community, but represented a major shift in policy. Similarly in Ghana, proposals were developed to promote the improvement of shallow dug-wells in low-income urban communities as it was recognised that these represented a significant risk to the health of the users. Other activities in Ghana focused on developing codes of practice for vendor supplies to improve maintenance of quality and improvement of performance.

One of the key lesson learnt from many projects worldwide is that there are no simple 'blueprints' for improving water supplies in low-income communities. Different communities may have very different perceptions about what is the real water supply problems in their community and the most appropriate solution. It is important to recognise that community-based strategies need flexibility in policy and implementation that allows for appropriate solutions for each community to be identified and implemented.

The need for a more participatory approach in the delivery of water supplies in under-served areas is increasingly recognised as being essential for sustained service delivery. This means that there should be greater dialogue with communities about the problems and preferred solutions in water supplies. This may include discussions between communities, surveillance agencies and water supplier to make piped water supply more attractive through greater flexibility regarding connection costs and payment. The use of private contractors to undertake small-scale works may offer opportunities both to reduce costs, increase local incomes and improve efficiency. This will allow communities and local authority staff time to monitor the construction process rather than implement construction themselves. This was done in an NGO supported project to rehabilitate protected springs and construct public taps in Kampala.

12.1.2 Source protection, minimum treatment requirements and distribution management

A further area where policy interventions may be required cover the basic components of source protection, minimum treatment requirements and distribution management. These are critical components in ensuring that water supplies continue to provide high-quality drinking water. The technical issues related to such issues are discussed in the following chapter, but the policy issues are briefly discussed here.

Source protection norms should be incorporated within policy documents as a statutory instruments that defines the protection codes that are expected and identify the responsible bodies for defining and implementing source protection norms. Such documents may also spell out the requirements placed on water suppliers to purchase land to provide adequate source protection and for environmental protection bodies to implement pollution and land-use control measures around water sources and any financial compensation that may be required for farmers or industry. In addition to broader source protection norms, the policy documents may also define the immediate sanitary completion norms through reference to sanitary completion norms and appropriate statutory instruments.

It is always preferred that water treatment employs the multiple barrier principle discussed in the next chapter. The development of water supply policies in relation the supply of potable water supply from surface water should indicate that the multiple barrier principle should be employed, whilst leaving choice of technologies up to water suppliers and local regulatory bodies. A similar approach should be followed regarding distribution management, which should typically cover aspects such as repair and rehabilitation strategies, flushing and cleaning schedules as well as control of leakage and continuity. Policy statements referring to the need to good distribution management and making reference to the appropriate norms and schedules that form the statutory instruments.

12.2 Using zoning approaches and surveillance data in policy and planning

The zoning of urban areas, the collection of water usage data and the water quality and sanitary risk data can all be used effectively in the policy and planning processes. The zoning of urban areas provides an effective mechanism by which to target resources on the areas where there is greatest risk from water-related disease as it classifies different parts of the urban area and allows priority areas to be identified. By comparing the zones developed and rates of infectious disease, a vulnerability map can also be developed that should allow better planning for response to outbreak situations.

The water quality and sanitary inspection data provide a good overview of current performance of water sources and indicate clearly where interventions are required. For instance, if water quality results indicate persistent failure of parts of a distribution system to maintain adequate free chlorine residuals despite adequate dosing at the works, this may lead to a policy decision that booster chlorination should be installed.

The planning of maintenance and rehabilitation programmes should also use sanitary inspection data as a key planning tool. These data provides valuable information regarding the deterioration in water supply service and water quality and therefore the need for action to be taken. Where point sources are used, the combined analysis of water quality and sanitary inspection data allows decisions to be made regarding whether point sources should be constructed within urban areas, and where they already exist, whether rehabilitation is justified. This may be combined with water usage data.

Water usage studies may also provide useful policy information in relation to the costs of water and whether these are perceived as affordable by low-income groups. This can be combined with other data relating to cost that influence specific components of policies relating to the cost of water, such as connection charges, minimum charges or billing arrangements. Other data incorporated in water usage studies, such as household water handling, storage and treatment practices can all be used to evaluate current approaches to water supply provision and hygiene education and be used to re-orientated policies so that they encourage greater uptake of higher-quality services by low-income communities.

12.3 Disease surveillance, epidemic preparedness and outbreak management

Water supply surveillance should link closely with disease surveillance, preparing strategies for dealing with epidemics and managing outbreaks when they occur. The transfer of routine quality data of water sources and households to agencies undertaking disease surveillance is an important component of identifying both the health burden derived from poor water and in indicating areas where disease surveillance may be particularly required. This process involves indicating the areas where populations are at greatest risk from infectious diarrhoeal disease.

When cases of notifiable diseases, such as cholera, dysentery or typhoid occur, it is important that water sources and household water is tested and inspected to establish whether it is likely that water is a cause of the disease. This can be critical in the early stages of an epidemic where decisions may need to be made regarding initial interventions in reducing the risk of transmission of the disease and in locating services within easy reach of those most likely to be affected. Whilst it would be preferable that this testing involves looking for the pathogen itself, in reality this may not always be possible. In this case, the usual water quality parameters and in particular thermotolerant coliforms or *E.coli* can be used, providing sanitary inspection is also undertaken to identify possible risks.

Epidemic preparedness typically involves identifying vulnerable areas and ensuring that the materials and logistics required for a rapid response are available and close to the areas at greatest risk. The zoning methodology discussed at the start of the manual is one way in which preparations can be made for epidemics as it identifies the most vulnerable areas. The routine testing of all sources used by the population will also allow preparations to be made as this may indicate greater than usual contamination of particular sources that represents an elevated risk and again will identify the areas at most risk.

Once an epidemic is underway, the testing of water sources and household water will become even more important in order to determine whether intervention is required at the source in the home. Such interventions may include provision of alternative water supplies, such as taps, or by chlorinating water at point sources and within the home. An example of this was seen in Kampala in 1997/98 when evidence of the degree of contamination of springs was important in the setting up of public taps in affected areas and chlorination of water collected from springs by Red Cross volunteers. The testing of sources and households in areas where the epidemic has not yet reached will also be important as this will help to indicate whether measures are required for emergency improvements to water supply in these areas to prevent the spread of the disease.

The linkage between water supply and disease surveillance systems is to be encouraged in all countries as a mechanism to limit the health impact from poor water supply. However, it should be noted that these are complementary activities and neither can replace the other. In some cases, the incidence of infectious diarrhoeal disease or an outbreak of epidemic disease may not be linked to water, but to other routes such as contaminated food. Therefore, in order to implement the most appropriate intervention requires information which both disease surveillance in terms of pathogen identification and water supply surveillance in terms of risk of transmission from water supply play an intrinsic part.

13.

Engineering and environmental interventions

Recommendations on technical and environmental protection interventions are key outputs of any surveillance programme. Both sanitary inspection and water quality data provide quantifiable assessments of supply performance and can indicate the protection norms required for different water source types. Furthermore, the collection of other data such as costs and access provide a sound basis for evaluating technical options and their sustainability. Routine surveillance should also contribute to the improvement in operation and maintenance of existing infrastructure.

13.1 Source protection

In order to ensure that water supplies can provide water that represents a limited risk to health, adequate source protection measures should be in place that limit the potential for pathogens or harmful chemicals from entering the supply. Source protection measures are required for all water sources that are used for domestic consumption and different measures will be required at different levels. A key use of sanitary inspection data should be to identify what basic measures are required at local and broader scales, and to identify the people responsible for undertaking protection work. This may include communities and users as well as water suppliers, planners and environment protection bodies.

13.1.1 Groundwater sources

As groundwater in its natural state is often of good microbiological quality, it is often the preferred source for drinking water. In many cases, groundwater sources do not receive any form of treatment, as they are low-cost supplies designed for community-management. Where boreholes or other groundwater sources are linked to piped distribution, limited disinfection is usually carried out prior to consumption. Thus groundwater sources are often lower-cost that comparable surface water sources. However, despite this, groundwater sources, whether small community-managed point sources or utility-operated boreholes supplying distribution networks, often become contaminated. This may result from widespread contamination of an aquifer from pollutant sources or in because the point of abstraction or discharge has been poorly protected or maintained and allows direct routes for contaminated surface water to enter the source.

The first level of source protection is the immediate sanitary protection works at the source. These are primarily designed to prevent contaminated surface water or wastewater from directly entering the water source and preventing other hazards that may allow direct contamination of the aquifer being established close the source. This will include measures such as casting concrete aprons on the ground surface and sealing of upper levels of boreholes and dug wells, and the construction of diversion ditches and covering of the backfill area of springs. Good source protection at this level depends in part on good design and construction, but the maintenance of such measures when put in place is extremely important. Well-designed sanitary protection measures may easily deteriorate if they are not maintained. For many small community-managed supplies, this may be the limit of feasible protection, but it is preferable that other source protection measures are put in place. Such protection measures should also be applied to mechanised boreholes serving piped distribution systems.

The next stage of source protection is to define areas where land-use and in particular the release of contaminants will be controlled - a process usually referred to as groundwater protection zones. Several zones may be defined, typically including an inner zone to protect against microbiological contaminants, a second zone to control chemical contamination and a final zone to protect recharge. All zones zone are usually determined by a travel time – i.e. the time expected for a microbe to reach a water source from the ground surface. Such zones must take into account the vulnerability of the aquifer, the nature of the hydrogeological regime and the likely hydraulic load applied. In many low and middle-income countries, the lack of knowledge of aquifer and unsaturated zone properties may hamper the development of protection zones and in these cases, a figure based on known groundwater flow rates could be used.

For the inner zone, a value of 50 days is often used. It should also be stressed that whilst 50 days will be adequate to remove many pathogens, there are some, for instance viruses, which may survive for much longer periods of time. In this case a balance must be struck between the likelihood of an infective dose being delivered and the need to develop excreta disposal facilities to improve health. The hydrogeological department in the national water resource management body should define travel time safety zones based on hydrogeological surveys. Information about protection zones may be found in the documents listed in Annex 6.

The development of good sanitary completion measures and the control of land use within the microbiological protection zone will usually significantly reduce treatment costs, by ensuring that most pathogens have been either inactivated or attenuated before they can reach the groundwater source. However, increasing evidence for extended survival of viruses suggests that greater attention is needed on providing contact time for chlorine rather than simple terminal disinfection as discussed later.

The further zone may be defined for chemical contaminants, again based on an estimated travel time that will reduce contaminants to acceptable levels. Where natural chemicals represent a problem, it is important to identify whether certain parts of the aquifer represent a higher risk and to define depths of abstraction that may reduce the problem. A final zone may be defined to cover the recharge area to provide protection for both quality and quantity of water. The purpose of all these zones is to control land-use in such a way that it does not create a significant deterioration in source water quality.

The surveillance agency, by monitoring groundwater-fed systems, can also provide evidence of the need for source protection and for disinfection needs for groundwater supplies. The evidence of water quality failure of groundwater sources, as opposed to distribution, can indicate improved sanitary protection norms both in the immediate area and broader scale on the basis of sanitary risk data analysis.

13.1.2 Surface water

Surface water sources are always more vulnerable to contamination and as a result is should always be treated before consumption. Whilst protection measures are less effective than for groundwater, is still important that catchments for reservoirs, river and lakes are protected as

146

far as possible from polluting activities. Typically pollutants will include microbiological contamination, suspended solids, inorganic and organic pollutants.

Defining protection of surface water catchments is often difficult as they often draw water from large areas and a certain degree of compromise will be necessary. Critical components, however, should include the prevention of excessive logging in upper reaches of rivers and lake catchments, prevention of untreated discharges of domestic and industrial wastes, control of urban run-off and prevention of encroachment into the immediate area around an intake or a reservoir. The latter is often a particular problem in developing countries and represents a major source of pollution.

In many water bodies, there are natural mechanisms that may reduce the pollutant load such as aquatic plants and the formation of heavy metal complexes in sediments. However, whilst these often provide reasonable protection, it should be stressed that a pollution-reduction strategy should be developed. Aquatic plants may die, or if not harvested may release contaminants during decay. Sediments may become disturbed and release pollutants back into the water. Changing pH and redox conditions may also affect whether contaminants move into an aquatic phase or remain in complexes.

The responsibility for ensuring surface water sources are adequately protected is primarily a responsibility of the water resource management body, through their pollution control department. However, both water suppliers and surveillance agencies should ensure that reasonable measures are put in place to protect surface and groundwater sources.

13.2 Minimum treatment requirements

All surface water and some groundwater requires treatment before it is consumed. The principal aim of most treatment is to remove microbiological contaminants and substances that influence the survival of microbes or that affect the aesthetic quality of water. Typically, greatest attention is placed on removal of microbes, reduction of suspended solids and colour problems and maintaining a pH consistent with effective disinfection.

For surface waters, the underlying principle of treatment should be to ensure that there are several stages of treatment – this is called the multiple barrier principle. Several stages of treatment provide greater safety both in terms of effective removal of contaminants and by ensuring that should one step fail, untreated or poorly treated water is not produced. All water going into piped distribution should be disinfected prior to pumping into the supply network and this is usually done using chlorine. For surface water a minimum of 30 minutes contact time is required with a free residual maintained to provide ongoing protection. For groundwaters, traditionally disinfection is usually limited to terminal disinfection with little or no contact time. However, there is now increasing evidence that viruses in particular may survive for at least 150 days in groundwater and probably considerably longer. Viruses have also been found in deep groundwater with limited evidence of direct by-pass routes. Therefore, in order to ensure the quality of water, consideration should be given to providing a 30-minute contact time with chlorine for groundwater supplies.

Removal of chemical contaminants is typically more difficult although many existing processes are effective in chemical removal – for instance slow sand filters for heavy metal removal, coagulation for fluoride removal and aeration for iron and manganese removal.

147

Some chemicals, notably organics, may require specialist and expensive treatment such as activated carbon filters.

The surveillance agency should check that all treatment plants operate a multiple barrier principle, that this is operated properly and that all water piped into distribution is disinfected with a residual left for the network.

13.3 Technology selection, rehabilitation and improved design

13.3.1 Technology selection

In terms of technology choice the role of surveillance is to indicate where existing technologies have failed to meet adequate performance targets and what improvements are required to improve performance. It may also provide information as to whether the type of technology used is appropriate or whether it exceeds the technical or financial resources of users or suppliers to maintain.

For instance, many small town supplies rely on conventional treatment plants with a high reliance on chemical treatment using coagulants for turbidity removal. Many supplies find it difficult to sustain such treatment processes as the costs of the coagulant are high and as a result the coagulation-flocculation-settling stage is by-passed, leading to less effective treatment. For such supplies, alternative methods such as multi-stage filtration that rely more on physical and biological processes may be more sustainable and provide more effective treatment of water.

Water quality in distribution occurs world-wide and whilst much of this may be related to poor operation and maintenance, materials selection and system design may influence water quality profoundly. By working closely together, the supplier and surveillance agency can identify technical problems in the system that need to be overcome. This may include the pipe materials used, as evidence may emerge of increased bursts or water quality failure in certain types of pipe material. Commonly this will include the use of supply mains whose pressure rating is too low.

Although the surveillance agencies themselves may not be able to easily identify whether the pipe materials are the cause of increased bursts, the recording of supply risks such as leakage and reported pipe breaks in sanitary inspection allows the surveillance agency to identify vulnerable areas. They can the work with the water supply agency to review the possible causes of failure and agree a programme of improvement. A similar process can be undertaken with regard to chlorine loss by zoning of the piped system and then evaluating where chlorine loss is most common and evaluate the potential causes. These may include bulk system storage, but also certain pipe materials (in particular GI pipe) that exert a greater chlorine demand.

13.3.2 Improved designs

For communal systems, technical improvements can be made. For public taps, a common problem is that the water coming from the tap is widely dispersed, leading to wastage of water. This is a particular problem where containers such as Jerrycans are used that have a narrow opening. As charges typically relate to a container, no revenue can be gained for the lost water leading to problems with sustaining the tap. As a result, many communities attach a small length of rubber hosing to the tap in order to direct the flow of water directly into the container. These attachments often lead to contamination of otherwise good quality water. To overcome this, improved designs can be developed that either use a tap with a more controlled flow, or reduce the height difference between the tap and container by lowering the riser pipe or building a small plinth to support the container. A further problem commonly found is that public taps have no support for the riser, this may lead to damage to the pipe and weakening of the joint to the supply pipe. Thus designs that provide a support to the riser pipe should be used.

All the above problems would be routinely identified through surveillance activities and discussions with communities by surveillance staff. Through use of the surveillance data and a community-orientated approach, many of these simple problems may be overcome and better water supplies result.

Technical improvement in the design of point sources may also be required. In urban areas, the intensity and scale of pollution within the environment is typically much greater than that found in rural areas. Thus designs that are effective in rural areas in preventing contamination may not work as well in an urban environment. A good example is the design of protected springs in Uganda, which traditionally used a very large aggregate to backfill the area behind the outlet. This allowed virtually no filtration of water entering the spring protection area and therefore little opportunity to attenuate any contamination entering from the groundwater. The design was improved by using a finer gravel aggregate to above the level of the water in the backfilled area and covering this with a layer of fine sand, clay and then murram. This design offered greater attenuation capacity in the backfill area and allows filtration of any surface water that enters the protected area. As a solid fence and diversion ditch was also constructed, surface water inundation was limited.

A further problem at point source may be congestion at peak collection times, a problem that may be identified through a water usage study or by observation. This may be overcome for springs by building a spring box with multiple outlets that allow greater number of people to collect water at one time. Such spring boxes have an additional value in that they permit chlorination of source water to be carried out using a porous pot chlorinated when risks are elevated, such as during an epidemic.

13.3.3 Rehabilitation

Rehabilitation of point sources may be an appropriate response to poor water supply in circumstances where water quality is poor and represents a risk to public health and in particular as a vehicle for epidemics. It may also be appropriate where public taps have a record of poor sustainability; or where increases in access to piped water at yard or in-house level are unlikely to be realised in the short to medium term.

Communities should be fully involved in the process of planning and implementation of rehabilitation works. The beneficiary community should also make contributions towards the cost of the rehabilitation works. Operation and maintenance issues should be dealt with from the start and awareness raised in the community of the impact of poor operation and maintenance on the quality of water. Wherever possible, commitments should be obtained from the community about operation and maintenance prior to the rehabilitation works being initiated.

The proper planning of improvement in community-managed water supply must address building capacity within the community to sustain the water supply once it is constructed. The most appropriate approach to develop new communal water facilities is to respond to requests from communities for the development of the facility. However, in some communities, there may be limited awareness of the potential to develop a new water facility. They may lack information about the process of obtaining a water source or may believe that their requests may not be supported by planners or local authorities. There may be weak community organisation and demand limited. Other issues may also include the limited working capital available to low-income communities, which precludes gaining access to an improved water supply without external support.

Community-based water supplies may take several forms, including bulk purchase of water for distribution within a community, establishment of community-managed public taps and a variety of point sources. The critical component for sustainable community-managed water supplies of whatever type, is the need for full involvement of communities at all stages of the project, the building of capacity to operate and maintain a community water supply and the link to external agencies for support in terms of information about water quality, good management practices and training.

Involvement of communities in the process of improvement should be ensured at all stages. Critical to this is their involvement in selecting the type of water supply desired as the imposition of an external solution frequently leads to failure. Such failure may be disconnection from the piped water supply, breakdown of a handpump or deterioration in a protected spring. In order for communities to make informed decisions, it is essential that they have the knowledge about short and long-term financial and management implications as well as technical or environmental problems that may restrict the options available. For instance, there may be a demand for a public tap in an area where the nearest supply main is distant and the pressure is unlikely to be able sustain continuous running and the cost prohibitive. Long-term implications in terms of paying utility tariffs and likely consequences for non-payment must be discussed and the need for good internal financial management stressed. This is often a particular problem for public taps where revenue is collected from users but the manager of the tap fails to remit payment for bills presented. The setting up of bank accounts for water supply is often essential in urban areas to ensure money can be saved to pay bills.

There is much evidence also to suggest that when communities do not have to contribute to the implementation of water supply improvement, the facilities provided often fail, as there is a lack of perceived ownership of the supply. In rural areas, such contributions typically take the form of donation of labour. However, in urban areas, it is often more effective to ensure that a monetary contribution is made because urban communities typically have access to funds but may have more limited time. Ensuring a contribution is made helps a sense of ownership to develop that often enhances sustainability. However, this is not always the case and the ownership of a supply is better ensured when there has be full and active participation in the whole process.

In urban areas community-managed facilities may be constructed by contractor rather than by community-labour with technical support. The management of small contracts is essential to ensure that work is carried out in a timely manner and at an adequate quality. In some countries, communities have themselves managed small contracts successfully and this may be appropriate in some settings.

The final component for community-managed supplies is to ensure that members of the community have the skills for routine operation and maintenance and financial management. A caretaker or vendor should be appointed for each facility and a management committee established. The caretaker should receive training in simple maintenance of the facilities and should have the equipment required to undertake these tasks. Tools may be purchased as part of a community contribution. The committee requires training in simple accounting procedures and suitable formats developed to allow accounts to be kept in a transparent manner.

13.4 Operation and Maintenance

Routine surveillance is a key element in operation and maintenance (O&M) of all forms of water supply and should form part of the O&M strategy. This requires an interaction between operational staff and water quality staff in the water supply agency, surveillance staff and communities. The important elements in using surveillance in operation and maintenance involve the rapid identification and reporting of faults and action taken to repair faults and to promote sustained operation and maintenance practices of importance for water quality and continuity such as leakage control, flushing of distribution systems and simple maintenance of point sources.

13.4.1 Utility supplies

Much of the use of surveillance data in improving water supply relates to regulation as already discussed. The failure in critical parameters should be a trigger for action and also provides a measure of performance by the water supplier.

There are practical ways in which surveillance should be used to improve the performance of operation and maintenance in piped water supplies. Surveillance and monitoring data can be used to improve performance during the production stage. By undertaking evaluations of treatment plant operation using the forms shown in Annex 3, critical failures can be identified and appropriate action taken such as training, preparing guidance materials or by ensuring that operators understand must follow standard operating procedures. Typically this will be the primary responsibility of the water supplier and it is not likely to be a routine surveillance activity. However, the surveillance agency may undertake such an evaluation when they have doubts about the plant operation or where the water supply agency lack the skills required, for instance in small supplies.

Within distribution systems, surveillance data should be used to improve operation and maintenance through identifying key supply faults and ensuring action is taken to reduce these. This will include aspects such as leakage, continuity and condition of pipes (including exposure). All these risks indicate operation and maintenance problems and the role of surveillance in reporting on performance and suggesting improvements in practice is important. This may be done through enforcement procedures where these lay down standards to be achieved or can be done through working closely together with the supplier to identify and rectify faults in a timely and effective manner. A example of the latter case comes from Soroti in Uganda, where sanitary inspection identified a major leak in distribution and a dirty service reservoir as the key elements leading to water quality failure and an plan of action was agreed with the water supply office to address these problems.

The routine monitoring of water quality parameters such as thermotolerant coliforms, free chlorine and colour should also be used to improve cleaning and flushing schedules for piped water. Losses in free chlorine residual or increased colour should immediately trigger cleaning of service reservoirs and flushing of distribution lines. For best practice, both should be carried out frequently and not simply rely on the results of monitoring. Dead-ends in particular require frequent flushing as chlorine loss and other water quality problems typically occur in such areas. Again, much of this work should be done by the water supplier, but the surveillance agency can provide advice on frequencies of cleaning and flushing required and monitor whether these are being undertaken. Failure may result in enforcement action where a regulatory system has been established.

The loss of pressure leading to discontinuity or reduced availability of water can also be identified through routine surveillance and community surveys. The surveillance agency can ensure that pressure is maintained at critical points in the system, such as public taps or where vendors collect water. Attention should be placed on those areas where the majority of people use piped water from a yard or communal supply as these people have much more limited capacity to store water within the home. Attention should also be paid to areas where contamination may be more likely such as in low-lying areas or high-density areas.

13.4.2 Community-managed facilities

Community-managed facilities are likely to be common in most urban areas and encompass a wide range of water points including public taps, point sources and rainwater collection at household levels.

As discussed in Chapter 6, sanitary inspection data provide an effective mechanism in assessing operation and maintenance performance of point water supplies and can be used to highlight improvements required. In many cases, improvement of operation and maintenance is critical to the improvement of water supplies as many of water supply problems (breakdown, deteriorating quality and decreasing yield) are due to poor operation and maintenance rather than design or construction faults.

The underlying causes of poor operation and maintenance may be vary but typically will include some or all of the following:

1. Lack of community participation in the provision of the sources and a limited sense of ownership. Responsibility for maintaining and improving the source is often perceived by the community as lying with the local authority or the source provider.

2. Poor understanding of the work required for operation and maintenance or its importance. Many communities may view work to be carried out on the supply as required only in times of complete breakdown and have a limited understanding of the need for ongoing preventative maintenance to reduce the likelihood of complete source failure.

3. Poor understanding of the water quality problems caused by poor operation and maintenance and lack of awareness about the quality of water provided by the source.

4. Poor community organisation and financial management. Community-managed facilities tend to be more effective when there is a defined group of people within the community that takes responsibility for managing the water supply and for employing a caretaker. In many cases, failures also occur because there are insufficient funds raised to cover the costs of labour and materials. In the case of public taps, this may translate into non-payment of water bills and disconnection from the public supply. However, raising funds is often important for point supplies as in many urban communities, contributions may be financial rather than as labour or provision of tools as would usually be the case in rural areas.

5. Loss of skills in managing the water supply. In some situations the water supply may have been provided many years previously and had a water committee and caretaker responsible for operation and maintenance. With time, however, these people may have moved and new inhabitants arrived into the community who lack the skills to manage the water source effectively or who are less willing to accept responsibility for the water source management.

In many cases operation and maintenance as assessed by the levels and types of risk is weak. In these cases, work can be initiated with the community to significantly improve maintenance of the water source but it is critical that this maximises the participation of the community. The role of the surveillance body is to act as a facilitator of the process rather than the principal force improving operation and maintenance.

Public taps
Public taps are a common feature in most urban areas and are commonly the preferred method of providing water to low-income settlements by planners and the option preferred by many communities. However, sustaining public taps has often proved difficult in urban settings where utilities demand regular payment for the services provided. Non-payment of water bills is often a problem and the rates of disconnection may be high. Sound, accountable and transparent financial management of public taps is essential if these are to be maintained.

The surveillance body can assist this process by working with communities to identify how water finances can be managed and what charges should be levied. The users should also review and discuss the payment of caretakers to ensure that the presence of a caretaker does not lead to an excessive cost, whilst ensuring that basic operation and maintenance is carried out. The community should also discuss whether they want to use the water supply to generate additional funds for future activities within their community or would prefer to see the water kept to a more affordable level. This may be an important point for the community. There is limited benefit in setting prices that in principle allow a community fund to be established, if this then makes water unaffordable. Furthermore, the surveillance agency can work with the community to establish simple accounting procedures that are transparent.

Public taps that are functioning are often at risk from water quality failure due to poor management of the environment around the tap. The surveillance body can work effectively with the community to resolve such problems through using sanitary inspection, water quality and hygiene education tools. The types of intervention fall into two broad categories:

1. Minimising risk to health caused by failures within immediate area around the tap and its use

2. Identifying the process of reporting faults to utilities and surveillance bodies.

In Uganda, many failures in water quality are caused by poor maintenance of the infrastructure in the immediate area of the public tap. Leaks in customer mains, the presence of stagnant water around the customer main and tap, the use of additional pipes on the ends of taps may all cause water to be contaminated.

In these cases, surveillance staff worked with communities to discuss the importance of these factors and to identify the activities required to prevent local contamination from occurring. This included encouraging communities to provide support to riser pipes and ensuring that the base of the riser pipe had a small raised concrete apron to allow spilt water to drain away from the tap.

Surveillance agencies should also work with communities to identify major supply faults and to report such faults to both the supplier and the surveillance agency. This is an important task for communities in terms of leakage control, as part of the reasons why so many leaks are allowed to continue for extended periods of time is that they are rarely reported. Given that routine inspection the system by the supplier is often weak and remote monitoring methods are in general not used, water suppliers are often highly dependent on the public to report faults. However, initial perceptions by communities may be that leaks are not detrimental to them. It is important for surveillance bodies to work with communities to ensure they understand that breaks and leaks in the main pipe system may affect the water they drink and therefore the need to report such problems and demand action. They should also understand the need to report discontinuity in supply and to demand action to improve the supply.

Point sources
The problems with operation and maintenance of point sources are often more profound than those of public taps. Whilst piped water may be contaminated, it is commonly less contaminated than point source water. Furthermore, the control over the sanitary protection of point sources will fall entirely on the community with limited input from outside agencies.

Operation and maintenance of point sources is often poor. Communities have often failed to keep water sources in the condition that they were designed for and often simple tasks are not undertaken. In part this reflects on a lack of participation within the construction phase and a limited sense of ownership. Such problems are often found to a greater extent in low-income areas receiving significant changes in the population, with new migrants moving into areas and homes vacated by previous migrants who have increased their economic status.

To improve the operation and maintenance of point sources, approaches that are participatory and emphasise the identification and problems and solutions within the user community are in general more effective. Again, the use of water quality and sanitary risk data as health education tools is important as these provide the evidence for communities to consider the nature of the problem and the ways in which this may be overcome.

The first step in improving operation and maintenance should be to facilitate a community discussion on the problems of the source, the possible causes of the problems and what solutions exist to improve the source. This then leads to identifying the major shortfalls in community operation and maintenance and a start point for reviewing and identifying the

154

possible solutions. Many of the basic operation and maintenance tasks are low-cost and are well within the grasp of communities. As with public taps, a critical problem in many communities that use point sources is that funds are unavailable for routine maintenance and money is only raised in times of compete breakdown. Furthermore, in urban areas unlike their rural counterparts, it is less likely that reliance can be placed on donation of labour for operation and maintenance. Therefore, establishing a small tariff on the users of point sources may be an essential component to improve operation and maintenance.

During community discussions, the first area to explore is whether a water source committee exists and who takes responsibility for maintenance of the spring, the degree to which the tasks are undertaken and whether those responsible have any accountability to the wider community. Where water source committees do not exist, their formation should be encouraged within communities, although care should be taken to generate the demand for such a committee from within the community rather than imposition from outside.

Once a committee has been formed, a caretaker should be identified and the tasks expected and remuneration to be provided for the work carried out. The committee should make a proposal for payment for use of the source and a set of regulations governing the use of the source. Responsible behaviour may be a critical element in this as many point sources suffer from congestion, particularly where the piped water supply in unreliable and this may lead to damage to the structure and harm to individuals.

The tasks for routine maintenance of point sources are relatively simple. They typically include: maintaining and repairing fences, ensuring that drains are regularly cleaned and kept clear of blockages and that the general environment is kept clean. Tables 13.1 and 13.2 below illustrate typical tasks for a caretaker of point sources in Uganda and the frequency of action. This was translated in local languages and provided to the caretaker to act as a reference document and to allow the committee and community to monitor the performance of the caretaker.

Activity	Dry season	Wet season	
		Routine	After heavy rainfall
Clear uphill diversion ditch	At least once per month	At least once per week	Clean if required
Clear drainage ditch from outlets	At least once per month	At least once per week	Clean if required
Slashing grass inside fence	At least once per dry season	At least once per month	Not necessary
Make sure steps are clean and not broken	At least once per week	At least once per week	Clean if required
Clear rubbish away from area around spring, particularly uphill	At least once per week	At least once per week	Clean if required
Keep paths and grassed areas above springs clear of rubbish	At least once per month	At least once per month	Clean if required
Trim hedge once it reaches a height of 4 feet	Do not trim in the dry season	When hedge reaches 4 feet	Not necessary
Carry out regular inspections of the spring and note any faults	At least twice per week	Daily	After every heavy rains

Table 13.1: O&M tasks for a protected spring

Activity	Dry season	Wet season	
		Routine	*After heavy rainfall*
Grease working parts of the handpump	At least once per week	At least once per week	At least once per week
Check handpump to see whether worn parts need replacement	At least once per quarter	At least once per quarter	At least once per quarter
Make sure fence is in good condition and make repairs	At least once per quarter	At least once per quarter	At least once per quarter
Check drainage channels and clean	At least once per month	At least once per week	Clean if required
Clear rubbish away from area around borehole, particularly uphill	At least once per week	At least once per week	Clean if required
Keep paths and grassed areas above borehole clear of rubbish	At least once per month	At least once per month	Clean if required
Check whether any water collecting close to the borehole and clear if required	At least once per month	At least once per week	Clean if required
Carry out regular inspections of the borehole and note any faults	At least twice per week	Daily	After every heavy rains

Table 13.2: O&M tasks for a borehole

14.

Hygiene education

A general experience from many countries is that any programme for the improvement of drinking water should be accompanied by educational programmes in order to ensure that the services are properly used and lead to benefits in health. As already discussed in many developing countries there is likely to be a significant amount of community-managed supplies within urban areas, including public taps and point sources. The users of such facilities may require additional inputs in terms of health and environmental education to ensure that water sources are well maintained. Furthermore, water collected from safe sources may become re-contaminated and thus hygiene education programmes often represent the most appropriate response to these problems. Surveillance of water supply can be a critical part of the delivery of hygiene education programmes through identification of key problems in water supply, identification of the causes of such problems and suggest appropriate solutions. The results of surveillance programmes therefore represent a key entry point in defining the focus of water hygiene programmes and in particular in promoting community-based responses to poor water supply and helping communities to overcome problems faced.

14.1 Selecting remedial actions

The critical questions that need to be asked for determining the remedial actions required within a water supply programme are listed in Figure 14.1

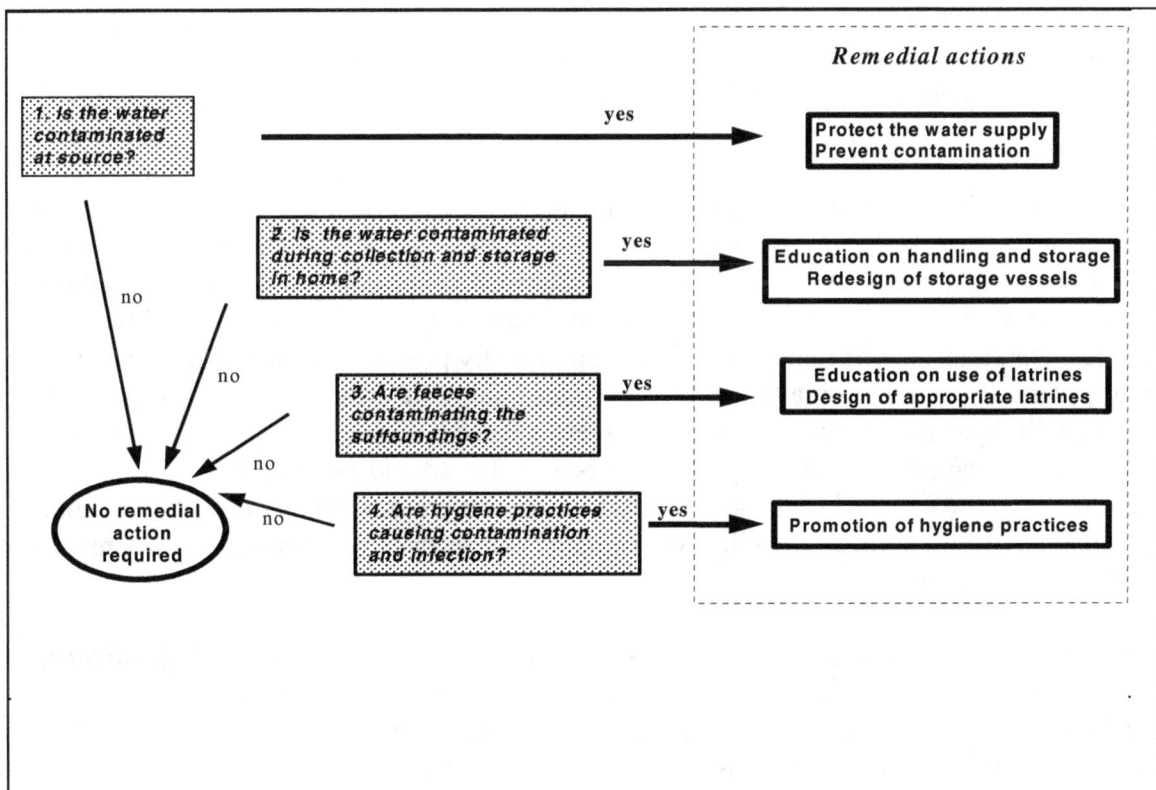

Figure 14.1 Critical questions for determining education/communication actions

This figure illustrates some of the key issues that must be addressed in the development of a communication/education programme on improving water supply and water quality. There are several key questions that should be answered as follows:

Is the water contaminated at source - from entry of faeces/pathogens during transit to the community or at the actual water point?
Is the water contaminated during collection and storage in the home e.g. by dirty containers, open water tanks, contamination by hands when scooping out the water?
In the first case, the education activities should focus on environmental protection and improved operation and maintenance. Such interventions are usually best achieved through community-based activities and discussion of problems and potential solutions to those problems.

As already noted, although the water at a source may be free of contamination, water stored within the home may be contaminated due to micro-organisms entering during handling. Hygiene education programme should therefore focus on the ensuring that the collection point and containers used for water collection, transport and storage are well-designed and that handling practices do not increase the risks of contamination. The education component in this case will focus on promoting the use of containers that are covered, that are cleaned using soap or disinfectant and promoting the use of containers with a tap for withdrawing the water. The strategy may also involve advice on treating water within the home and to locate storage containers away from easy contamination.

Care should be taken when advocating boiling of drinking water, as this may not always be the most appropriate response to water quality problems within the home. If the water at source is free of pathogens and is not contaminated during handling and storage there should be no need to boil drinking water prior to use. Therefore if certain sources are known to be safe it may be better to focus on promoting safe collection and storage techniques rather than promote further treatment.

There is evidence that messages on boiling that are repeated may lose their effectiveness and become a 'socially desirable' response rather than a routine activity. It should be remembered that in-house treatment of water is usually relatively expensive and that the additional financial burden of treating water within the home may be significant for low-income families, who thus may be reluctant to follow such costly practices. This has many dangers as an urgent need for boiling may arise due to water quality deterioration and this may not be followed. If hygiene education programmes are planned where treatment of water in the home will be included, consider carefully whether this should be restricted to cases when risks are increased (e.g. during rainy periods or an outbreak is underway). Other, routine messages could then focus on selection of safe sources and prevention of contamination through good handling.

Are faeces disposed of safely? Do the community have access to latrines? Are these latrines adequate, well maintained and clean? Are the latrines used by children?
Use of latrines is particularly important in urban communities where space is limited. It is especially important that children use latrines and that the faeces of very young children and infants are disposed in latrines as they contain the pathogens that will infect other children. Not only do faeces in the environment lead to other transmission routes for infectious micro-organisms, but may also represent a serious concern for water quality both of the source and

within the home. Faecal matter that is not disposed of properly can often enter into point water sources and may also affect piped water, particularly within the immediate area of the tap. Again this will require a focus on environmental education within the community to ensure that the environment is kept as clean as possible and that faeces are disposed of properly.

Are hygiene and child care practices causing contamination and infection?
Where water is supplied through communal supplies or if communities have experienced severe shortages of water or high charges they will have developed low water-usage habits. Even if they start to receive improved water systems these habits may persist and they will not increase their water consumption to the level that is required for adequate personal hygiene. It may be necessary to encourage the community to increase their water consumption and also to promote handwashing with soap or local agents after defecating and before preparing food or eating may be required. Effective handwashing may also contribute to a reduction of contamination of water stored within the home by preventing the transfer of faeces from hands into drinking water containers. Evaluations have shown that many local handwashing agents such as ashes or traditional soaps are as effective as soap. The washing of children's faces, especially around the eyes, will prevent the disease trachoma that causes blindness. Whilst in both hand and face washing quantity of water available is an important factor, it may be more essential to encourage the best use of water by ensuring that what water is available is used for critical tasks like bathing.

14.2 Determining influences/entry points

Information on the community is needed in order to determine factors that might hinder or help the adoption of particular hygiene behaviours including 'entry points' including topics of community concern, influential persons support groups etc. These are listed in table 14.1.

Important Issues	Strategy for situation assessment
	WHO? Size and location - The size of the target population. Where do they live, carry out water, sanitation and hygiene behaviours? Where would be the best place to reach them?
	WHO? Social/cultural characteristics: ethnic/linguistic background, age range, literacy/education, religion, political grouping, occupation, income; sub-groups within the target population? Networks of contacts and influence; mobility?
	WHAT? Risk behaviours: Detailed and specific descriptions on the nature and extent of practice of risk behaviours e.g. water collection, storage, use of latrines, disposal of children's faeces, existing water consumption, handwashing, face washing use of soap, food preparation, breastfeeding, weaning of infants. Language and vocabulary used to describe the risk behaviour and norms and values associated with them. Willingness and ability to pay for water and sanitation.
Kinds of information required	**WHY? Individual and cultural determinants of risk behaviours** e.g. perception of risk/susceptibility; levels of awareness and knowledge, their ability/power to change current behaviours; community felt needs. Gender issues - role of men and women in decision-making on water, sanitation and hygiene.
	WHY? Enabling factors outside the individual's control: What are the factors outside the individual's control that would make the needed behavioural changes difficult to carry out? e.g. employment, settlement rights, access to land, child care facilities
	WHY? Levels and quality of service provision. Technical support for latrine construction, maintenance of water systems, availability of soap
	Entry points and channels of communication: Possible channels of communication to the target population e.g. organisations, key individuals, patterns of listening to mass media e.g. radio/television/newspapers; patterns of interpersonal communication e.g. community networks, opinion leaders, existing health/community development and other services/NGOs.
Sources of information	**Surveillance, records and previous research**; including health records, surveillance and monitoring reports, newspaper reports, minutes of meetings, previous resource etc. can provide a useful background and help define what additional information you need to gather.
	Street work - walking around informally talking to target audience and making a map of how the target audience is laid out.
	Interviewing key informants: speaking to people with in depth knowledge of the target community.
	Focus group discussions; Forming groups of 8-12 of the target community and holding a structured interview using a trained facilitator. It can also be useful to show them samples of existing educational materials and inviting comments and reactions.
	PRA- (participatory rapid appraisal). This involves working with target audiences over a series of visits or in a workshop to describe their situation and identify solutions. This can involve preparing maps of the community.

How to ensure quality of data	Surveys; Interviews with a sample of the target community collecting both qualitative and quantitative information.
	Community participation in data gathering: A small informal committee of interested persons can be formed e.g. local leaders, women's groups can serve as your "panel of experts" in matters of appropriate language, pilot testing, sampling etc.
	Pre-testing data collection instruments: Trying out questionnaires with samples of the target group to ensure that they are understood and acceptable.
	Careful attention to sampling: Avoiding bias by choosing samples for data-gathering that are representative of the target population.
	Triangulation – comparison of information received from different sources
	Explaining the purpose of the situation assessment, giving guarantees of confidentiality and creation of a climate of trust: The community are more likely to give you an honest answer if they trust you, believe that the information will benefit them and that information will be confidential.

Table 14.1 Determining influences and entry points

14.3 Community participation in health education

There is increasing evidence that people learn most effectively when the learning experience is participatory and the target audience is involved in the process of problem definition, identification of solutions and identifying the steps or process that will lead them to their preferred situation. This approach underpins the PHAST (Participatory Hygiene and Sanitation Transformation) approach. As discussed in Chapter 2, many urban areas are composed of a collection of smaller communities, many of whom are more homogenous that would appear at first when considering community-based actions.

As much of the water supply utilised by the urban poor will be community managed in some form and because contamination of all sources is often related to problems within the immediate area of the sampling point, the resolution of water quality problems of sources and within homes requires community-based action. The role of hygiene education programmes in this regard should be to work closely with communities to identify problems and to facilitate actions through identifying solutions and implementing a plan of action.

Participatory approaches emphasise the importance of community involvement in the learning process. Rather than education from outsiders it is designed to help communities and families to improve water supplies through their own decision-making processes and actions. This does not mean that participatory approaches do not involve an element of information transfer and knowledge-building, but rather that the way that this done is different from more didactic approaches.

Critical to community participation is ensure that the health education process addresses the following issues:

- Drawing on the experiences, insights and understandings of the local community on the nature of their problem and possible solutions.

- Involvement of the community in identifying local resources, solving problems and the creation of sustainable and effective solutions. The development of a sense of ownership in the water supply system will lead to greater involvement in implementation, monitoring and maintenance.

- The creation of a climate of trust and understanding between service providers and the community which can be built upon in follow-up activities.

The process of community participation is often seen as going through the stages shown in figure 14.2.

```
┌─────────────────────────────────────────────────────────────────────────┐
│                                  Entry                                    │
│                                                                           │
│                       Dialogue with the community,                        │
│                                                                           │
│   Learning about community structures, felt needs, participatory learning activities to introduce and │
│                                    ↓                                      │
│                            Setting priorities                             │
│                                                                           │
│   Action planning with community, decisions on technical inputs, installation, procedures for use, │
│   notifying faults and maintenance. Identification of community contributions including labour and │
│   money. Setting up of community structures e.g. water committees, training of community-based │
│   volunteers e.g. water minders, maintenance workers. Identifying the need for accompanying hygiene │
│                                 behaviours.                               │
│                                    ↓                                      │
│                                  Action                                   │
│                                                                           │
│        Initial activities chosen to bring people together on common issues│
│                                                                           │
│           Further actions build on the confidence and trust generated     │
│                                    ↓                                      │
│                  Evaluation, reflection, further activities               │
│                                                                           │
│   Evaluation becomes an opportunity for everyone to reflect on achievements, shortfalls and need for │
│                               further action                              │
└─────────────────────────────────────────────────────────────────────────┘
```

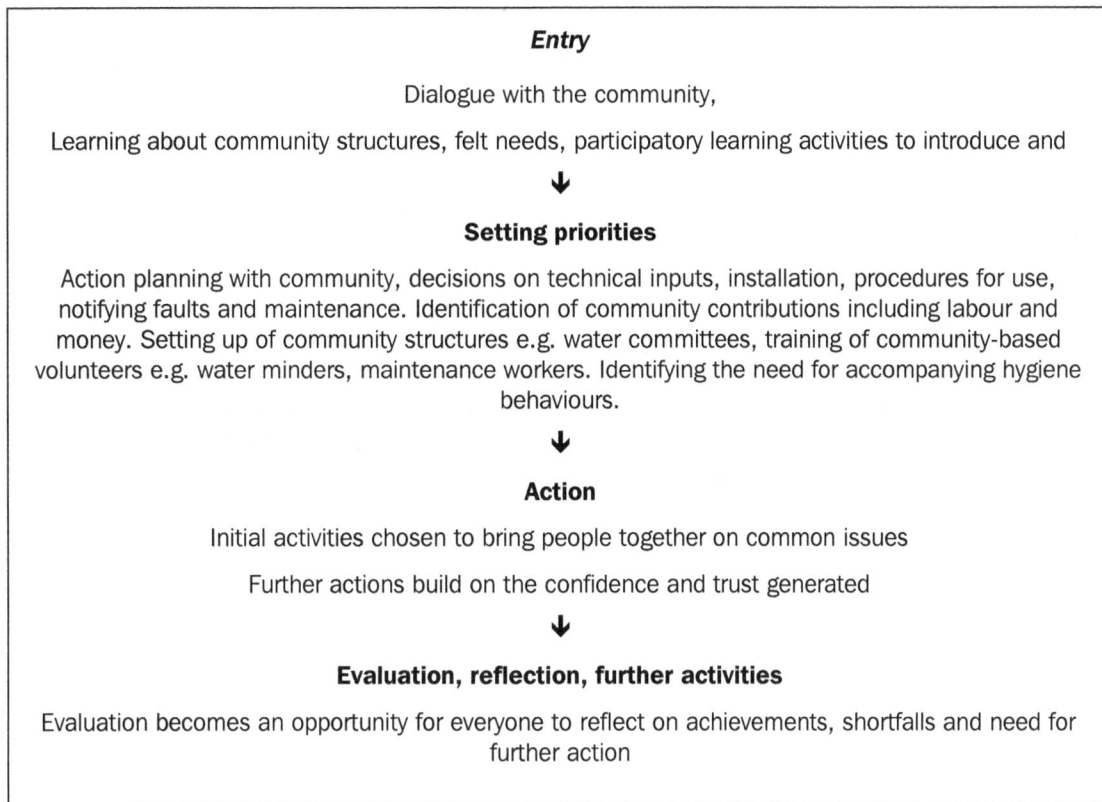

Figure 14.2: Community participation processes

Lessons from community programmes suggest that the following issues need to be taken into account when planning community participation programmes:

- It is important to begin with issues that the community feels strongly about, as they will be motivated to participate on these. While there is usually a strong community felt need for water, the need for sanitation and hygiene practices may be less widely appreciated. It is important to explain the importance of these inputs at an early stage while there is still strong enthusiasms for action.

- It is always important to work through existing community structures and organisations and build upon what already exists. In some newly formed urban communities such as squatter communities these may not be well developed. In that case you may need to bring people together and encourage the formation of community structures.

- Care is needed to identify any divisions and disagreements e.g. political, religious or cultural differences that might exist. Where disagreements exist avoid taking one side. Choose initial actions that everyone agrees with, which are easier to accomplish and which will unite the community and build up community confidence and awareness of the benefits of working together.

- Community structures such as water committees need support and encouragement to remain active and be effective.

- The processes of getting to know a community, dialogue and participation can take time. It is important to ensure that you have field staff trained to carry out this sensitive work and that there is time allocated in your schedule to carry out community participation.

14.3.1 Developing an intervention

The development of a health education intervention needs to consider which communities are priorities, where interventions are more likely to be effective, what barriers may be faced in uptake of good hygiene that is beyond community control and who will undertake the intervention. Some of these are discussed below.

- *Field staff:* Field staff used in community programmes should have training in educational and communication methods as well as having a sensitive and understanding approach to the community. Both male and female field workers will be needed with an emphasis on those who share cultural values and language with the community.

- *Entry points:* These might include issues that are already of concern to the community and existing initiatives that can be built on - for example existing women's health promotion activities, urban heath initiatives, pre-school initiatives.

- *Local resource organisations:* These are that local organisations that such as existing NGOs working in the community, churches and mosques, women's organisations, clinics etc. Involve all relevant local organisations in hygiene education.

- *Target groups:* These might include persons with influence over household decisions, community leaders, and persons who are responsible for looking after children.

- *Educational methods and support materials:* Choose educational methods that are appropriate to the community and relevant to the topic. The three options are use of mass media, outreach and facility-based education. The impact of educational methods will be increased with well designed support materials such as leaflets and participatory learning materials. These should be pre-tested with the community to ensure that the language and content is appropriate, acceptable and easily understood.

It is important that interventions focus on those communities of greatest need, but consideration should be given the nature of the community and the selection of suitable communities. One mistake often made is that health education activities are initiated on a large scale by field staff. This may make achievement of targets difficult as the resources are spread too thinly. Furthermore, communities may be selected at the outset that may be particularly difficult to work with because they are illegal or transitory and have little faith in local government. The impact of the health education programme may therefore be limited, possibly leading to discouragement and abandonment of the health education component. It is therefore usually better to plan a programme of health education which starts with initial pilot areas and then develops in a systematic manner and allows each community to receive the input required to achieve the aims of the intervention.

Where health education programmes are being developed, there is also often a better chance of success in communities that are more stable and these could be targeted first to gain experience that can be transferred to other, more difficult communities. This does not mean that difficult to work with communities should not benefit from such programmes, but rather they are best handled once experience has been developed and skills and tools refined.

Experience of field programmes suggests that educational interventions are most effective when the methods used address the following issues:

- **Promote actions that are realistic and feasible within the constraints faced by the community.** There is little point in promoting behaviours that are governed by external factors or relate to intrinsic problems As it is likely that only limited quantities of water will be collected from communal sources, an emphasis may need to be placed on good use of water rather than increasing quantities collected. The same is also likely to be true in situations where water must be purchased. The benefits of household water treatment must be set against the costs of this and an emphasis on using safe water sources and maintaining a safe water chain may be more effective.

- **Build on ideas, concepts and practices that people already have and respond to perceived priorities.** The introduction of completely alien concepts will take a great deal of time and in non-literate populations it may be difficult to convince target groups on the reliability of this information. Equally, responding to external priorities rather than community priorities often results in failure, as there is little or no commitment to the change required. The process of dialogue and priority setting with the community is essential.

- **Repeated and reinforced messages over time using different methods.** This may be important to ensure that the message is taken up and accepted. However, caution should be exercised to prevent indifference from setting in and therefore it is important to make the message interesting. Furthermore, when using different methods, it is essential that coherence in the underlying information is maintained and care must be taken to avoid confusing or contradictory messages are not sent out. Bear in mind that some behaviours have financial implications for the household and therefore excessive emphasis on these behaviours may lead to people feeling disgruntled and that the health education programme is out of touch with the realities of the urban poor.

- **Adaptable approaches that use existing channels of communication - for example songs, drama, story telling and community meetings.** The latter is particularly important in participatory approaches where the involvement of the community is most important in defining solutions.

- **Entertaining and attracts community's attention.** Health education approaches that are uninteresting will lead to indifference within the community. The use of participatory approaches can again overcome such problems by ensuring that there is dialogue and community participation in the decision-making process.

- **Use clear simple language with local expressions.** The critical component of any education or communication strategy is to ensure that the message being transmitted is clear, concise, comprehensible and coherent. Where messages are unclear or have contradictions, different conclusions can be drawn by different people, some of which may be in direct conflict with the message desired.

- **Health education should emphasise short-term benefits and other benefits not related to health, such as social status and greater household savings.** This is sometimes called social marketing. Where benefits are long-term, many people will lose interest as they have immediate concerns that take priority. They may also not see the value of long-term benefit when they would hope to move within a shorter time period to a better area. The use of non-health benefits is particularly useful as the importance ascribed by communities to the incidence of diarrhoea, for instance, may not be that high. However, by convincing people that savings due to reduce health care spending or lost days of work will be significant may have a greater impact.

- **Use demonstrations to show the benefits of adopting practices.** This is often one of the best ways of creating interest, particularly where the demonstration is in a setting that is relevant to the community. This may therefore include things such as visits to communities that have implemented similar interventions at a community or household level and encourage them to describe what they did, how they did it, the benefits, what problems were encountered and how these were overcome. An alternative approach is to focus on a few households within a community who can act as models for the rest of the community and who can undertake promotion of improved hygiene within their community.

14.4 Using routine water quality surveillance data in hygiene education

A key use of surveillance data is to inform health education programmes in order to reduce the risk of contamination as water is collected, transported and stored within the home. Surveillance can be a very effective tool in this, particularly when you use water quality sampling and analysis as a health education tool. The use of on-site equipment means that the community can become involved in the collection of the sample and analysis. A particular useful approach is to read the plates with community members and explain what the yellow colonies mean. This can then also be used as a discussion point within the community about how contamination may be prevented and what simple actions can be taken to reduce contamination risks. This can be a very good entry point to discussing the problems of poor water quality on health and effective in promoting better water handling. This has been successfully implemented in several countries and has yielded significant improvements.

The same process can be used for sources of water, with sanitary risk factors incorporated within the discussion. A good idea is to review the sanitary inspection data and look for risks that are related to operation and maintenance or other aspects that you would expect the community itself to be able to resolve. Discussion of these problems can then allow the community to identify what failures there have been in maintaining and managing the source and how these may be overcome in the future.

In order to ensure that health education focuses on a safe water chain, make sure you review the data on household and source water. There is little point in initiating health education programmes if the results of samples taken over significant amount of time (for instance 6 months or more) in a particular community have not been contaminated. In addition to checking whether contamination of household water is found, also check whether this is restricted to certain communities or use of particular sources. If you find that in a particular community, samples always show no contamination, it is a good idea to meet with the community and discuss why and how they keep their water clean. This may yield very useful information when designing a health education intervention in other communities.

In many cases, water collected at sources of good microbiological quality becomes contaminated once it reaches the home. This may be because the containers used are not clean, are open or because people must dip hands, fingers or utensils into the container in order to get water to drink. It is therefore important to look at the sanitary inspection results from household water using the survey report by category to see whether there are any particular factors that are strongly positively associated with increasing levels of contamination. For instance in one town in Uganda, factors such as the cleanliness of the outside of the container, households not using soap to clean the inside of the container and unhygienic storage of the utensil to draw water showed the strongest association. Thus these are critical factors to focus on.

Caution should be applied, however, when promoting particular types of storage container for collecting water. In principle, the best containers are those where water from drinking is drawn through a tap, as this prevents dirty hands and other contamination from entering the container. In many cases, such containers may actually already be available, but if they are not, it is worth considering encouraging manufacture of such container.

Where such containers are not used, it is common to find that the use of containers with a narrow opening is promoted. However, be aware that such containers may be more difficult to clean than containers with wide mouths. This can be overcome by promoting the use of diluted bleach to clean the inside of the container. In this case, water would be left in the container with the dilute bleach for 30 minutes to one hour, in which time most micro-organisms will have been inactivated. Where wide–mouthed vessels are used, the health education should focus ensuring that the potential for contamination is minimised. This should include promoting the hygienic storage of the utensil used to draw the water from the vessel (for instance by always keeping it in the vessel itself), that a lid is kept in place at all times when water is not actually being drawn and that the container and utensil are cleaned regularly (weekly or daily) using soap. The use of vessels with smooth surfaces on the inside (for instance plastic or glazed clay) should also be promoted as rough surfaces may encourage the growth of biological communities in the vessel.

A critical element of the health education programme will be the promotion of handwashing, particularly after defecation. This is an important factor in reducing contamination of drinking-water being introduced from dirty fingers and hands. Any hygiene education programme that focuses on improvement of water quality from source to the household, should be integrated in wider hygiene education programmes dealing with a broader range of healthy behaviours. It is important that where different departments take responsibility for different aspects of hygiene education, messages are consistent between different departments. If you decide to use mass media as a means to disseminate hygiene education messages, make sure that these are attractive, can reach your target audience and are relevant to the audience. Thus, any materials developed should be thoroughly pre-tested before they are used on a large scale.

When using water and sanitary inspection data, however, it is important that hygiene education or surveillance staff focus attention within communities on priority problem areas and on simple and positive actions that the community themselves can undertake to reduce the risk of contamination. It is important that the discussion about poor water quality does not lead to either an expectation that the surveillance body will provide a new water supply (unless this can be fulfilled) or that there is nothing that the community can do to improve their water supply. In particular, make sure that hygiene education staff have a clear understanding of what the controlling factors in contamination for different sources so that this can be used in a constructive manner to improve local response to water supply problems.

14.4.1 Using water usage data to inform interventions

Water usage data provides much useful information that also be used to develop health education programmes as it provides information about practices and, through the analysis of reasons for source selection, important indications as to what communities view as being most important about water.

The reasons for use of different sources may provide an indication of the types of health education messages that will be effective and the approach to promotion of improved water supply that will yield the greatest results. If quality is a reason provided by a significant numbers of people participating in the study, then this provides a good entry point for a hygiene education programme to promote improved water quality. This can be linked to water handling practices such as the type of storage container used and the need for covers on storage containers within the home.

The reported frequency of treatment of water within the home can provide an early indication of the degree to which the community has accepted certain key concepts in the safe water chain. However, water quality data may indicate a gap between knowledge and practice, thus the hygiene education programme can focus on translating knowledge into sustained action.

It should be remembered that water usage data not only provides useful information about how people view water supply and water quality and what importance people attach to high-quality water in preventing disease. It also provides a starting point for looking at how local solutions to local problems can be found and often provides the impetus for a discussion within a community about what can be done to improve water supply.

14.4.2 Translating surveillance information into hygiene education

As with using surveillance data to inform appropriate technical interventions, if the surveillance programme is to be able to inform hygiene education programmes, it is essential to be clear about how the information generated during surveillance activities can be incorporated into hygiene education.

Much of this will relate to how information is reported back to communities as this process will be critical to the uptake of surveillance information and the translation of this information into hygiene practices. Where information is fed back to the community in a simple and comprehensible form, then this can provide an impetus for behaviour change. Where communities have not received the information or the information is provided in a way that makes little sense, then it may not allow communities and households to initiate actions. By using the water quality and sanitary inspection data, the process of evaluating likely causes of water quality failure and thus how these can be overcome is an important mechanism of promoting hygiene improvement. The use of the data is shown in Table 14.2 below.

Focus of activity	Types of message	Surveillance data
Operation and maintenance of a water source	Point sources: maintain protection works; maintain and clear diversion ditches; clear wastewater drains; drain stagnant water; maintain fences. Taps: paying water bills; keeping area around tap clean; reporting faults to the water supplier	Sanitary inspections Water quality results Costs of water and reconnection
Environmental hygiene	Clearing environment of rubbish and faeces; keeping pit latrines away from sources; keeping environment around taps clean	Sanitary inspection data
Promoting safe sources	Use of sources know to be safe for drinking and food preparation	Water quality data Water usage studies
Promoting safe water handling	Using clean containers; using containers with lids	Sanitary inspection data Water quality data
Promoting safe water storage and treatment	Using clean containers; using containers with lids, pouring or using a tap to get water; treatment of water	Sanitary inspection data Water quality data Water usage studies

Table 14.2: Health education message using surveillance data

By developing simple methods of sanitary inspection that are amenable to use by communities to monitor their own water supply, ongoing improvements in water quality can be made. This may cover both personal as well as community hygiene. A key element may be to identify and train a number of community members in basic assessment techniques as a way to promote improved hygiene.

14.5 Monitoring and evaluation

As with any intervention, monitoring and evaluation is important to assess whether the health education programme is being effective and what refinements are required. Monitoring involves collecting information as during implementation of the programme to assess whether it is meeting the objectives or there needs to be changes. The data required for monitoring can come from:

- Routine surveillance information e.g., water quality monitoring, diarrhoea data from clinics

- Water usage studies that evaluate pre and post intervention behaviours

- Supervision reports from staff visiting field workers and community workers

- Feedback from communities through community meetings, field visits and correspondence

Evaluation is the assessment of the overall impact at the end of the programme to find out if the situation has improved over the baseline level at the beginning of the activity. This again may use water quality data collected as well as the other data collection methods indicated above.

The most important decision in planning evaluation is the choice of indicators. Indicators should be measurable by simple and objective methods, be feasible to collect - ideally it should be possible to collect the information as part of routine data collection by field workers - and be a meaningful measure of an important programme activity. Some examples of indicators that could be used for the evaluation of hygiene education activities are shown below in Table 14.3.

It is essential that from the outset of the programme realistic targets are set and that you are aware of the limitations of some indicators. It may not be realistic to set high targets from diarrhoeal disease reduction within a short period of time as the uptake of the behaviour may not be immediate and may take some years to become the standard household or community practice. Where water sources have been improved through education, it may be more effective to assess the reduction of risks associated with poor water source management and the degree of contamination. The same may be true for household water storage and proper disposal of faeces and uptake of good hygiene practices.

Where diarrhoeal rates are used, it is important to be aware that data from medical facilities may be highly inaccurate, as most people will initially treat milder cases within the home. Recall methods may be used, but bear in mind, recall is often limited once it is beyond a short period of time (one week at most). Furthermore, health education programmes, because they increase awareness, may lead to an apparent increase in diarrhoea because medical treatment is sought. It may be more effective to concentrate on the reduction of epidemic diseases, where outbreaks have been previously common or a reduction in stunting over several years.

Some common indicators for evaluation	
▪ Health outcomes	Diarrhoea deaths
	Diarrhoea cases
▪ Behaviours	Use of particular sources for drinking water
	Use of household treatment techniques
	Lack of faecal contamination of water storage containers
	Cleanliness of water points
	Days lost through non-functioning water systems
▪ Preconditions for behaviour change	Understanding of the link between faeces and diarrhoea
	Recognition of symptoms of dehydration
	Awareness of importance of removal of children's faeces

Table 14.3 Common indicators for evaluating health education programmes

In many cases, it is better to select indicators that are more easily and reliably measurable and this would often focus on indicators of behaviours or the pre-conditions for behaviour change. One good method for collecting data in such an evaluation will be to carry out pre and post-intervention water usage studies. For instance, a key component of a hygiene education strategy may be to introduce a 'rationality' factor into source use. Therefore the use of sources of known higher quality for drinking is promoted within the community with a concurrent promotion of the use of alternative sources for non-consumption uses of water.

By undertaking a water usage study before and after the intervention, you should be able to assess whether there has been significant uptake of the use of particular sources for drinking and food preparation. The same approach could be used when the hygiene education programme promotes treatment of water within the home.

Annexes

Annex 1:

Inventory forms

Urban and Peri-Urban Water Supply Surveillance Project
Inventory observation sheet and questionnaire

Water source No. ☐

Name of water source	
Location	
Parish	
Division	
Town	
Interviewer's name	
Date	

1 What is the water source:
   Tick 1 box

Public standpost	☐
Private tapstand - water selling	☐
Landlord provided tap	☐
Protected spring in good condition	☐
Protected spring requiring repair	☐
Unprotected spring	☐
Borehole with handpump	☐
Dug well with no handpump/windlass	☐
Dug well with windlass	☐
Dug well with handpump	☐
Rooftop rainwater catchment	☐
Unprotected scoop well	☐
Pond/stream/swamp/lake	☐

f the source is a pond, stream, swamp, lake, unprotected spring or unprotected scoop well, only answer uestions 1-5 and 14-22

2 Who owns the water source:
   Tick 1 box

Private owner	☐
NWSC	☐
Community	☐
Local Councils (LCI/II)	☐
City/Town Councils (LCIII-V)	☐
Project	☐
No-one	☐

3 Who supervises the water supply
   Tick 1 box

Owner	☐
Community caretaker	☐
Other community representative	☐
Project staff	☐
Other	☐
No-one	☐

4 Is the water provided: Free of charge   ☐

Cost per bucket/jerry can

Meter/flat rate

If water is free go to question 6

5 How much is charged for the water   USh [   ]   per [   ]
   Get information from source caretaker   USh [   ]   per [   ]

6 Who did the actual construction of the
   water supply
   Tick one box - get information from source
   caretaker or from your records

   Community
   NGO/Donor [   ]
   Contractor
   Govt agency [   ]
   Other (who)
   City/Town/District council (LCIII-V)

7 Which Project/Organisation sponsored
   the design and construction
   Get information from source caretaker or from
   your records

8 When was it constructed
   Tick one box - get information from source
   caretaker or from your records

   0-6 months
   6-12 months
   More than 1 year
   Don't know/don't remember

9 Has any repair or rehabilitation work
   been carried out on the water supply
   Tick one box - get information from
   source caretaker

   Yes
   No
   If 'no' go to question 14

10 What was the most recent repair
   Get information from source caretaker

11 Who did this
   If more than one organisation tick all the
   appropriate boxes

   Community
   City/Town/District Council (LCIII-V)
   Govt Agency [   ]
   NGO/Donor [   ]
   Owner

12 When was it done
   Tick one box - get information from
   source caretaker

   0-6 months
   6-12 months
   More than 1 year
   Don't know/remember

13 Who paid for the work to be done	Community	
If more than one organisation tick all the	City/Town Council (LCIII-V)	
appropriate boxes	Govt Agency	
	NGO/Donor	
	Owner	

14 Who is responsible for maintenance of	Community	
the source	City/Town Council (LCIII-V)	
If more than one organisation tick all the	Govt Agency	
appropriate boxes	NGO/Donor	
	Owner	
	Don't know	
	No-one	
	If 'don't know' or 'no-one' go to question 17	

15 Who pays for maintenance work	Community	
If more than one organisation tick all the	City/Town Council (LCIII-V)	
appropriate boxes	Govt Agency	
	NGO/Donor	
	Owner	
	Don't know	
	No-one	

16 How often is this done	Daily	
Tick one box - get information from	More than once a week	
source caretaker	Weekly	
	More than once a month	
	Monthly	
	Less than once a month	
	Don't know	

17 Who is responsible for cleaning the area	Community	
around the source	City/Town Council (LCIII-V)	
If more than one organisation tick all the	Govt Agency	
appropriate boxes	NGO/Donor	
	Owner	
	No-one	
	Don't know	
	If no-one go to question 19	

18 How often is this done	Daily	
Tick one box - get information from	More than once a week	
source caretaker	Weekly	
	More than once a month	
	Monthly	
	Less than once a month	
	Don't know	

19 Do you restrict how much water each
person can take

Yes

No

If 'no' go to question 21

Tick one box - get information from source caretaker. NB: does not include restriction because of lack of money)

20 Why is there a restriction
*Tick one box - get information from
source caretaker*

Source has low flow

Too many people use source

Limited time for caretaker

Non-domestic uses of water

Other (specify)

Don't know

21 Does the source dry up

Yes

No

If 'yes' answer question 22

Tick one box - get information from source caretaker. NB: does not include disconnection)

22 If the source does dry up, does this happen
*Tick one box - get information from
source caretaker*

Daily

Monthly

Seasonally

Occassionally

Annex 2:

Examples of surveillance reports

Environmental Health Division, Ministry of Health

Urban and Peri-Urban Water Supply Surveillance: Monthly Point Source Water Quality Results by Division

Town　　Kampala

Division　Rubaga Division

Month　September 1999

| Source Name | Source No. | Category | Samples | Date | Faecal coliforms per 100ml | | | | Turbidity | Appearance | Risk% |
					Min	Max	Mean	Median			
Mukiibi, Nakulabye	KRA006	PRTSP	1	22/09/99	1	1	1	1	<5	Clear	10
Kalymutina	KRA008	PRTSP	1	22/09/99	18	18	18	18	<5	Clear	40
Dr Bogere	KRA009	PRTSP	1	22/09/99	2	2	2	2	<5	Clear	50
Beth, Lusaze	KRA010	PRTSP	1	22/09/99	11	11	11	11	<5	Clear	60
Mapera, Lusaze	KRA011	PRTSP	1	22/09/99	4	4	4	4	<5	Clear	70
Lwamulungi, Wakaliga B	KRA023	PRTSP	1	23/09/99	4	4	4	4	<5	Clear	60
Wambizzi, Nakukolongo	KRA024	PRTSP	1	23/09/99	3	3	3	3	<5	Clear	60
Aggrey, Aggrey zone	KRA033	PRTSP	1	23/09/99	4	4	4	4	<5	Clear	30
Nabunya, Pope Paul	KRA057	PRTSP	1	23/09/99	7	7	7	7	<5	Clear	30
Aggrey, Aggrey Nr Star Se	KRA058	PRTSP	1	23/09/99	12	12	12	12	<5	Clear	40

Number of samples　10

Average contamination FC/100ml with TNC results　7
Average contamination FC/100ml minus TNC results　7

Note: 30,000 is equivalent of a result of too numerous to count

Note: PRTSP = protected spring; BHHP = borehole with handpump; DWHP = dug well with handpump

Environmental Health Division, Ministry of Health

Urban and Peri-Urban Water Supply Surveillance: **Monthly Household Water Quality Results by Division**

Town **Kampala**

Division Rubaga Division

Month September 1999

| Source Name | Source Risk | Samples | Date | *Faecal coliforms per 100ml* | | | Turbidity | Appearance |
				Min	Max	Median		
Household water, Rubaga	Nsereko,	2	22/09/99	0	0	0		0
Household water, Rubaga	Mukasa,	4	23/09/99	0	0	0	<5	Clear 0
Household water, Rubaga	Musa, Ka	4	27/09/99	0	2	0	<5	Clear 0
Household water, Rubaga	Mukiibi,	2	28/09/99	0	0	0	<5	Clear 0

Total Number of samples **12**

Average contamination FC/100ml including TNC results **1**
Average contamination FC/100ml minus TNC results **1**

Note: 30,000 is equivalent to a result of too numerous to count
Note: JCHHS = jerrycan and household water

SanMan Risk Management Software Robens Centre for Public and Environmental Health

184

Environmental Health Division, Ministry of Health

Urban and Peri-Urban Water Supply Surveillance: Monthly Piped Source Water Quality Results by Division

Town   **Kampala**

Division   Kawempe Division

Month   September   1999

Source Name	Source No.	Date	Samples	*Faecal coliforms/100ml*		Turbidity	pH	*Chlorine*		Appearance	Risk%
				Min	Max			Free	Total		
Bwaise III piped	KKE059	17/09/99	1	0	0	<5	7.2	0.3	0.5	Clear	0
Bwaise II piped	KKE062	17/09/99	1	0	0	<5	7.3	0.2	0.5	Clear	10
Kazo piped	KKE063	17/09/99	1	0	0	<5	7.4	0.3	0.6	Clear	0
Kawempe I piped	KKE076	17/09/99	3	0	0	<5	7.2	0.2	0.4	Clear	0
Kanyanya piped	KKE061	24/09/99	1	0	0	<5	7.1	0.3	0.6	Clear	20
Kyebando piped	KKE066	24/09/99	2	0	0	<5	7.3	0.4	0.5	Clear	10
Mulago II piped	KKE067	24/09/99	2	0	0	<5	7.4	0.2	0.4	Clear	0
Wandegeya piped	KKE068	24/09/99	1	0	0	<5	7.2	0.3	0.6	Clear	20
Kikaya piped	KKE060	30/09/99	1	0	0	<5	7.4	0.3	0.6	Clear	0
Makerere I piped	KKE069	30/09/99	1	0	0	<5	7.2	0.4	0.6	Clear	0
Makerere II piped	KKE075	30/09/99	3	0	0	<5	7.3	0.3	0.4	Clear	20

Total Number of samples   **17**

Note: 30,000 is the equivalent of a result of to numerous to count

Note: PIPEW = piped water; GFSPP = gravity-fed piped water

SanMan Risk Management Software Robens Centre for Public and Environmental Health

185

Urban and Peri-Urban Water Supply Surveillance Project

Town:

Date: **Area:**

Staff from the Public Health Department recently came to your community and took water quality samples and carried out sanitary inspection at sites shown below. The results of the survey are shown in the table.

Sample site	Source type	Faecal contamination	Sanitary risk score	Major risk points noted	State of water source
		Yes No			

Notes:

1 If faecal contamination is yes, this means your water is contaminated with excreta and is a risk to the health of those who drink this water

2 Sanitary risk score shows the level of risk of contamination in your supply.

3 Risk points noted show the major problems with your water supply.

The following recommendations are made for your community on the basis of the above results:

186

Annex 3:

Report forms; Sanitary inspection forms; Pollution risk appraisal forms

Division

Date

Daily Report Sheet
Town/City

Analyst

Sample No.	Sample source	Source code No.	SI score	Time	Colour	Turbidity TU	Chlorine		pH	Faecal coliforms		
							Free	Total		Vol ml.	No. colonies	FC/100ml

Comments

Signature of analyst

189

I.   **Type of Facility   PIPED WATER**

1.   General Information :   Zone:

                                   :   Area

2.   Code Number

3.   Date of Visit

4.   Water samples taken? ……..   Sample Nos. ………

II   Specific Diagnostic Information for Assessment

	Risk	**Sample No**
(please indicate at which sample sites the risk was identified)		
1. Do any tapstands leak	Y/N	…………
2. Does surface water collect around any tapstand?	Y/N	…………
3. Is the area uphill of any tapstand eroded?	Y/N	…………
4. Are pipes exposed close to any tapstand?	Y/N	…………
5. Is human excreta on the ground within 10m of any tapstand?	Y/N	…………
6. Is there a sewer within 30m of any tapstand?	Y/N	…………
7. Has there been discontinuity in the last 10 days at any tapstand?	Y/N	…………
8. Are there signs of leaks in the mains pipes in the Parish?	Y/N	…………
9. Do the community report any pipe breaks in the last week?	Y/N	…………
10. Is the main pipe exposed anywhere in the Parish?	Y/N	…………

                                   Total Score of Risks   …./10

Risk score: 9-10 = Very high; 6-8 = High; 3-5 = Medium; 0-3 = Low

III   Results and Recommendations:
The following important points of risk were noted: (list nos. 1-10)

Signature of Health Inspector/Assistant:

Comments:

I. **Type of Facility**   **PIPED WATER WITH SERVICE RESERVOIR**

1. General Information :   Zone

                                :   Area

2. Code Number

3. Date of Visit

4. Water samples taken? ……..   Sample Nos. ………

II **Specific Diagnostic Information for Assessment**

	Risk	**Sample No**
(please indicate at which sample sites the risk was identified)		
1. Do any standpipes leak at sample sites?	Y/N	………….
2. Does water collect around any sample site?	Y/N	………….
3. Is area uphill eroded at any sample site?	Y/N	………….
4.Are pipes exposed close to any sample site?	Y/N	………….
5. Is human excreta on ground within 10m of standpipe?	Y/N	………….
6. Sewer or latrine within 30m of sample site?	Y/N	………….
7. Has there been discontinuity within last 10 days at sample site?	Y/N	………….
8. Are there signs of leaks in sampling area?	Y/N	………….
9. Do users report pipe breaks in last week?	Y/N	………….
10. Is the supply main exposed in sampling area?	Y/N	………….
11. Is the service reservoir cracked or leaking?	Y/N	………….
12. Are the air vents or inspection cover insanitary?	Y/N	………….
Total Score of Risks	..../12	

Risk score: 10-12 = Very high; 8-10 = High; 5-7 = Medium; 2-4 = Low; 0-1 = Very Low

III **Results and Recommendations:**
The following important points of risk were noted: (list nos. 1-12)

Signature of Health Inspector/Assistant:

Comments:

I   **Type of Facility**   **HYDRANTS AND TANKER TRUCKS**

1.   General information   :   Sub-Metro

                                     :   Community

2.   Code Number:

3.   Date of visit:

4.   Is water sample taken?………Sample No……Thermotolerant Coliform Grade………

II   **Specific Diagnostic Information for Assessment**   **Risk**

1.   Is the discharge pipe dirty?   Y/N

2.   Can the discharge pipe touch the ground?   Y/N

3.   Is the delivery nozzle dirty or in poor condition?   Y/N

4.   Are there any leaks close to the riser pipe of the hydrant?   Y/N

5.   Is the base of the riser piped for the hydrant sealed with a concrete apron?   Y/N

3.   Is the tanker ever used for transporting other liquids?   Y/N

7.   Is the inside of the tanker dirty?   Y/N

8.   Does the tanker fill through an inspection cover on the tanker?   Y/N

9.   Is the discharge nozzle dirty or in poor condition?   Y/N

10.   Does the tanker leak?   Y/N

                                     Total Score of Risks   …./10

Contamination risk score: >8/10 = very high; 6-8/10 = high; 4-7/10 = intermediate; 0-3/10 = low

III   **Results and Recommendations:**

The following important points of risk were noted: (list nos.1-10)
And the authority advised on remedial action

Signature of inspector:

Comments:

I.   Type of Facility   **GRAVITY-FED PIPED WATER**

1.   General Information :   System name:

2.   Code Number

3.   Date of Visit

4.   Water samples taken? ……..   Sample Nos. ………

II   Specific Diagnostic Information for Assessment

	Risk	Sample No
(please indicate at which sample sites the risk was identified)		
1. Does the pipe leak between the source and storage tank?	Y/N	
2. Is the storage tank cracked, damaged or leak?	Y/N	
3. Are the vents and covers on the tank damaged or open?	Y/N	
4. Do any tapstands leak?	Y/N	………….
5. Does surface water collect around any tapstand?	Y/N	………….
6. Is the area uphill of any tapstand eroded?	Y/N	………….
7. Are pipes exposed close to any tapstand?	Y/N	…………
8. Is human excreta on the ground within 10m of any tapstand?	Y/N	………….
9. Has there been discontinuity n the last 10 days at any tapstand?	Y/N	………….
10. Are there signs of leaks in the main supply pipe in the system?	Y/N	………….
11. Do the community report any pipe breaks in the last week?	Y/N	………….
12. Is the main supply pipe exposed anywhere in the system?	Y/N	………….

Total Score of Risks   …./12

Risk score: 10-12 = Very high; 8-10 = High; 5-7 = Medium; 2-4 = Low; 0-1 = Very Low

III   Results and Recommendations:
The following important points of risk were noted: (list nos. 1-12)

Signature of Health Inspector/Assistant:

Comments:

I. **Type of Facility**   **DEEP BOREHOLE WITH MECAHNISED PUMPING**

1. General Information :   Supply zone
                       :   Location:

2. Code Number

3. Date of Visit

4. Water sample taken? ……..   Sample No. ……… FC/100ml ………..

II **Specific Diagnostic Information for Assessment**

	Risk
1. Is there a latrine or sewer within 100m of pumphouse	Y/N
2. Is the nearest latrine unsewered	Y/N
3. Is there any source of other pollution within 50m	Y/N
4. Is there an uncapped well within 100m	Y/N
5. Is the drainage around pumphouse faulty	Y/N
6. Is the fencing damaged allowing animal entry	Y/N
7. Is the floor of the pumphouse permeable to water	Y/N
8. Does water forms pools in the pumphouse	Y/N
9. Is the well seal insanitary	Y/N
Total Score of Risks	..../9

Risk score: 7-9 = High; 3-6 = Medium; 0-2 = Low

III **Results and Recommendations:**
The following important points of risk were noted: (list nos. 1-9)

Signature of Health Inspector/Assistant:

Comments:

I.   Type of Facility   BOREHOLE WITH HANDPUMP

1.   General Information :   Zone
                                              :   Location

2.   Code Number

3.   Date of Visit

4.   Water sample taken? ……..   Sample No. ……… FC/100ml ………..

II   Specific Diagnostic Information for Assessment

Risk

1. Is there a latrine within 10m of the borehole?   Y/N

2. Is there a latrine uphill of the borehole?   Y/N

3. Are there any other sources of pollution within 10m of borehole?   Y/N
      (e.g. animal breeding, cultivation, roads, industry etc)

4. Is the drainage faulty allowing ponding within 2m of the borehole?   Y/N

5. Is the drainage channel cracked, broken or need cleaning?   Y/N

6. Is the fence missing or faulty?   Y/N

7. Is the apron less than 1m in radius?   Y/N

8. Does spilt water collect in the apron area?   Y/N

9. Is the apron cracked or damaged?   Y/N

10. Is the handpump loose at the point of attachment to apron?   Y/N

                                              Total Score of Risks   …./10
Risk score: 9-10 = Very high; 6-8 = High; 3-5 = Medium; 0-3 = Low

III   Results and Recommendations:
The following important points of risk were noted: (list nos. 1-10)

Signature of Health Inspector/Assistant:

Comments:

I.   Type of Facility   PROTECTED SPRING

1.   General Information :   Zone:
                                          :   Location

2.   Code Number:

3.   Date of Visit:

4.   Water sample taken? ……..   Sample No. ……… FC/100ml ………..

II   Specific Diagnostic Information for Assessment

                                                                                     Risk

1. Is the spring unprotected?   Y/N

2. Is the masonary protecting the spring faulty?   Y/N

3. Is the backfill area behind the retaining wall eroded?   Y/N

4. Does spilt water flood the collection area?   Y/N

5. Is the fence absent or faulty?   Y/N

6. Can animals have access within 10m of the spring?   Y/N

7. Is there a latrine uphill and/or within 30m of the spring?   Y/N

8. Does surface water collect uphill of the spring?   Y/N

9. Is the diversion ditch above the spring absent or non-functional?   Y/N

10. Are there any other sources of pollution uphill of the spring?   Y/N
        (e.g. solid waste)

                                  Total Score of Risks   …./10
Risk score: 9-10 = Very high; 6-8 = High; 3-5 = Medium; 0-3 = Low

III   Results and Recommendations:
The following important points of risk were noted: (list nos. 1-10)

Signature of Health Inspector/Assistant:

Comments:

I.   **Type of Facility**   **DUG WELL WITH HANDPUMP/WINDLASS**

1.   General Information   :   Zone:
                                 :   Location

2.   Code Number

3.   Date of Visit

4.   Water sample taken? ……..   Sample No. ……… FC/100ml ………..

II   **Specific Diagnostic Information for Assessment**

                                                                 Risk

1. Is there a latrine within 10m of the well?   Y/N

2. Is the nearest latrine uphill of the well?   Y/N

3. Is there any other source of pollution within 10m of well?   Y/N
       (e.g. animal breeding, cultivation, roads, industry etc)

4. Is the drainage faulty allowing ponding within 2m of the well?   Y/N

5. Is the drainage channel cracked, broken or need cleaning?   Y/N

6. Is the fence missing or faulty?   Y/N

7. Is the cement less than 1m in radius around the top of the well?   Y/N

8. Does spilt water collect in the apron area?   Y/N

9. Are there cracks in the cement floor?   Y/N

10. Is the handpump loose at the point of attachment to well head?   Y/N

11. Is the well-cover insanity?   Y/N

                                 Total Score of Risks   …./11
Risk score: 9-11 = Very high; 6-8 = High; 3-5 = Medium; 0-3 = Low

III   **Results and Recommendations:**
The following important points of risk were noted: (list nos. 1-11)

Signature of Health Inspector/Assistant:

Comments:

I.   **Type of Facility**   **RAINWATER COLLECTION AND STORAGE**

1.   General Information :   Zone
                       :   Location

2.   Code Number

3.   Date of Visit

4.   Water sample taken? ……..   Sample No. ……… FC/100ml ………..

II   **Specific Diagnostic Information for Assessment**

                                                                     Risk

1. Is rainwater collected in an open container?   Y/N

2. Are there visible signs of contamination on the roof catchment?   Y/N
        (e.g. plants, excreta, dust)

3. Is guttering that collects water dirty or blocked?   Y/N

4. Are the top or walls of the tank cracked or damaged?   Y/N

5. Is water collected directly from the tank (no tap on the tank)?   Y/N

6. Is there a bucket in use and is this left where it can become contaminated?   Y/N

7. Is the tap leaking or damaged?   Y/N

8. Is the concrete floor under the tap defective or dirty?   Y/N

9. Is there any source of pollution around the tank or water collection area?   Y/N

10. Is the tank clean inside?   Y/N

                                Total Score of Risks   …./10

Risk score: 9-10 = Very high; 6-8 = High; 3-5 = Medium; 0-3 = Low

III   **Results and Recommendations:**
The following important points of risk were noted: (list nos. 1-10)

Signature of Health Inspector/Assistant:

Comments:

I. Type of Facility   WATER TREATMENT PLANT

Date of survey: _____

Survey carried out on: Source   Intake   Plant
(circle all those inspected)

Inspector: _____

Name of plant: _____

Name of Principal Operator: _____

Name of Responsible Engineer/Manager: _____

Years in operation: _____   Area served (Km2): _____

Population served: _____

Design capacity (m3): _____   Current production (m3/day): _____

Fence around plant? Y/N   Fencing in good condition? Y/N   Security guard? Y/N

II. Source (circle one): Reservoir   Stream   River   Well   Other

III Intake:
1. Condition of intake works: Good   Average   Poor

2. Problems with aquatic vegetation?:   Y/N

3. Spontaneous settlement close to intake: None   Small-scale   Significant   Serious

4. Industrial pollution close to source

5. Agricultural pollution close to source:

6. Sewage discharge/urban run-off close to intake?

IV Treatment processes (circle all those used):

Fine screen   Grit chamber   Oil/grease trap   Pre-sedimentation   Pre-disinfection

Activated carbon   Aeration   Coagulation/flocculation – Lime Alum Polyelectrolyte

Sedimentation: Rectangular   Circular   Other

Filtration: Rapid   Slow   Granular carbon

Disinfection: Chlorine   Ozone   Other
Other processes: _____

V. Sedimentation:

1. No. of sedimentation tanks: _____

2. Frequency of desludging: _____

3. Type of desludging facility: _____

4. Method of sludge disposal: _____

5. General appearance of final water: _____

6. Turbidity at inlet: _____   Turbidity at outlet: _____

7. Retention time: _____

VI Filtration

1. No. of filters: _____

2. Filtration rate: _____

3. Filter run (time): _____

4. Depth of gravel: _____

5. Depth of sand: _____

6. Turbidity at inlet: _____   Turbidity at outlet: _____

7. Criteria for backwashing:

Air scour: Rate_____   Duration: _____

Water scour: Rate_____   Duration: _____

8. Is air and water supply distribution in sand bed even? Y/N

9. Capacity of clean water for backwash: _____

10. Any mud balls or cracks in filter: Before backwash - Y/N   After backwash – Y/N

11. How is wash-water disposed of? _____

VIII: Disinfection

1. Any failures/interruption in disinfection: Y/N

2. Frequency of interruption: _____

3. Cause of interruption: _____

4. Disinfectant used: _____

5. Dosage of disinfectant: _____

6. Dosing method: _____

7. Safety equipment and measures adequate: Y/N

8. Reserves of disinfectant available? Y/N Quantity: _____

9. Storage conditions: Good   Average   Poor

IX Clear water tanks
1. No. of tanks: _____

2. Capacity of each tank: _____

3. Concentration of free residual at outlet: _____

4. pH: _____

5. Chemical used for pH adjustment and dosage: _____

6. Are any tanks leaking? Y/N

7. Are tanks properly covered and locked? Y/N

8. Is the inside of the tank clean? Y/N

9. Are air vents and overflow pipes protected by screens? Y/N

X Process control

1. Jar test	Yes	No	Frequency: _____
2. pH	Yes	No	Frequency: _____
3. Free chlorine:	Yes	No	Frequency: _____
4. Colour:	Yes	No	Frequency: _____
5.Turbidity:	Yes	No	Frequency: _____
6. Faecal coliforms:	Yes	No	Frequency: _____

XI Record keeping

1. Chemical consumption	Good	Poor	Updated: _____
2. Process control tests	Good	Poor	Updated: _____
3. Bacteriological quality:	Good	Poor	Updated: _____
4. Residual chlorine:	Good	Poor	Updated: _____

XII Maintenance:

1. Screen:	Good	Poor
2. Pumps:	Good	Poor

3. Chlorine dosing:	Good	Poor
4. Instrumentation:	Good	Poor
5. Cleanliness:	Good	Poor
6. Chemical storage:	Good	Poor

XIII Personnel
1. No. of present staff: Permanent_____   Casual_____

2. Educational level of plant superintendent or principal operator: _____

3. Years at this plant: _____

4. Total experience in water treatment: _____

XIV Problems recorded with:
1. Treatment processes: _____
(please list processes and describe problems)

2. Customer complaints: _____
(please indicate how many complaints, nature of complaints and frequnecy)

XV Flow diagram of treatment works: *(insert diagram)*

XVI Actions
1. Suggested remedial actions:
(please indicate priorities)

3. Have previously identified problems been rectified? Y/N

Signature:

Household water quality inspection

1.   Is drinking water kept in a separate container (ask to be shown this)?

☐ Yes   ☐ No

2.   Is drinking water container kept above floor level and away from contamination?

☐ Yes   ☐ No

3.   Do water containers have a narrow mouth/opening?

☐ Yes   ☐ No

4.   Do containers have a lid/cover?

☐ Yes   ☐ No

5.   Is this is in place at time of visit

☐ Yes   ☐ No

6.   How is water taken from the container?

☐ Poured   ☐ Cup   ☐ Other utensil

7.   Is the utensil used to draw water from the container clean?

☐ Yes   ☐ No

8.   Is the utensil used to draw water the container kept away from surfaces and stored in a hygienic manner?

☐ Yes   ☐ No

9.   How often is the container cleaned?

☐ Every day   ☐ Every month   ☐ Never

☐ Every week   ☐ Rarely

10.   How is the container cleaned?

....

11.   Is the inside of the drinking water container clean?

☐ Yes   ☐ No

12.   Is the outside of the drinking container clean?

☐ Yes   ☐ No

Rapid Environmental Risk Appraisal Form

Name of Town/scheme   **Project Ref:**

Please have the form as complete as possible by ....2000.
The information from this form will be used to assess the risk of pollution to the water source (current and future) so that measures to prevent or control it can be recommended.

Please use blank sheets to add any additional information in answering the questions.
Where possible, indicate the location of the pollution source on a photocopy of an existing map or on a sketch map (an example is attached)
Please fill in the boxes below or tick where appropriate.

1. Does the water source have any pollution problems?		Yes		No	

2. Does the water source have any of the following water quality problems?					
Colour Y/N	Turbidity Y/N	Coliforms Y/N	Iron Y/N	Algae Y/N	

3. Please list any other pollution problems with the water source.

4. If there are any problems, when do the occur?

Jan	Feb	Mar	Apr	May	Jun	July	Aug	Sept	Oct	Nov	Dec	am	pm

5. For each of the following POTENTIAL sources of pollution indicate whether it is present (Yes/No) and how far it is from the water source.

Potential source of pollution	Yes	No	Distance	Comment
Residential				
• settlement (town/village)				
• construction				
• encroachment				
Other:				
Agricultural activity				
• livestock				
• crops - commercial				
• crops - small scale				
• chemical storage				
• other				
Industrial activity				
• food processing				
• textiles				
• tanneries				
• brewery				
• small scale industry (including garages				
• abattoir (slaughter house)				
• mining				
Miscellaneous				
• deforestation				
• erosion				
• other				

Annex 4:

Aseptic technique evaluation form

Aseptic technique evaluation form

Quality control factors	Assessment	Comments
1) Was the kit and apparatus clean (including incubator)	Yes No	
2) Is the media stored in a dark and preferably cool place	Yes No	
3) Was the media fresh and uncontaminated	Yes No	
4) Was the pad placed in the petri-dish correctly	Plates: Fail:	
5) If pad not successfully placed in dish, did staff member use sterilised forceps to replace pad	Plates: Fail:	
6) Was filtration apparatus and sample cup sterilised before each analysis and was this done correctly	Tests: Fail:	
7) Was filtration & sample cup left for 5 minutes after sterilisation	Tests: Fail:	
8) Were forceps sterilised before each use, including if touched	Tests: Fail:	
9) Are forceps kept away from contamination when in use	Tests: Fail:	
10) Were filters sealed before use	Tests: Fail:	
11) Was the filter touched by staff member	Tests: Fail:	
12) Was the filter laid on the pad correctly	Tests: Fail:	
13) Was the sample cup rinsed before sample taken	Tests: Fail:	
14) Did staff member only read the yellow colonies on filter	Plates: Fail:	
15) Did staff member correctly state the number of coliforms per 100ml	Plates: Fail:	

Annex 4:

Water usage questionnaires

Water Usage Questionnaire – Short Form

Interviewer Name	[blank]	Date	[blank] / /
Parish	[blank]	Subject No.	[blank]
Zone/Cell	[blank]	Respondent: Male Female Child	

Section 1: Water Sources

A: Main Water Source
I would like to learn about the different places you or someone in your family gets water from,
NOT INCLUDING RAINWATER AND VENDORS

1. Firstly I Would Like To Know Where You Most Often Get Your Water From?
*[If the person says "spring", ask **if it is a protected or unprotected spring**. TICK the number of the type of source]*

TYPE OF SOURCE		TICK
Spring	Protected	1
	Unprotected	2
Tap		3
Other		4

NAME OF SOURCE:

2. What Do You Use This Water For?
*[If only one use is given say **"do you use this water for anything else?"** Tick **EACH** answer the person gives]*

USE	TICK	
Consumption	1	Drinking, Cooking and food preparation
Other domestic use	2	Bathing, laundry etc

3. What Kind Of Container Do You Use To Collect Water And How Big Is It?
[Ask person to show you if you are not clear]

Type of container [blank]   *Approximate Litres* [blank]

4. How Many Jerry Cans (Other Vessel) Of Water Do You Collect From This Source Each Day?

[blank]   *Number of Jerry Can/other container*

B: Second Water Source

Often people use more than one place to get their water from

1. **Are There Are Any Other Places You Get Water From, NOT INCLUDING RAINWATER AND VENDORS? [IF NO, GO TO SECTION 2]**

   ❏ Yes   ❏ No

2. **Which Is The Place You Get Water From Most Often After (*Say* <u>Name Of Primary Water Source</u>)**

TYPE OF SOURCE		TICK
Spring	Protected	1
	Unprotected	2
Tap		3
Other		4

NAME OF SOURCE:

3. **What Do You Use This Water For?**

   *[If only one use is given say "**do you use this water for anything else?**" Tick **EACH** answer the person gives]*

USE	TICK	
Consumption	1	Drinking, Cooking and food preparation
Other domestic use	2	Bathing, laundry etc

4. **What Kind Of Container Do You Use To Collect Water And How Big Is It?**

   [Ask person to show you if you are not clear]

   Type of container [　　　　　]   *Approximate Litres* [　　　]

5. **How Many Jerry Cans (Other Vessel) Of Water Do You Collect From This Source Each Day?**

   [　　　　　]   *Number of Jerrycan/other container*

C: Other sources

Do You Use Any Other Water Sources, NOT INCLUDING RAINWATER AND VENDORS? [IF NO, GO TO SECTION 2]

❏ Yes   ❏ No

[More than one source can be ticked, state name of source]

❏ Tap   Name [　　　　　　　　　　]

❏ Protected Spring [　　　　　　　　　　]

❏ Unprotected Spring [　　　　　　　　　　]

❏ Other [　　　　　　　　　　]

Section 2: Other water

A: RAINWATER
Do You Ever Collect Rainwater?

    ❏ Yes   ❏ No

Observation: *Is There Guttering And Tank/Drum For Rainwater Collection?*

❏   Yes   ❏   No

B: VENDORS

1. **Do You Buy Water From Vendors [IF NO GO TO SECTION 3]**

    ❏ Yes   ❏ No

2. **How Often Do You Buy Water From A Vendor?**

    ❏ Every day   ❏ At least once a month

    ❏ At least once a week   ❏ Very occasionally

3. **How Much Water Do You Buy On Each Occasion?**

Type of Container [   ]   *Number* [   ]

Section 3: Socio-demographic Information

Finally I would like to ask you some information about your household

1. **How Many People Live In Your Household?**

No. Women [   ]   No. of Men [   ]   No. of Children [   ]

FOR OFFICE USE ONLY:

                Total No. SOURCES   [   ]

                No. external SOURCES   [   ]

Water Usage Questionnaire – Long form

Interviewer Name	[blank]	Date	[blank] / /
Parish	[blank]	Subject No.	[blank]
Zone/Cell	[blank]	Respondent:	Male Female Child

Section 1:   Water Sources

PART A: Primary Water Source

To start with, I would like to learn about the different places you or someone in your family get water from, NOT INCLUDING RAIN WATER AND VENDORS

1. Firstly I Would Like To Know Where You Most Often Get Your Water From?

[If the person says "spring", ask if it is a <u>protected</u> or <u>unprotected</u> spring. TICK the number of the type of source]

TYPE OF SOURCE		TICK
Spring	Protected	1
	Unprotected	2
Tap		3
Other		4

NAME OF SOURCE:

2. Why Do You Choose To Get Water From This Place?

*[If only one reason is given say **"are there any other reasons why you get water from this place?"** TICK **EACH** answer the person gives]*

TICK	REASONS	TICK	REASON
1	Distance	6	Only source
2	Cost	7	Only tap
3	Quality	8	Personal/family reasons
4	Reliability	9	Other ....
5	Available		....

3. What Do You Use This Water For?

*[If only one use is given say **"do you use this water for anything else?"** Tick **EACH** answer the person gives]*

TICK	USE	TICK	USE
1	Bathing	5	Animals
2	Cooking	6	Gardening
3	*Drinking*	7	Laundry
4	Cleaning house	8	Other..................... ....

4. What Kind Of Container Do You Use To Collect Water And How Big Is It?
[Ask person to show you if you are not clear]

Type of container [   ]   *Approximate Litres* [   ]

5. How Many Jerry Cans (Other Vessel) Of Water Do You Collect From This Source Each Day?

[   ]   *Number of Jerry Can/other container*

6. Do you pay for the water from this source? [IF NO GO TO QUESTION 8]
❑ Yes   ❑ No

7. How much do you pay for a Jerry Can? [   ]

8. Are there times when you find no water at this source? [IF NO GO TO PART B]
❑ Yes   ❑ No

9. How often is there no water at this place?
❑ At least every day   ❑ In the dry season
❑ At least once a week   ❑ Only occasionally
❑ At least once a month

PART B: Second Water Source
Often people use more than one place to get their water from

I Would Like To Know If There Are Any Other Places You Get Water From, NOT INCLUDING RAINWATER AND VENDORS? [IF NO, GO TO PART D]
❑ Yes   ❑ No

1. Which Is The Place You Get Water From Most Often After (*Say* Name Of Primary Water Source)

TYPE OF SOURCE		TICK
Spring	Protected	1
	Unprotected	2
Tap		3
Other		4

NAME OF SOURCE:

216

2. Why Do You Choose To Get Water From This Place?

*[If only one reason is given say **"are there any other reasons why you get water from this place?"** TICK **EACH** answer the person gives]*

TICK	REASONS	TICK	REASON
1	Distance	6	Only source
2	Cost	7	Only tap
3	Quality	8	Personal/family reasons
4	Reliability	9	Other ....
5	Available		....

3. What Do You Use This Water For?

*[If only one use is given say **"do you use this water for anything else?"** Tick **EACH** answer the person gives]*

TICK	USE	TICK	USE
1	Bathing	5	Animals
2	Cooking	6	Gardening
3	Drinking	7	Laundry
4	Cleaning house	8	Other......................... ....

4. What Kind Of Container Do You Use To Collect Water And How Big Is It?
[Ask person to show you if you are not clear]

Type of container [　　　　　　　] *Approximate Litres* [　　　　　]

5. How Many Jerry Cans (Other Vessel) Of Water Do You Collect From This Source Each Day?

[　　　　　　　] *Number of Jerry Can/other container*

6. Do You Pay For The Water From This Source? [IF NO, GO TO QUESTION 9]

❑ Yes   ❑ No

7. How Much Do You Pay For A Jerry Can?

USh: [　　　　　　]

8. Are There Times When You Find No Water At This Source? [IF NO, GO TO PART C]

❑ Yes   ❑ No

9. How Often Is There No Water At This Place?

❑ At least every day   ❑ In the dry season

❑ At least once a week   ❑ Only occasionally

❑ At least once a month

Part C: Other sources
Do You Use Any Other Water Sources, NOT INCLUDING RAINWATER AND VENDORS? [IF NO, GO TO PART D]

❏   Yes   ❏   **No**

[More than one source can be ticked, state name of source]

❏ Tap   Name |_____|

❏ Protected Spring |_____|

❏ Unprotected Spring |_____|

❏ Other |_____|

Part D: Rainwater
Do You Ever Collect Rainwater?

❏ Yes   ❏ No

Observation: *Is There Guttering And Tank/Drum For Rainwater Collection?*

❏   Yes   ❏   No

Part E: Proximity

Which Of The Source You Have Mentioned Is Nearest To Your Home, Which Is The Next Nearest And Which Is The Furthest?
[Write type of source and name]

Nearest |_____| **Second Nearest** |_____|

Furthest |_____|

Section 2: Vendors
I would now like to ask you about whether you ever buy water from a vendor.

1. **Do You Buy Water From Vendors [IF NO GO TO SECTION 3]**

   ❏ Yes   ❏ No

2. **How Often Do You Buy Water From A Vendor?**

   ❏ Every day   ❏ At least once a month

   ❏ At least once a week   ❏ Very occasionally

3. **How Much Water Do You Buy On Each Occasion?**

   Type of Container |_____| *Number* |_____|

4. How Much Do You Pay Per Container?

Ush ……………… per container

5. Why Do You Buy From The Vendor?
*[If give only one reason, ask "**is there any other reason?**". Tick **EACH** answer given]*

TICK	REASON	TICK	REASON
1	Lack of assistance in the home	5	No other source/restricted access
2	Proximity/Time	6	Personal/family/health problems
3	Cost	7	Quality
4	Inadequacy	8	

Section 3: Water Collection and Storage

I would now like to ask you about how you collect and store your water

1. Which People Collect Water In Your Family?

☐ Children   ☐ Women   ☐ Men

2. Where Do You Keep Or Store Your Water?
[Type of container and place]

3. Do You Do Anything To Your Water Before You Drink It?

☐ Yes   ☐ No

If yes what do you do to it?

Section 4: Socio-demographic Information

Finally I would like to ask you some information about your household

1. How Many People Live In Your Household?

No. Women ☐   No. of Men ☐   No. of Children ☐

2. How Many Rooms Do You And Your Family Live In? ☐

3. Has Anyone In Your Family Had Diarrhea Within The Last Week?

☐ Yes   ☐ No
☐

Section 5: Observations by Health Worker

Floor Material

❑ Earth

❑ Wood/Stone

❑ Cement Screed

❑ Concrete/Brick

Roof Material

❑ Tile/Concrete

❑ Iron Sheet

❑ Asbestos

❑ Papyrus/Grass

Wall material

❑ **Concrete**

❑ **Burnt bricks**

❑ **Unburnt bricks**

❑ **Pole and mud**

❑ **Stone/Cement/Block/Wood**

FOR OFFICE USE ONLY: *Total No. SOURCES*

No. external SOURCES

Annex 6:

Further reading

References and further reading

Almedom, A and Odhiambo, C. 1994. *The rationality factor: Choosing water sources according to uses.* Waterlines, 13 (2): 28-31.

Almedom, A M, (1996) *Recent developments in hygiene behaviour research: an emphasis on methods and meaning.* Tropical Medicine & International Health 1(2):171-182, 1996.

Andreasen, J. 1996. *Urban tenants and community involvement.* Habitat International, 20(3): 359-365.

Barrett, H and Browne, A (1996) *Health, hygiene and maternal education: evidence from The Gambia.* Social Science & Medicine 43(11):1579-1590.

Bartram, J and Balance, R (1996) *Water quality monitoring: a practical guide to the design and implementation of freshwater quality studies and monitoring programmes,* E&FN Spon, London, UK.

Boot, M. (1991) *Just stir gently - the way to mix hygiene education with water supply and sanitation,* The Hague: IRC International Water and Sanitation Centre.

Boot, M and Cairncross, S (Eds) (1993) *Actions speak: the study of hygiene behaviour in water and sanitation projects,* IRC/LSHTM, Delft, The Netherlands.

Bradley, D, Stephens, C, Harpham, T and Cairncross, S (1992) *A review of environmental health impacts in developing country cities,* Urban Management Program, Washington DC, USA

Carter, R, Tyrrel, SF and Howsam, P, 1993. *Lessons Learned from the UN Water Decade.* Journal of the Instution of Water and Environmental Management, 7(6): 646-650.

Chowdury, M.A.I, Ahmed, M.F, Bhuiyan, M.A and Rahman, M.H, 1997. *Unaccounted-for water management states in Bangladesh.* Journal of Water Supply Research and Technology – Aqua, 46(5): 235-241.

Cotton, A P and Tayler, W K. 1994. *Community management of urban infrastructure in developing-countries.* Proceedings of the Institution of Civil Engineers-Municipal Engineer, 103(4): 215-224.

Deb, B C, Sircar, B K, Sengupta, P G, De, S P, Mondal, S K, Gupta, D N, Saha, N C, Ghosh, S, Mitra, U and Pal, S C (1986) *Studies on interventions to prevent eltor cholera transmission in urban slums.* Bulletin of the World Health Organ 64(1):127-131.

Defaria, A L and Alegre, H. 1996. *Paving the way to excellence in water-supply systems -a national framework for levels of service assessment based on consumer satisfaction.* Journal of Water Supply Research and Technology-Aqua, 45(1): 1-12.

Dinar, A and Subramanian, A. 1997. *Water pricing experiences.* World Bank Technical Paper No. 386. The World Bank, Washington D.C. USA.

Esrey, S A , Feacham, R G and Hughes, J M, 1985. *Interventions for the control of diarrhoeal diseases among young children: improving water supplies and excreta disposal facilities.* Bulletin of the World Health Organization, 63(4): 757-772.

Esrey, S A, Potash, J B, Roberts, L and Shiff, C, 1991. *Effects of improved water supply and sanitation on ascariasis, diarrhoea, dracunculiasis, hookworm infection, schistosomiasis, and trachoma.* Bulletin of the World Health Organization, 69(5): 609-621.

Esrey, S A, 1996. *No half measures – sustaining health from water and sanitation systems.* Waterlines, 14(3): 24-27

Esrey, S.A, 1996. *Water, waste and well-being: a multicountry study.* American Journal of Epidemiology 143 (6): 608-623.

Clark, R M, Goodrich, J A and Wymer, L J, 1993. *Effect of the distribution system on drinking-water quality.* Journal of Water Supply Research and Technology – Aqua, 42(1): 30-38.

Ford, T E. 1999. *Microbiological safety of drinking water: United States and global perspectives.* Environmental Health Perspectives, 107 (S1): 191-206.

Franceys, R, 1990. *Paying for water – urban water tariffs.* Waterlines, 9(1): 9-12.

Friedman-Huffman, D and Rose, J. 1998. *Emerging waterborne pathogens.* Water Quality International, December 1998: 14-18.

Franceys, R (1997) *Private sector participation the water and sanitation sector: Private waters? - a bias towards the poor,* DFID Occasional Paper No. 3, Londo

Gale, P. 1996. *Coliforms in drinking-water supply: what information do the 0/100ml samples provide?* Journal of Water Supply Research and Technology – Aqua, 45(4): 155-161.

Gamble, D R. 1979. *Viruses in drinking-water: reconsideration of evidence for postulated health hazard and proposals for virological standards for purity.* Lancet, 24th February 1984: 425-428.

Geldreich, E E, Fox, K R and Clark, R M. 1991. *Microbial quality of water supplies during the 1991 cholera outbreak in Peru.* Paper presented at the Conference on Public Health Issues in Peru and International Assistance, Rickville, Maryland.

Geldreich, E E(1990) *Microbiological quality of source waters for water supply,* **in** McFetters, GA (ed), 1990, *Drinking water microbiology.* Springer-Verlag, New York, USA.

Gelinas, Y, Randall, H, Robidoux, L and Schmit, J (1996) Well water survey in two districts of Conakry (Republic of Guinea), and comparison with the piped city water. Water Research. 30, 2017-2026.

Gerba, C P and Rose, J B (1990) *Viruses in source and drinking water,* **in** McFetters, GA (ed), 1990, *Drinking water microbiology.* Springer-Verlag, New York, USA.

Grabow, W O K, (1996) Waterbore diseases: Update on water quality assessment and control, Water SA, 22(2):193-202

Haas, C N and Heller, B, 199? *Statistical approaches to monitoring,* **in** McFetters, GA (ed), 1990, *Drinking water microbiology.* Springer-Verlag, New York, USA.

Haas, C N. 1999. *Benefits of employing a distribution residual.* Journal of Water Supply Research and Technology – Aqua 48 (1): 11-15.

Hardoy JE, Satterthwaite, D (1989) *Squatter citizen: life in the urban third world.* Earthscan Publications, London.

Hazen, T C and Toranzos, G A (1990) *Tropical source water,* **in** McFetters, GA (ed), 1990, *Drinking water microbiology.* Springer-Verlag, New York, USA.

Henry, FJ and Rahim, Z (1990). *Transmission of diarrhoea in two crowded areas with different sanitary facilities in Dhaka, Bangladesh.* Journal of Tropical Medicine & Hygiene 93(2):121-126, 1990.

Howard, G (1996) *Urbanisation, sanitation and environmental health.* Commonwealth Secretariat, London.

Howard, G (1997) *Healthier values – realistic approaches to improving drinking-water quality,* Waterlines, 16(1):2-4

Howard, G and Luyima, P G (1999). *Urban water supply surveillance in Uganda.* In Pickford, J (ed), *Integrated Development for Water Supply and Sanitation, Proceedings of the 25th WEDC Conference, Addis Ababa, 1999*, pp290-293.

Howard, G, Bartram, J K and Luyima, P G (1999). *Small water supplies in Urban Areas of Developing Countries.* **in** Cotruvo, J A, Craun, G F and Hearne, N (eds) *Providing safe drinking water in small system: technology, operations and economics.* Lewis Publishers, Washington, DC. USA, pp83-93.

Howard, G. (*in press*). *Challenges in increasing access to safe water in urban Uganda: economic, social and technical issues.* To be published in the Monograph of the 2nd International Conference on the Safety of Water Disinfection, Miami, November 1999.

Howarth, D A, 1998. *Arriving at the economic level of leakage: environmental aspects.* Journal of the Chatered Institution of Water and Environmental Management, 12: 197-201.

Howe, C W and Smith, M G. 1994. *The value of water supply reliability in urban water systems.* Journal of Environmental Economics and Management, 26: 19-30.

Hubley, J. (1993) *Communicating health: an action guide to health education and health promotion*, Basingstoke and London: Macmillan.

Ince, M. and Howard, G. (1999) *Developing realistic drinking water standards.* In Pickford, J (ed), *Integrated Development for Water Supply and Sanitation, Proceedings of the 25th WEDC Conference, Addis Ababa*, 1999, pp294-297.

Jones, J. 1997. *Urban water supplies for developing coutnries: The French approach.* WEDC Institutional Development Series. Loughborough University.

Kaltenthaler, E C and Drasar, B S (1996) *The study of hygiene behaviour in Botswana: a combination of qualitative and quantitative methods.* Tropical Medicine & International Health 1(5):690-698.

Kayaga, S M. 1997. *Marketing of Watsan services: NWSC Uganda.* WEDC Institutional Development Series. Loughborough University.

Kiene, L, Lu, W and Levi, Y. 1998. *Relative importance of the phenomena responsible for chlorine decay in drinking water distribution systems.* Water Science and Technology, 38 (6): 219-227.

Lewin, S, Stephens, C and Cairncross , S. 1996. *Health impacts of environmental improvements in Cuttack and Cochin, India: Review prepared for the Overseas Development Administration by the London School of Tropical Medicine and Health.* London School of Torpical Medicine and Health.

Lightfoot, N F, Tillet, H E, Boyd, P and Eaton, S. 1994. *Duplicate spilt samples for internal quality control in routine water microbiology.* Letters in Applied Microbiology, 19: 321-324.

Lloyd, B, Bartram, J, Rojas, R, Pardon, M, Wheeler, D and Wedgewood, K. 1991. *Surveillance and improvement of Peruvian drinking water supplies.* Robens Institute, DelAgua and ODA. Guildford.

Lloyd, B and Bartram, J, 1991. *Surveillance solutions to microbiological problems in water quality control in developing countries.* Water, Science and Technology, 24(2): 61-75.

Maul, A, El-Shaarawi. A H and Block, J C (1990) *Bacterial distribution and sampling strategies for drinking water networks,* **in** McFetters, GA (ed), 1990, *Drinking water microbiology.* Springer-Verlag, New York, USA.

McCommon, C S, Perez, E A and Rosensweig, F. 1998. *Environmental Health Programme Applied Study No. 7: Providing urban environmental services for the poor:*

Lessons learned from three pilot project. Environmental Health Project. Washington, USA.

McCauley, A P, Lynch, M, Pounds, M B, and West, S (1990) *Changing water-use patterns in a water-poor area: lessons for a trachoma intervention project*. Social Science & Medicine 31(11):1233-1238.

McGranahan, G, Leitman, J and Surjadi, C. 1997. *Understanding environmental problems in disadvantaged neighbourhoods: Broad spectrum surveys, participatory appraisal and contingent valuation*. Urban Management Programme Working Paper 16. Stockholm Environment Institute. Stockholm.

Moe, C, Sobsey, M D, Samsa, G P and Mesolo, V. 1991. *Bacterial indicators of diarrhoeal disease from drinking-water in the Philippines*. Bulletin of the World Health Organization, **69** (3): 305-317.

Narayan, D. 1993. *Participatory evalution: tools for managing change in water and sanitation*. World Bank Technical Paper No. 207. World Bank. Washington, USA.

Nixon, A (1996) The public-private mix in urban water supply. Web page of the International Development Department, School of Public Policy, University of Birmingham, UK.

Ongley, E. 1998. *Modernisation of water quality programmes in developing countries: issues of relevancy and cost efficiency*. Water Quality International, September/October 1998, 37-42.

Payne. G, 1997. *Urban Land Tenure and Property Rights in Developing Countries: A review*. IT publications and ODA, London.

Payment, P, Richardson, L, Siemiatycki, J, Dewar, R, Edwardes, M and Franco, E.1991. *A Randomised trial to evaluate the risk of Gastrointestinal disease sue to consumption of drinking water meeting current microbiological standards*. American Journal of Public Health 81(6): 703-708.

Pedley, S and Howard, G, 1997. *The public health implications of microbiological contamination of groundwater*. Quarterly Journal of Engineering Geology. 30: 179-188.

Pegram, G C, Rollins, N and Espey, Q. 1998. *Estimating the costs of diarrhoea and epidemic dysentery in KwaZulu-Natal and South Africa*. Water SA, 24(1):11-20.

Pinfold, J.V. (1990) *Faecal contamination of water and fingertip-rinses as a method for evaluating the effect of low-cost water supply and sanitation activities on faeco-oral disease transmission. II. A hygiene intervention study in rural north-east Thailand*. Epidemiology & Infection 105, 377-389.

Pipes, O, 1990 *Microbiological methods and monitoring of drinking water*, **in** McFetters, GA (ed), 1990, *Drinking water microbiology*. Springer-Verlag, New York, USA.

Rahman, A. 1996. *Groundwater as source of contamination for water supply in rapidly growing megacities of Asia: Case of Karachi, Pakitstan*. Water Science and Technology, 34(7-8): 285-292.

Rahman A, Lee H K and Khan M A. 1997. *Domestic water contamination in rapidly growing megacities of Asia: Case of Karachi, Pakistan*. Environmental Monitoring and Assessment, 44 (1-3): 339-360

Ramteke, P W, Bhattacharjee, J W, Pathak, S P and Kaira, N, 1992. *Evaluation of coliforms as indicators of water quality in India*. Journal of Applied Bacteriology, 72: 353-356.

Ramteke, P W, 1995. *Comparison of standard most probable number method with 3 alternate tests for detection of bacteriological water-quality indicators.* Environmental Toxicology and Water Quality, 10(3): 173-178.

Sharma, N P, Damhang, T, Gilgan-Hunt, E, Grey, D, Okaru, V and Rothberg, D 1996. *African Water Resources: Challenges and opportunities for sustainable development.* World Bank Technical Paper No. 331.World Bank. Washington, USA.

Stephens, C, Akerman, M, Avle, S, Maia, P B, Campanario, P, Doe, B and Tetteh, D. 1997. *Urban equity and urban health: using exisitng data to understand inequalities in health and environment in Accra, Ghana and Sao Paulo, Brazil.* Environment and Urbanisation, 9(1): 181-202.

Stephens, C, 1995. *The urban environment, poverty and health in devloping countries.* Health Policy and Planning, 10(2): 109-121.

Stephens, C, 1996. *Healthy cities or unhealthy islands? The health and social implications of urban inequality.* Environment and Urbanization, 8(2): 9-30.

Stranlund, J K. 1995. *Public mechanisms to support compliance to an environmental norm.* Journal of Environment Economics and Management, 28: 205-222.

Subramanian, A, Jaggannathan, N V and Meinzen-Dick, R. 1997. *User organizations for sustainable water services.* World Bank Technical Paper No. 354. The World Bank, Washington D.C. USA.

Trussell, R R. 1999. *An overview of disinfectant residuals in drinking water distribution systems.* Journal of Water Supply Research and Technology – Aqua 48 (1): 2-10.

Vanderslice, J and Briscoe, J, 1993. *All coliforms are not created equal: a comparison of the effects of water source and in-house water contamination on infantile diarrheal disease.* Water Resources Research 29(7): 1983-1995.

Vanderslice, J and Briscoe, J, 1995. *Environmental interventions in developing countries: interactions and their implications.* American Journal of Epidemiology, 141(2): 135-141.

West, S, Lynch, M, Turner, V, Munoz, B, Rapoza, P, Mmbaga, B B, and Taylor, H R (1989) Water availability and trachoma. *Bulletin of the World Health Organ.* 67(1):71-75.

WHO, 1987. *Drinking-water quality and health-related risks.* WHO Regional Office for Europe. Copenhagen, Denmark.

World Bank, 1993. *Water Resources Management.* World Bank Policy Paper. World Bank. Washington.

WHO, 1993. *Guidelines for drinking-water quality: Volume 1 Recommendations.* WHO, Geneva.

WHO, 1993. *Guidelines for drinking-water quality: Volume 2 Health Criteria and other supporting material,* WHO, Geneva.

WHO, 1992. *Report of the panel on urbanization.* WHO, Geneva.

WHO, 1995. *Report of the Co-ordinating Committee on the Rolling Revision of the Guidelines for Drinking-water Quality.* WHO.

World Resources Institute, *World Resources: A Guide to the Global Environment: The Urban Environment*, Oxford University Press, New York, 1996, 365.

Xie, M, Kuffner, U and Le Moigne, G. 1993. *Using water efficiently: Technological options.* World Bank Technical Paper No. 205. World Bank. Washington, USA.

Annex 7:

Index

Index

233